D1715444

Legacy of Faith
collection

Marilyn Hickey

Harrison House
Tulsa, Oklahoma

The Life, Ministry, and Legacy of Marilyn Hickey
Legacy of Faith Collection
ISBN: 978-1-60683-028-4
Copyright © 2011 by Marilyn Hickey

Published by Harrison House Publishers
P.O. Box 35035
Tulsa, OK 74153
www.harrisonhouse.com

Contents

Part 4: *Know Your Ministry*

Part 5: *Healing*

Part 6: *Winning Over Weight*

Part 7: *End Times*

Part One

Introduction

Introduction

"Over forty years ago, God called me to 'cover the earth with His Word.' At the time, I couldn't imagine what that would mean and how He would send me around the globe preaching His Word. In the past three decades, the Lord has opened amazing doors for me in nearly 130 countries. There's truly nothing impossible with God."

—Marilyn Hickey

I n the height of the Charismatic revival of the 1970s God called Marilyn Hickey, an unassuming minister's wife, to worldwide ministry. From a global view, it was a time of great upheaval of the established principles of society, but from God's view it was an opportunity for openness like never before to pour out His Spirit on all denominations and cultures. Unbeknownst to her, Marilyn's passions, upbringing, education, and training had all been cultivated by God for such a time as this.

The healing revival of the mid-1900s introduced daring men and women of God to society including A. A. Allen, William Branham, Kathryn Kuhlman, Jack Coe, and others who were not afraid to proclaim God's power with bold demonstrations of salvation and healing. But as this revival began to wane, the counterculture of the 1960s started to take hold in America and Europe—promising freedom to its followers. In an attempt to gain this freedom, those affected found themselves in only greater bondage to deception, drug addiction, alcoholism, and unprecedented social pressure. God's next move would penetrate this era of supposed *free* philosophies with an amazing outpouring of the power of the Holy Spirit, unveiling the true freedom only found in Christ.

Referred to as the Charismatic movement, God revealed His Spirit in a fresh new way that brought down the walls of various religious denominations. Believers from all faiths came together and thousands were born again, healed, and filled with Spirit. It was during this great outpouring, God spoke to Marilyn Hickey.

From humble beginnings, Marilyn started with home Bible studies, teaching powerful truths from God's Word. With the encouragement of those she taught, she started a five-minute radio broadcast. Later, Marilyn felt led by the LORD to go on television and from there she began to receive invitations to speak, which she had not anticipated.

Marilyn says, "I began to fast and pray and I told the Lord, 'I can do a lot of good things and miss Your best. What do You want me to do?' And He said, 'I want you to cover the earth with the Word.' That's when I was called. Everything I do is a process of that call." The Lord gave Marilyn the Scripture Isaiah 11:9, "The earth shall be full of the knowledge of the Lord," and ever since it has remained her motto.

Today, Marilyn is president and founder of Marilyn Hickey Ministries, a worldwide Christian humanitarian organization based in Denver, Colorado. Working closely with her daughter, Sarah Bowling, Marilyn considers their work a powerful bridge builder for people of all cultures and religious backgrounds.

"A bridge by definition connects two adjacent elements to form one unified entity. Worldwide, people often forget about the bridge that fundamentally connects us; it is that we are all a part of mankind, the human race.

"Because the suffering of mankind from poverty, violence, racism, and deficiency is counteractive to the philosophy of a bridge, Marilyn Hickey Ministries is predominately focused on positively affecting negative circumstances in countries across the globe. At the heart of the organization lies the desire to connect people of all cultures, backgrounds, and religious beliefs with understanding, education, and humanitarian acts in order to benefit mankind," states Marilyn's ministry prospectus.

Marilyn ministers the Gospel through salvation in Christ Jesus and healing according to His Word, and she also works diligently to assist with feeding the hungry. She sees the Gospel as not only the saving of souls but also physically helping the needy. Recently, the First Lady of Cambodia expressed her gratitude for the six-ton gift of rice donated to Cambodia's poorest families by Marilyn Hickey Ministries. In Ethiopia, Marilyn was granted a private audience with President Girma Wolde-Giorgis and Sarah with the governor of Gondor for their humanitarian efforts within that country. In 2008, Dr. Hickey received a gift of recognition while in Egypt that only presidents and dignitaries receive and her healing meetings in Cairo were the largest gatherings on spirituality in the country's history to date.

Her mission has been effectively accomplished through various avenues of ministry, such as partnering with other ministries to ship thousands of Bibles into communist countries; to bring food and supplies to poor nations; and to hold crusades in places like Ethiopia, the Philippines, Korea, Haiti, Brazil, Malaysia, Japan, and Honduras.

Marilyn has in her heart to minister especially in Muslim nations, often putting her life in danger by proclaiming the Gospel of Christ. In 2008, her crusades in Sudan drew more than 150,000 people with 20,000 recorded salvations. Her message to believers is to remember the importance of ministering to your neighbor even if they are Muslim.

Marilyn is also one of the most respected and sought after lecturers on divine healing and biblical truth. Marilyn's program, *Today with Marilyn and Sarah,* is broadcast in more than 125 countries. She has produced over 1,500 CD and DVD lectures and published more than 110 books in over 25 languages.

Marilyn also served the body of Christ as the chairman of the Board of Regents for Oral Roberts University in Tulsa, Oklahoma, and is the only woman serving on the board of directors for Dr. David Yonggi Cho, pastor of the world's largest congregation, Yoido Full Gospel Church in Seoul, South Korea with over one million members.

In addition to her ministry, Marilyn is also a busy wife and mother of two grown children. She is married to Wallace Hickey, founding pastor of Orchard Road Christian Center in Greenwood Village, Colorado.

Marilyn's accomplishments are many, but her demeanor is still humble and compassionate. Now in her late seventies, Marilyn has remained stable, strong, and fixed on the mission God gave her so many years ago, to cover the earth with His Word. As a teacher, her concern is that those who hear her messages "really get it." Within the pages of this volume, some of Marilyn's best teachings are contained as well as personal insight from a woman who has learned to persevere through remarkable difficulties to achieve amazing things for the Kingdom of God.

What can you learn from her story? More than you can imagine.

Chapter 1

The Living Word

"Jesus is the most radical gift God could give. For He so loved the world He gave His only begotten Son" (John 3:16).

—Marilyn Hickey

Marilyn's ministry is "all about vision and destiny" perhaps because she recognizes God has been pushing her toward her destiny since she was a child. From her early years as young as 10-years-old, Marilyn remembers having a hunger for the Word of God. She was raised in a liberal denominational church that did not encourage much spiritual training, but that did not deter her. Marilyn was reading and memorizing scriptures all by herself—the Living Word drawing her close.

A few years later, Marilyn attended a youth camp where she heard a Baptist youth pastor speak. He asked the kids if they had Jesus in their hearts. It was the first time Marilyn heard you could have Jesus live inside. She remembers her reaction, "And I thought, *I don't. I know about Him, but I don't have Him inside.* So that's when I received the Lord. That was very, very transformational. I came home and I could not stay out of the Bible. I had the Author in my heart. My family was nice, but they didn't understand. They thought I was emotional—that it was my age. I was 16."

It was also at age 16 when Marilyn took her first airplane flight to visit her Aunt Ethel. Marilyn saw a confidant in Aunt Ethel, a woman who loved deeply and reached out to others. She was a faithful volunteer at a local hospital and was appreciated by many. Marilyn speaks of her aunt's "lavish generosity to those in need" that "allowed me to see what beauty really was."

The flight was an adventure and Marilyn, who was already drawn to see the world, determined she loved to travel. She even confided in Aunt Ethel her dream of becoming a foreign ambassador. Aunt Ethel replied that God had given Marilyn a strong wit and she could be whatever she wanted.

Marilyn was also learning to speak various languages, including six years of Latin by the time she graduated from high school. "In middle school, high school, and college I went on to study French and Spanish—I loved the romance languages—and I even took Greek," Marilyn says. "Thoughts of other cultures, and of adventures overseas, were always with me."

Marilyn graduated from the University of Northern Colorado in 1953 with a Bachelor of Arts in collective foreign languages. Marilyn recalls, "Now I felt ready to jet-set around the world on the way to becoming a foreign ambassador. But then, the Lord had other plans."

Charisma at Home

Marilyn's home life was not perfect. Her mother was an encourager and an anchor for Marilyn and her brother David, but her father, although a good provider, struggled with a mental illness. At times he would end up in the hospital and was quite abusive to Marilyn's mother.

When Marilyn was 19, her mother started going to a Charismatic church. Marilyn didn't care for it much, but went to please her mother. "They clapped their hands and they spoke in tongues. I thought they were way too emotional, too loud," states Marilyn. Looking back Marilyn says, "It was a really good church." As time went by, Marilyn's family began to see a change in their mother; she had a new confidence in her faith. Marilyn's father did not like it and he became even more verbally abusive.

On one occasion upon her mother's arrival home from church, Marilyn's father met her mother at the door threatening her with a knife. She stood firm and declared, "In the name of Jesus, you drop that knife!" Marilyn's father slumped back to the floor. He couldn't move for some time, overwhelmed by the power of God. Marilyn says, "I had never witnessed anything like that before, but I knew God was at work. The Lord became more relevant to me…after that encounter."

Filled with the Spirit

After college, Marilyn began teaching school in Pueblo, Colorado. She would visit her family often in Denver and had come up one particular weekend only to find her grandmother ill and her mother too busy to spend time with her. Marilyn recalls, "To me, it looked like the weekend was falling apart; but in reality, it was going to change my life." Some of her mother's friends invited her to spend the evening with them. Little did she know they had something up their sleeve; they had also invited a young man named Wally who had recently been Spirit-filled.

When Marilyn met Wallace Hickey she remembers, "He was a tall, fair, and very handsome man who was radically turned on to Jesus. I was instantly attracted to him, and the next thing I knew, he'd invited me to go to church with them the following Sunday—a Spirit-filled church."

Wally was hungry for God and wanted to be in church as much as possible. Although Marilyn was not very excited to visit a Spirit-filled church or even be in church all that frequently, she realized that if she wanted to spend time with Wally, it would have to be in church. Marilyn found out later that her mother, Mary Sweitzer, had been praying for her to be Spirit-filled. Marilyn thought she was going to church "for social reasons," but God was divinely ordering her steps.

All this church going led to several things, for one, a proposal. Wallace Hickey asked Marilyn to marry him and they were officially engaged. It also led to some soul-searching on both of their parts.

Wally was invited to dinner one evening at the Sweitzer house. Marilyn adds, "He loved my mother's cooking!" But this night, Wally called and told Marilyn he was not going to make it and he would see her later. Disappointed, she asked him why. He responded, "I'm fasting and praying for you to develop a greater hunger for God. Marilyn, I served the devil with all my heart and now I'm going to serve God with all my heart. I'm not going to marry a woman who is halfhearted. I don't know that this is the will of God for me. I'm fasting for three days."

Marilyn says she was a little insulted because she was saved and considered herself a Christian. For three nights she could not sleep and the third night the Lord spoke clearly in her heart and said, "If you turn the baptism of the Holy Spirit down now, I will never deal with you about this again. You will not marry Wallace Hickey. You will move to California, get your masters degree, marry a Christian, die, and go to heaven. But, I have something so wonderful for you, you cannot imagine." Marilyn recalls, "I went to an all-night prayer meeting at this wild church and I was Spirit-filled there about two days later." She was 23.

Knowing the Lord

Marilyn's salvation and spirit-infilling changed her forever. If you ask anyone at her ministry what Marilyn Hickey Ministries is about, they will tell you, "It's all about winning souls for Christ." Marilyn responds that she hangs out with sinners a lot. "I like to witness—all around the world, on planes, every place. I want my neighborhood saved." Marilyn knows people ubiquitously are deceived about salvation. "People say there are many ways to God. They think if you are sincere in your faith, you are going to heaven. They say the Hindus are going to heaven, the Muslims…if they are sincere. I heard that growing up in our church." But that is also the biggest question Marilyn is asked by unbelievers, "Do you think there is just one way to God?" Something does not ring true about sincerity getting you into heaven and many question if that is enough.

Marilyn explains, "If you tell them there's only one way to God, they get upset with you and argue." Because Marilyn travels so much, she has experienced this response frequently and the Lord showed her what to say. She recalls an incident when a rancher from Colorado was seated next to her. The rancher asked Marilyn what she did for a living. She responded, "I teach the Bible. I go to Muslims, Hindus, and Buddhist countries. I teach the Bible on television so I go all around the world."

"I'm glad you said that because I was raised to believe there is only one way to go to heaven—through Jesus," the rancher replied.

Marilyn thought, *Here we go again.* Right then the Lord spoke to Marilyn's heart, "Don't teach him about the Bible; tell him your experience."

Marilyn said to the rancher, "I don't really want to talk about Hindus, Buddhist, and Muslims. Let me tell you about how I have Jesus in my heart."

She proceeded to tell him about her salvation experience—she knew about God but did not have Him in her heart. She told him of her youth camp conversion and how it changed her life. The rancher broke down in tears and told Marilyn he had been diagnosed with cancer. He knew he was supposed to sit by her and he wanted to receive Jesus.

Marilyn adds, "If you tell them your experience—how you received Jesus or how you were healed—they will listen to you."

Marilyn has a little card with a sinner's prayer on it. When she witnesses to a person, she gives them a card so they know how to be saved. She says, "This prayer changed my life. May I leave it with you?" The ministry also has a little book titled *I Can Be Born Again* that Marilyn gives away when she ministers to help people understand salvation in Christ.

Sure About Heaven

How about you? Do you want to know God better? Do you want to know for sure that you have life after death in heaven? Do you want God's peace, protection, and provision in your life? You can have all of this by following these steps:

1. Recognize and admit that you *need God's help.*

You may be at the point where you realize some things can't

be changed through self-effort or hard work. Sometimes, you just need God to make things better. Whether you need physical or emotional healing, finances, friends, or peace of mind, God has it all. Are you ready to ask Him to make a difference in your life?

2. Believe in *Jesus.*

Have you heard the "good news?" The "good news" is this: "For there [is only] one God, and [only] one Mediator between God and men, the Man Christ Jesus, Who gave Himself as a ransom for all" (1 Timothy 2:5 AMP).
God sent Jesus Christ to be the Savior of the world. Romans 10:9-10 says, "For if you tell others with your own mouth that Jesus Christ is your Lord and believe in your own heart that God has raised him from the dead, you will be saved. For it is by believing in his heart that a man becomes right with God; and with his mouth he tells others of his faith, confirming his salvation" (TLB).

3. Say this *prayer.*
This simple prayer when prayed in sincerity will bring you into personal relationship with God.

Heavenly Father,
I acknowledge that I need Your help. I am not able to change my life or circumstances through my own efforts. I know that I have made some wrong decisions in my life, and I turn away from those ways of thinking and acting that are not producing positive outcomes in my life. I believe You have provided a way for me to receive Your

blessings and help in my life. That way is Jesus. Right now, I believe and confess Jesus as my Lord and Savior. I ask Jesus to come into my heart and give me a new life born of Your Spirit. Thank You for saving me and I ask for Your grace and mercy in my life. I pray this in Jesus' name.

If you just prayed this prayer, Marilyn and her staff would like to know. Please find the contact information at the back of this book and send them an e-mail or letter.

Chapter 2

Small Beginnings

"I remember, early on, Marilyn's concern that, if we went into the ministry, our family would struggle. God has long since laid that fear to rest…and worked His will through us in ways we could never have imagined."

—Wallace Hickey

On December 26, 1954, Marilyn and Wallace Hickey were married. They were both saved and filled with the Holy Spirit, but before they walked down the aisle, Marilyn had one final concern…was Wally planning on becoming a full-time minister? Marilyn had no desire to be a minister's wife and since Wally worked for a recording label and was a successful businessman, she felt confident she knew the answer.

Even though the couple was very involved in their church—singing in the choir and teaching Sunday school—Wally replied he had no plans to enter the ministry. It calmed Marilyn to know that she could pursue her dreams of becoming a foreign ambassador and see the world. Marilyn loved teaching but still held on to her thoughts of traveling around the globe. She was also hesitant about their financial future if ministry was in the picture. "Successful businessman" seemed much more stable that "full-time ministry."

Yet, the desire to minister was deep inside of both of them. Wally volunteered as a co-pastor of a summer church in the Rocky Mountains and also did some evangelistic work. Marilyn even taught a personal soul-winning course during the crusades. As time passed by, as much as they both thought they would not, ultimately they did feel a call to full-time ministry. Wally spoke to Marilyn about it. She recalls, "Astonished, I knew that this was something I could not fight. I, too, moved forward, asking God to lead me as well."

Three years after Marilyn voiced her concern of ministry as a career, the couple moved to Amarillo, Texas, where they accepted the positions of associate pastors. God has a way of moving in our hearts and bringing about His desire as our own. Trust in His leading allows us to experience the joy of what He has planned for us.

Marilyn, however, wasn't experiencing much joy at first. She did not like Texas and told Wally she wanted to move back to Denver—in Texas they had too small of a house and too many bugs! But with a little encouragement, Marilyn changed her attitude and was grateful for the work God did for the people in Texas.

Moving Up

After just a short time in the Lone Star State, a group of believers in Denver contacted the Hickeys about starting a new church. The couple sought the Lord and felt a release to go. They finished their work in Texas and moved back to Denver—a bittersweet day for Marilyn after making new friendships in Amarillo.

Wally and Marilyn were excited to be back in their hometown and forged ahead. They founded Full Gospel Chapel, later named Happy Church, which became a large, multicultural congregation. The church continues to this day under the name Orchard Road Christian Center.

During this time, Marilyn's ministry began to grow as well. As a gifted teacher, her profound insight into the Scriptures was easily understood and accepted by many believers. At one time she had more than 20 Bible study groups located in the greater Denver metropolitan area.

"Down through the years," Wally says, "Marilyn would occasionally remind the Lord that she was not 'called' by Him, but was simply aiding her husband in his call. She did this especially when she was 'strung out' and tired.

"She got away with this for quite a number of years until one day in the early 1970s when the Lord suddenly jerked her up on a 'short string.' He spoke directly to her in her heart and said *she* was called by Him—that He had called her for herself, not just as her husband's assistant. This was no surprise to me, but it was a wonderful and encouraging bit of news to her. At last, it assured her that she had a definite calling!"

Marilyn's supporters encouraged her to start a radio program. The program was only five minutes long but was widely accepted across the area. The radio program grew and not long after, Marilyn began to feel the Lord prompting her to start a television ministry. "I felt very led to go on television and not many ministers were on at that time except Oral Roberts," Marilyn explains.

It was a big step and Wally didn't feel he could handle a television ministry and the church. They talked it out and came to an agreement.

"I feel the Lord has called me to pastoral work, so I want to continue in His call," Wally told Marilyn. "If you want to go ahead with TV, fine. I'll do whatever I can to help, but I don't feel I can take the full burden."

Marilyn responded, "That's fine with me, but promise me one thing: that you will take your hands off and let me do it!"

Wally says Marilyn was putting it rather bluntly, but he understood what she was really saying. She was willing to do it all, but she wanted Wally's blessing. Wally recalls, "I knew the Lord was leading her. He had revealed His hand in so many ways. How could I say no? I had consecrated my life to Him and had prayed for Marilyn when she was somewhat rebellious (which is certainly an amusing thought when one sees how she is used of God today!) I love her dearly!"

Now more than 40 years later, Marilyn is seen on television around the world in more than 120 countries! Wally adds, "Marilyn has definitely been called and is being used mightily of God as a unique and precious woman of the Word."

Worldwide Ministry

When Marilyn began broadcasting on television, invitations to speak and minister came in from across her viewing area. As her viewing area increased, so did the invitations. The speaking engagements were unexpected by Marilyn and she sought the Lord if this was His will. Recording programs was very different from packing up and traveling away from her family. Of course, this was an answer to a long-time desire of her heart to travel and see the world—but in a different aspect, a beautiful aspect. She was to be a foreign ambassador— a foreign ambassador for Christ.

Marilyn first traveled abroad to minister in the early 80s when she journeyed to Ethiopia, of all places. The country was under a communist regime and there was a severe famine—no small beginnings this time! The need for the Gospel and for food was great and Marilyn felt compelled by God to take on the mission.

The Lord spoke to Marilyn's heart to take 10,000 Bibles and 10,000 pounds of food for the children. Because the ministry was not sure they could bring Bibles in, they contacted the ministry of affairs of Ethiopia. The minister said they could bring the Bibles, but he failed to send the visa.

Undaunted, Marilyn knew an Ethiopian woman who was saved at the church and contacted her about the situation. She just happened to know the minister of affairs—in fact, she was a former girlfriend. God was working behind the scenes! Marilyn finally received the visa and went in with food and Bibles. She was able to connect with an orthodox priest in the country who helped her, but the communist government was watching her every move. Marilyn calls it "a very dark time for Ethiopia."

The Lord had spoken to Marilyn telling her to have a healing meeting there. She requested an assembly from the government officials but they denied the request, adding they didn't even believe in God. Disappointed, the team headed home. Plans were made and the team went back in 1984 with more food and Bibles. Again, they were denied a meeting. Marilyn was not giving up and they went back one more time in 1985. There was no meeting granted. Then in 1987, communism was overthrown and the new government told Marilyn she could have a meeting if a religious denomination would sponsor her. That proved difficult for Marilyn Hickey Ministries since it is an independent ministry.

In the meantime, Marilyn's television outreach was increasing and she began to travel worldwide holding healing meetings and conducting humanitarian efforts. In 1997, Marilyn sent a team to Ethiopia again, but no meeting was granted. Finally in 2002, Marilyn was granted an assembly. The international team headed to Ethiopia one more time with high hopes. Everything had come together and the healing meeting was an amazing success with more than 40,000 people in attendance! The president of the country even invited Marilyn to the palace. Persistent, patient, or perhaps tenacious may be the best way to describe Marilyn Hickey. It was 19 years in the making, but Marilyn was able to fulfill what God put in her heart for Ethiopia.

Reaching the Lost

Marilyn will tell you God really didn't call her to her own ministry until she was 42. Although she was very involved in ministry with Wally at the church, she did not feel God spoke specifically to her until this time. Marilyn felt such a strong desire to witness and bring others to Christ. The Lord told her explicitly, "If you want to win the lost, you have to go where they are. They don't fall in on you."

Marilyn took that to heart. Her outreaches center on winning the lost all over the world, in countries that are not always friendly to Christians, women, or Americans. Although she has ministered in more than 120 nations, Marilyn says it is not about the number of nations, but about the souls that are reached and the lives that are eternally changed by the Word of God.

Often she invites believers to join her on her overseas ministry trips where she trains them to pray for the sick and minister salvation. It's a powerful strategy that turns out to be a blessing for all—Marilyn has a team big enough to handle the crowds, believers have an opportunity to minister and use their gifts to help others, and the lost are won and healed.

Humanitarian Efforts

Marilyn has traveled to the most impoverished corners of the world and has given generously to educate church leaders. When Jesus says to love your neighbor, Marilyn takes that as meaning to help those in crises. Marilyn has donated thousands of dollars towards tsunami relief, Hurricane Katrina, and the devastating earthquake of 2005 in Pakistan, which left 73,000 dead and 3.5 million homeless. She also has provided educational opportunities for Ethiopian children, and both food and water wells in places of famine and drought. In addition, Marilyn Hickey Ministries has supported Feed the Children, Samaritan's Purse, and relief after the Indonesian earthquake of 2006.

Marilyn Hickey ministries has made a dramatic impact on many countries worldwide; from disaster relief efforts in Haiti, Indonesia, and Pakistan to providing food for the hungry in Mexico, Costa Rica, Russia, and Manila. There are many real stories of genuine acts of love Marilyn has set out to do.

Muslim Nations

Although Marilyn travels to a great number of countries, more than 120, she feels a special calling to minister in Muslim nations. She has personally traveled to over 20 Muslim countries including Egypt, Turkey, Sudan, Morocco, United Arab Emirates (Dubai), Palestine, Lebanon, Jordan, Turkey, Pakistan, Malaysia, and Indonesia. Marilyn says, "A lot of my meetings are in Muslim countries. I don't have any question that God has told me to go there."

Marilyn has many stories of God's extraordinary favor as she has ministered in places that have been hostile toward Christians—even when her life has been threatened by radical regimes. She faces these instances with the kind of courage that can only be given by God. Marilyn explains, "Many times, God has given me peace and an assurance in my heart—often through Scriptures—that He would bring me home safely."

Marilyn believes in the power of prayer—even in areas of great evil. She knows it is a force that can stop the enemy from invading hearts and minds. Through prayer, Marilyn has found an inoffensive way to minister to practicing Muslims. It's simple really—she offers to pray for their healing. With a powerful healing testimony of her own and Scriptures showing a God who performs miracles, Marilyn's approach is irresistible. And she does not compromise her own faith but upholds Christian principles including praying "in Jesus' name." As healing testimonies come forth, people are overwhelmed with the goodness of the one true God and His Son, Jesus.

Building a Bridge in Cairo

Shortly after Anwar Sadat, the president of Egypt, was assassinated in 1981, Marilyn received a call from a consultant, asking if she might be able to help bring Bibles to Egypt in Arabic and air a satellite program from Cairo. Marilyn had taken a number of trips to the Holy Land, but at that time, her experience with Muslims was limited. Marilyn recalls, "I was told we could even sell Bibles in public places. I felt impressed to pursue this and prayed the Lord would provide the opportunities needed."

After planning with her international team, it was decided to do a satellite broadcast right out of Cairo; it would air in 29 cities to raise funds for the Bibles. Country officials told Marilyn she would need $5,000 to cover the cost of taping and airing the program, and for printing the Bibles.

"After I arrived, I found myself in a real dilemma," Marilyn remembers. "I had brought money to print the Bibles, but as I checked through customs, I was asked to give the money to the government, so I did. Well, I soon found out it was a foolish thing to do, and I needed help. Through the power of networking, I was able to get help. I had tea with Jehan Sadat (wife of the late president, Anwar Sadat) and was invited to her mansion on the Nile."

It was an amazing meeting that opened Marilyn's eyes to the Muslim world. Jehan made some calls and Marilyn was able to record and air her program as planned. "I told her I loved the people of Egypt. I knew she was grieving over her husband's death and asked if I could pray for her, and so we did," Marilyn explains. "The next thing I knew she was making a call to someone, and I was able to do the programs I set out to do. I was overwhelmed with gratitude and somewhat taken aback that she would go to this trouble."

Ministry in Sudan

Marilyn traveled to Sudan in December of 2008 to hold the first Christian meetings in a public stadium ever in that country. It had taken several years of overcoming setbacks and much negotiation to finally see the meetings come to pass. Marilyn says, "Getting back into the country was a miracle in and of itself."

The first night 37,000 people attended. Then the second night they had 45,000. The third night followed with 54,000 and more than 60,000 attended the final night with 10,000 plus outside the stadium!

The attendance at the pastors and leaders conference increased every day starting with 1,800 and ending with 3,700. There were over 20,000 salvations recorded and numerous healings and miracles. Government officials and dignitaries also attended every night. It was an amazing success and a testimony of the hunger for the saving message of Jesus Christ in Muslim nations. Marilyn adds, "We pushed and pressed for a long time, but *this* was the right time."

Marilyn believes her burden for Muslims began during a time of intensive intercession, more than 20 years ago. It was a time when she felt led to pray for every country of the world and as a result gained a greater sensitivity for the Muslim nations. Not long afterwards, opportunities began to open for Marilyn Hickey Ministries to hold meetings in these areas. Prayer is powerful and reveals the heart of God.

American Muslims

Marilyn is also intensely aware of the Muslim population in the United States that has been estimated to be anywhere from two to eight million. Marilyn's hometown of Denver has a Muslim population estimated at 20,000. Her heart is to build bridges between Christian believers and Muslims at home and abroad, which could be considered difficult in light of the 9/11 terrorist attack and continued terrorism by Muslim extremists. Marilyn realizes however that "for God so loved the world" includes all people groups. Jesus says we are to love our neighbors and if our neighbors are Muslims, we are to show the love of God. Marilyn believes that we should at least try to understand their culture and look for ways to minister and pray.

While Marilyn was speaking in Detroit, she learned the highest concentration of Muslims in the United States was located there—

estimated at 250,000. Through a Divine appointment, she was invited by Emam Elahi to lead a healing meeting at the International House of Wisdom, which is considered one of the largest mosques in the United States. A Christian woman leading a healing meeting in a mosque had never been done before—not in 1,400 years! Truly a breakthrough event, Marilyn's presentation included a film showing her ministry's outreach to Muslim countries such as Pakistan and Sudan, revealing her heart and God's love for the Muslim people. As she ministered to the sick, she prayed freely, "in Jesus' name" with two remarkable healings taking place during the meeting.

Marilyn is excited to see what God is doing in the lives of Muslims all over the world. She exclaims, "I have another invitation to a mosque in Jakarta for a healing meeting! And we were just in Morocco where I believe the Lord is going to open up a healing meeting with the Sufi Muslims. Some of these things are pretty radical."

This Generation

One of the ways God has been moving in recent years is through sincere, heartfelt worship, especially in young believers. Marilyn loves the way these believers enter into worship, but she does hold some concerns. "I love the way they worship, but if they don't get into the Word, they are not going to produce." Marilyn explains, "My passion is for people to get a love for the Word and the lost."

Especially in America, Marilyn finds many Christians haven't realized the power of prayer and how it instills a passion to win the lost—truly revealing the heart of God to save humanity. It becomes a natural reaction for believers to follow the Lord's leading in sharing with others when they have spent quality time in His presence—in worship and also getting to know God's heart in prayer and through

His Word. Marilyn councils that American believers have to come alive to this or the consequences for America could be devastating. Marilyn understands the gravity of the Body of Christ influencing a nation.

In some nations, the young Christians love to pray and don't think anything about all-night prayer meetings. They have prayer vigils and when it is time to study the Bible, they are excited. Marilyn is not deterred about America, however. She says, "We have to press in. I have a small group of people under 30-years-old I mentor and they help me to understand this generation. I feel very accepted by this generation and recognize they have a great need."

Many Christians struggle with how to get their prayers answered, whether it's prayers about a broken marriage, depression, financial trouble, or a new job. Marilyn's answer is much the same as what she encourages for young believers—spend time in the Word and prayer. It may sound basic, but it is key to God being able to reveal His answers to each person. Marilyn has a little book called *Speak the Word* she likes to give away that encourages believers to pray and know what the Scripture says about life's challenges. She explains, "Many Christians in this generation speak the problem. I tell them they need to speak the promise that goes with the problem. All the promises in Him are yes and amen to the glory of God through us, not to us. God says, Yes! In Christ you can do all things in Christ who strengthens you."

Marilyn has been a student of the Word for many years and has memorized much of the Bible. She knows the power of the Living Word—it or He, rather, produces life. The Scripture tells us Jesus is the Living Word. Marilyn adds, "I really try to get people to read and speak the Word. So unless they say 'yes' with what the Word says, it's not going to work for them."

Future Ministry

Marilyn and her daughter, Sarah, have a passion for lost souls that often leads them to difficult places, including lands oppressed by communism, cruel dictators, poverty, disaster, and disease. Year after year, they cross unfriendly borders with Bibles, teaching materials, food and supplies, often at great personal risk.

With a true humanitarian's heart, Dr. Hickey has helped millions of individuals overcome setbacks and come to the saving knowledge of Jesus Christ. Through her television and Internet ministry, books, audio messages, and healing outreaches, Marilyn will continue to answer the call. Her hope is that you too will answer the call God has given you.

Chapter 3

Women in Ministry?

"I am asked how it feels to have a traveling, part-time wife and how it feels to be the husband of Marilyn Hickey. I have no problem with it for I am super-proud of her. Marilyn's wide acceptance in the Body of Christ is a delight to me. Really, she's some lady!"

—Wallace Hickey

A s a woman in ministry, Marilyn has addressed the topic of how God views women and especially in a position of authority in ministry. Her little book titled *Women of the Word* has gone around the world and encouraged women everywhere that God has a place for them whether in full-time ministry or ministry to their family, neighbors, community, and local church.

Marilyn's husband Wally introduces this message with these words:

As Marilyn's teaching ministry has continued to grow under the blessing of the Lord, I've had an influx of questions asked of me regarding the Scripture: "I suffer not a woman to teach" (1 Timothy 2:12).

I react in varied ways to this question, sometimes going into long scriptural defenses and explanations. But my shortest treatment has been: "You know, when I look around and see the world dying and going to hell, I really don't believe God cares very much who brings the saving message!"

The following excerpts are taken from *Women of the Word*.

Women of the Word

Many times women have said to me, "Marilyn, I have the feeling God thinks women are second-class citizens." The more I dig into the Word of God, the more I want to respond with a shout, "Untrue! God loves women!"

The "bad guy" in the Bible is not God, but the devil! Satan began his devious methods on Eve in the Garden and he has never stopped harassing her ancestors. Let's look at God's real feelings and His abundant provisions for women by going back to the "seed plot" of the Bible—the Book of Genesis.

In Genesis 2:7, God formed man from the dust of the earth, and the Hebrew word for "formed" is *yatsar*, which means "to mold like a potter or squeeze into shape."

An entirely different word is used when it comes to Eve's construction in Genesis 2:22. When God made Eve, the Hebrew word *banah* is used and means "skillfully formed." Eve was not squeezed out, but skillfully formed and carefully molded. God's treatment of Eve from the beginning was super special, with care and gentleness.

When God gave His blessing in the Garden, He blessed both Adam and Eve with five blessings. He directed them: Be fruitful, and multiply, and replenish the earth, and subdue it: and have dominion (Genesis 1:28).

Both male and female were made in His image, and both were given power and dominion. God did not take woman from man's foot for man to trample upon her; she was to be his equal and near his heart. That is why she was taken from the very rib of man.

Protected by Families

God's tender, loving care is shown in His command in Genesis 2:24: "Therefore shall a man leave his father and his mother, and shall cleave unto his wife: and they shall be one flesh." Men were to leave their immediate families; women were not. This is shown very clearly in Genesis 24 and the account of the servant's search for Isaac's bride.

Abraham asked his faithful and wise steward to go back to his ancient homeland in Mesopotamia, unto the city of Nahor, to find a bride for Isaac. He was given specific instructions to bring back a bride for Isaac. Isaac was not to join his bride in Mesopotamia, even though it was customary for the new husband to leave his family and to join his wife's family.

The command was to be changed as Isaac's new bride joined him in God's Promised Land. If she refused (which she had the right to do), the servant would then be free from Abraham's charge to him. Rebekah, the bride he chose, could have refused because of God's marriage law, but she did not; she went willingly to meet her new husband, Isaac.

It is also interesting to note that Jacob did not require Rachel and Leah to return with him to his homeland. He "requested" they go with him for he knew he was to leave his parents, but they were not to leave theirs.

In Judges 15 we find Samson's wife stayed with her family; and in Matthew 25 the virgins waited at the home of the bride. Why did God call men to leave their homes? Why didn't He call women to leave their parents? Because He wanted the bride's parents to watch over her in order to add protection should her husband become abusive.

Enmity with the Woman

Eve's sin in the Garden was no greater than Adam's. In Genesis 2:15, Adam was commanded to dress and keep the Garden. In verse 18, God said, "It is not good that the man should be alone: I will make him an help meet for him." From this context we can see that Adam was not only to dress the Garden, he was also to protect it; but Adam did not protect the tree on that infamous day when Eve ate from it.

From that dreadful moment on, there has been a burning enmity between Satan and the woman. God commanded in Genesis 3:15: "I will put enmity between thee and the woman, and between thy seed and her seed; it shall bruise thy head, and thou shalt bruise his heel." Satan knew his days were numbered. A Seed was to come through woman to give him an eternal bruising. Through the virgin birth, God was to send a Savior—Jesus Christ—and through faith in Him, salvation would be open to all who believed. Satan persecuted woman in child-bearing for she was his enemy, but her Seed-to-come would be his greatest enemy.

It is interesting to note here that God intervened on woman's behalf. First Timothy 2:15 declares she would be saved in child-bearing.

The words of God struck deep into the heart of Eve. They also brought hope out of trouble to the defeated Adam, for he knew there would come redemption through the woman's Seed.

Women and Prophecy

Genesis 3:20 tells us Adam called his wife's name "Eve" because she was the mother of all living. Her name means "the mother of the living one." When Eve gave birth to her first son, Cain, she boldly confessed her faith: "I have gotten a man from the LORD" (Gen. 4:1). I believe that at that moment, the Spirit of prophecy rested upon her.

God also looked down the ages of time and gently touched a frustrated, barren wife—Hannah (1 Samuel 1). Through her barrenness, she cried out to God and received a son, Samuel. She then prophesied a prayer and spoke another title of the coming Son of God. She called her Lord the Anointed One, which is another word for Messiah (1 Samuel 2:35). Hannah was the first to use it, the first ever to utter the revelation of the Messiah; and her revelation would rock the world throughout the eons of time.

Centuries passed. Then God sent His special angel on a mission to a young virgin girl named Mary, revealing to her the Name above every name (Luke 1:26-33). Things in heaven, on earth, and even under the earth, would bow to that Name. Again, a woman would speak that Name of all power—Jesus!

Three women had received the major revelation of His Name. A fallen Eve knew there was a Lord God; a faith-filled Hannah saw a coming Messiah; and a young virgin would give birth to Jesus, the Savior of the world!

The Lineage of Jesus

God called Abram to become a "Father of Altitude." The word Abram comes from the Hebrew word *abar* which means "altitude." Because of his living in the altitude of God's Word, he would become Abraham, which means the "Father of Multitudes." His wife Sarai, meaning "dominative" or contentious, would become Sarah, meaning "princess or beautiful." She would become the mother of kings and nations (Genesis 17).

First Peter 3:6 tells us Sarah obeyed Abraham and called him "lord." Yet God told Abraham in Genesis 21:12 he would profit from his wife's counsel, so they became a team of faith. Abraham received faith to expect and receive a child; Sarah received faith to expect and conceive a child.

Years later when Isaac received his lovely virgin bride, Rebekah, he took her into Sarah's tent. Perhaps he wanted her to experience the faith of his beautiful mother, Sarah.

So Rebekah became the matriarch, appearing in the Messianic lineage along with Leah, Rahab, Ruth, and others. God had a special relationship with these women, for He placed them in the lineage of Jesus Christ, His very own Son, even though they were of foreign blood.

No male could be found in the lineage of Jesus Christ unless he met two very important conditions: He had to be a descendant of Abraham, and he had to be circumcised. Yet God took women of other nations and circumstances and wrote their names for eternity in the lineage of His first-begotten Son.

Women Receive God's Revelations

God brought His revelation to Rebekah concerning her turbulent pregnancy, revealing to her the plan of two nations in her womb. He also saw fit to bring revelations to Hagar and Hannah during their pregnancies, revealing His purpose to the wife, rather than the husband.

Rachel was a gorgeous young wife with a problem. Her sister Leah bore their mutual husband one child after another, but Rachel was barren. Her problem stimulated her prayer life, for Genesis 30:22 declares: "God remembered Rachel, and God hearkened to her (prayers), and opened her womb."

Rachel conceived and bore a son, calling him Joseph, which means "adding," for later she declared, "I know God will add another son to me" (v. 24). Joseph drew on the treasure of her faith; and through his position in the wealthy nation of Egypt, he was able to save the nation of Israel from starvation.

Jacob prophesied on his deathbed that Joseph's seed would multiply and be fruitful. Rachel's two grandchildren, Ephraim and Manasseh, did become famous, for each would receive a tribal heritage of the two largest tribes of Israel. In later years, ten tribes of the North would adopt the name of Ephraim as their national name. Truly, Rachel's seed was a "fruitful bough" for instead of adding, God multiplied her seed many times!

Women as Prophetesses

Next we see God's women used as prophetesses. We see their ministries varied and flexible, combining unique personality traits.

Miriam was the prophetess sister of Moses and Aaron. In Exodus 15:20, her prophecy was sung and she joined the other women of Israel to dance in joyous abandonment before the Lord after He had parted, then closed, the Red Sea. God declared in Micah 6:4 that He sent Moses, Aaron, and Miriam before Israel as leaders of the Israelites' journey to the Promised Land.

Judges 4 gives the account of another singing prophetess, Deborah, who saved her nation. Her name means "buzzing bee," and her words carried a sting to Barak, urging him to fulfill his duty as the military leader of Israel (Judges 4:6). She was happily married to Lapidoth and did her judging in an unusual environment—by sitting under a palm tree!

Isaiah, the prince of prophets, married a prophetess who bore him a son with one of the longest names in the Bible: "Maher-shalal-hash-baz" (Isaiah 8:3).

Huldah was another prophetess of the Old Testament, who was not a singer, but a teacher. Second Chronicles 34:22 describes her as the scholarly type, who dwelt in a college in Jerusalem, and was held in high esteem for her knowledge of the Word.

There were also false prophetesses, even as there were false prophets. Ezekiel 13:17 states: "Likewise, thou son of man, set thy face against the daughters of thy people, which prophesy out of their own heart; and prophesy thou against them." Nehemiah 6:14 declares: "My God, think thou upon Tobiah and Sanballat according to these their works, and on the prophetess Noadiah, and the rest of the prophets, that would have put me in fear."

Jeremiah spoke concerning the women prophetesses of his day: "…send for cunning (wise) women, that they may come" (Jeremiah

9:17). In Jeremiah 9:20 he said: "Yet hear the word of the LORD, O ye women, and let your ear receive the word of his mouth, and teach your daughters wailing, and every one her neighbour lamentation."

In the New Testament, Philip the evangelist had a house full of prophetesses. He had four daughters called into this special ministry of God (Acts 21:8-9).

God's Compassion for Women

There is a beautiful tenderness in both Testaments in relation to God's concern for the physical needs and feelings of women. After all, He had carefully constructed them, and they would need special care.

In Leviticus 20:18 is a warning against unhygienic conduct which is forbidden in marriage relationships: "If a man shall lie with a woman having her sickness, and shall uncover her nakedness; he hath discovered her fountain, and she hath uncovered the fountain of her blood: and both of them shall be cut off from among their people."

Also, in Leviticus 15:19 God saw that special care was taken during a woman's menstrual time. Rachel is seen taking special care during her menstrual time in Genesis 31:35.

In God's eyes, women were of equal value as men. The law of "an eye for an eye and a tooth for a tooth" was applied to women as well as men in Exodus 21:22-25.

God was even concerned about provisions made for captive women (Deuteronomy 21:10-14). He also made special provisions concerning a woman's inheritance and possessions (Numbers 27:1-11), and special laws were set aside to protect women from jealous husbands (Numbers 5).

Jesus loved women in a very special way and spoke of their importance to God. He was greatly concerned about the pregnant women during the end-time disaster that is to come, for He said in Luke 21:23, "Woe unto them that are with child, and to them that give suck, in those days!" He speaks of this concern in three of the Gospels.

In John 8:3, when a woman was taken in the very act of adultery and thrown before a mixed jeering crowd, Jesus stood with her and would not allow the angry mob to cast stones at her.

During His agony on the cross, Jesus was still concerned enough for women to ask His disciple, John, to care for His mother, Mary, in her later years (John 19:26-27).

Both the Old and New Testament directed women to submit to their husbands, but never to be slave to them. The word subjection does not mean "to obey," but "to arrange in order."

In 1 Samuel 25, Abigail does not obey her husband, but instead brings food to the enemy of her husband and her household. The Bible tells us to feed our enemies. Because of Abigail's obedience to the Word, she saved her entire household and later became queen as the wife of David.

Women are Anointed by God

God pointed to a special anointing for His "carefully constructed creation." A certain number of feast days were required for all men to attend, but there was also one special festival for women—the

Feast of Pentecost—which was to have much bearing on their future. Deuteronomy 16:11 reads:

And thou shalt rejoice before the Lord thy God, thou, and thy son, and thy daughter, and thy manservant, and thy maidservant, and the Levite that is within thy gates, and the stranger, and the fatherless, and the widow, that are among you, in the place which the Lord thy God hath chosen to place his name there.

Isaiah prophesied that women would be Spirit-filled; and Joel—the mighty prophet of Pentecost—spoke concerning the details and manifestations of these Spirit-filled women (Isaiah 32:9-15, Joel 2:28-29).

Chapter 2 of Acts describes the day of Pentecost when a group of 120 men and women were assembled—including Mary, the mother of Jesus. Suddenly, God poured out His Spirit as was promised by Moses, Isaiah, and Joel; and Peter stood in boldness before the world to declare this as the "outpouring" prophesied by Joel. From then on, the world could not attack God's "chosen" men or women and be guiltless.

The church that silences women silences the Holy Spirit, for both men and women are God's anointed. Psalm 105:15 declares, "Touch not mine anointed, and do my prophets no harm."

Are Women to be Silent?

Women have been used of God to speak His oracles down through the centuries. The Apostle Paul stated that women were to keep silence in the church because the law commanded it (1 Cornthians 14:34-35); however, it must have been a law of Paul's day for there is not one place in the Old Testament where God commands women to keep silent in His house.

Paul admonished women not to ask questions of their husbands during a church service, but total silence was never commanded in the Old Testament, neither was it commanded in the New Testament, by Jesus or Paul.

Women were spiritually active from the very beginning in God's worship center—the tabernacle. The Bible tells us women assembled there for prayer and fasting and were active in the spiritual life of the Jews. It was while in the tabernacle that Hannah prophesied of God's Anointed, the coming Messiah.

Nehemiah 7:67 also describes many women singers in the temple, which would seem to rule out women's "silence" in the church!

Jesus never told women not to speak; He encouraged them to do so.

Luke 8:47 describes the declaration of joy from the woman who was healed of an issue of blood: "And when the woman saw that she was not hid, she came trembling, and falling down before him, she declared unto him before all the people for what cause she had touched him, and how she was healed immediately."

On another occasion, we read in Luke 11:27: "A certain woman of the company lifted up her voice, and said unto him, Blessed is the womb that bare thee." Jesus answered, "Yea rather, blessed are they that hear the word of God, and keep it" (vs. 28).

Jesus had a very special entourage of women who testified of His resurrection. In fact, women were the first ones present at the tomb to bear record after His resurrection. Luke 24:1-2 reads: "Now upon the first day of the week, very early in the morning, they (the women) came unto the sepulcher…and they found the stone rolled away from the sepulcher."

It was the witness of these women that brought the good news of the Resurrection to the world. If these women had kept their silence, we would not have read their glorious account in all four of the Gospels!

Women continued to witness after Jesus' resurrection, and they were thrown in prison for doing so. In Acts 8:3, we read of Saul who made havoc of the Church, entering into every house, taking men and women, and committing them to prison.

Women in the Home

Special commands and ministries were given to women in the home, for women were to be builders of the home. Proverbs 14:1 declares: "Every wise woman buildeth her house: but the foolish plucketh it down with her hands."

Judges 13 gives the account of God's angel appearing to Manoah's wife with special instructions on how to raise the son she would soon bear. Not only was her son to be a Nazarite, she was also to take a Nazarite vow during her pregnancy. She boldly named her newborn son, Samson, which means "like the sun."

Being true to his name, Samson brought rays of light to the hopeless situation facing the Hebrews, for God used his life to deliver Israel from their dreaded enemy, the Philistines.

Samson was one of the most eminent of the Hebrew judges (Judges 14-16). The Spirit of the Lord had moved early upon him in the camp of Dan between Zorah and Eshtaol; but almost from the outset, he showed a weakness of character—a passion for women. Even though he had godly parents who carefully watched their son grow and be blessed, they also questioned certain areas of Samson's life, especially his choice of a wife.

The life of Samson was like a roller coaster, rising and falling with gladness and sadness, until finally his life ended tragically, but victoriously "like the sun."

Women in Marriage Relationships

In regard to the institution of marriage, God's Word makes it clear that there is to be one wife to a household. Exodus 20:17 states, "Thou shalt not covet...thy neighbour's wife" (not wives). Deuteronomy 28:54 speaks of the "wife of his bosom" (not wives). Psalm 128:3 declares: "Thy wife (not wives) shall be as a fruitful vine." Then in Ephesians 5:22, Paul exhorts the woman to submit, not to every man, but to one man—her very own husband.

God's Word points out that divorce could harm a home, so why did Moses allow divorce? He permitted it, not because it was right to do so, but because there was "wrong" in men. Jesus answered this question also in Matthew 19:8: "Moses because of the hardness of your hearts suffered you to put away your wives: but from the beginning it was not so."

The Old Testament did not sanction polygamy, but there were laws to protect "lesser" wives who were victims of death or divorce. Deuteronomy 21:15-18 refers to the birthright law: If a man hated his first wife, he could not transfer the birthright from the first wife's eldest son to the favored wife's son.

Many times in the Old Testament, circumstance showed closer ties between a child and its mother than with the father. Samuel's mother, Hannah, had more to do with him than his father, perhaps because of the two wives in the household. Because of the love of a godly mother, Samuel was raised in godly fashion and became the "Seer of Israel." He anointed the first king and was instrumental in establishing a school for prophets, which would produce some of the greatest prophets of the Old Testament. Hannah had built her house well!

Wisdom for Women

God has allowed me to find many Scriptures that have been applicable in my own life. Sometimes when my husband and I would be spending a quiet evening together in our home, I might be studying and preparing for my Sunday school lesson. As I would dig into God's Word, I would find many precious treasures and become very excited about some new nugget of truth God had just revealed to me.

When I would eagerly try to share these with my husband, thinking he would be as excited as I, many times he would react with a "ho-hum" attitude, totally disconnected with the truth I was sharing. Yet, if he happened to slip into my Sunday school class and hear me explain the same truth, he would be ecstatic after the class: "Marilyn, where did you get that revelation? It was outstanding!"

What was the explanation for his former attitude? The Holy Spirit gently revealed the truth of this unusual circumstance to me; and I learned when and how to share revelations with my loving husband. I want to share this truth with you. Maybe it can help you, too.

In our home, I am Wally's wife. I am called to love him, not teach him. However, when I stand behind the pulpit, I am neither male nor female—I am God's messenger with God's message.

Christian women have a very special birthright. They are divine citizens with a divine heritage and birthright. In Genesis 25, Esau treated his birthright lightly and finally sold it for a bowl of stew. Women can sell their spiritual birthrights also by feeling that their only place is in a kitchen, cooking stew! We can be good cooks, and should be, but we also have a divine heritage to minister in our own unique situation.

Allow me to challenge the faith of every woman who reads this book. Don't despise the birthright God has given you, for you, too, can be a woman of the Word!

Part Two

Breaking Generational Curses

Chapter 4

In the Beginning

One of Marilyn's most popular books is *Breaking Generational Curses,* with hundreds of thousands of copies sold all over the globe. This message resonates with people worldwide who have struggled with sin and iniquity in their personal life or in members of their family. The following passages are highlights from this best-selling book.

In the Beginning

In the beginning, God created the perfect family. He created Adam and Eve and placed them in a utopian setting in the Garden of Eden with a charge to be blessed and live an abundant life:

> *And God blessed them, and God said unto them, Be fruitful, and multiply, and replenish the earth, and subdue it: and have dominion over the fish of the sea, and over the fowl of the air, and over every living thing that moveth upon the earth.... I have given you every herb bearing seed, which is upon the face of all the earth, and every tree...to you it shall be for meat. And to every beast of the*

earth, and to every fowl of the air, and to every thing that creepeth upon the earth, wherein there is life, I have given every green herb for meat.

Genesis 1:28-30

Adam and Eve walked in the fullness of God's provision until Satan deceived them and they lost their dominion over the earth. Prior to their fall, their family was blessed. After the fall, however, the curse of sin, death, and destruction entered, and the family as God originally created it has not been the same since.

Because of their transgression, Adam and Eve placed themselves under a curse that not only impacted their family, but all of the families that have come after them. God pronounced a curse upon the serpent and the land. Adam was sentenced to a life of hard labor, and Eve's pain during childbearing was greatly increased. Adam and Eve went from a place of great abundance, prosperity, and peace to a place of death, disease, and fear. Every undesirable, hereditary trait that seems to "run in the family" came directly from the sin of Adam and Eve. They are directly responsible for what is known today as the "generational curse."

To the woman he said, "I will greatly increase your pains in child-bearing; with pain you will give birth to children"... To Adam he said..."Cursed is the ground because of you; through painful toil you will eat of it all the days of your life. It will produce thorns and thistles for you, and you will eat the plants of the field. By the sweat of your brow you will eat your food..."*

Genesis 3:16-19 NIV

If there is anything that you and I want, it is for our families to be strong, healthy, and blessed. Yet, from the beginning, we see the degeneration of the family structure. As we trace Adam and Eve's family tree, we discover that after they were evicted from the Garden, Eve gave birth to two sons, Cain and Abel.

Cain became jealous of his brother, Abel, and murdered him. (Genesis 4:5, 8.) Cain's descendant, Lamech, followed in his forefather's footsteps and also murdered a man (Genesis 4:23), There is a definite hereditary trait that passed from one generation to the other.

Sins Revisited

In Exodus 20:5, we discover a profound truth having to do with these hereditary traits or family weaknesses that are passed from generation to generation:

> *Thou shalt not bow down thyself to them [idols], nor serve them: for I the Lord thy God am a jealous God, visiting the iniquity of the fathers upon the children unto the third and fourth generation of them that hate me.*

I'm sure all of us can think of certain families who have been ripped apart by such problems as alcoholism, obesity, or teenage pregnancy. You may be able to examine your own family tree and recognize a pattern of disease or infirmity. Or you may see a certain characteristic, such as adultery or child abuse, and think, *Wow, my family tree is a mess.* Don't panic! God has made a provision for you and your future generations.

Isaiah 53:12 says Jesus bore our sins. The Bible makes a distinction between the terms sin, iniquity, and transgression. Not only did Jesus bear our sins on Calvary, but He also bore our transgressions and iniquities: "He was wounded for our transgressions, he was bruised for our iniquities: the chastisement of our peace was upon him; and with his stripes we are healed" (Isaiah 53:5).

Sin means to miss the mark or a "deliberate violation of moral principle." So when you sin, you miss the mark or fall below the mark of what God has called you to do. We all have been guilty of missing the mark at some time in our lives: "For all have sinned, and come short of the glory of God" (Romans 3:23).

Transgress, when used with an object, on the other hand, means to trespass or overstep pre-established boundaries. We can trespass against man and God. If I were to come up to you and purposely step on your foot or violate your "No Trespassing" sign by entering onto your property without permission, I'd be transgressing against you.

But Jesus was wounded for our transgressions (Isaiah 53:5). If you look at the body of Christ, you'll see seven times Jesus' blood was shed: He was circumcised at birth; His beard was plucked; a crown of thorns was pressed on His head; His hands, feet and side were pierced; and His back was beaten. Seven is the number of completion, and I believe God is telling us that Jesus has completely provided for every kind of weakness, infirmity, and transgression that we could have through the seven wounds He endured. We can truly say Christ's provision is full and complete.

The Mystery of Iniquity

The word "iniquity" means to bend or to distort (the heart) or "gross injustice or wickness." It also implies a certain weakness or predisposition toward a certain sin. Isaiah says Christ was "bruised for our iniquities" (53:5).

If you commit a certain sin once and repent of it and never do it again, then that's the end of it. However, your sin becomes an iniquity when you keep committing that same act; it goes from being a sin to an iniquity, something that is practiced over and over again until it becomes spontaneous. Given certain circumstances or the "right" environment, you will "bend" in that direction.

If a sin is repeatedly committed, it becomes an iniquity that can be passed down through the bloodline. When a person continually transgresses the law, iniquity is created in him and that iniquity is passed to his children. The offspring will have a weakness to the same kind of sin. Each generation adds to the overall iniquity, further weakening the resistance of the next generation to sin.

Exodus 20:5 speaks very specifically about the iniquities of the forefathers. If the family tree is not cleansed of this iniquity, then each generation becomes worse and will do what their parents, grandparents, and great-grandparents did. The next generation will bend in the same way of the past generations, and it becomes a bond of iniquity or a generational curse in that family.

We have all seen where one or both parents or grandparents were alcoholics, and one or more of the offspring became alcoholics, too. And to think it all started as a sin with that one person who overindulged; but because he practiced it and did not repent, his drinking became an iniquity. Consequently, that family begins to bend or have a predisposition toward alcoholism.

Let me give you an example. My father had two nervous breakdowns. I didn't know this until later, but my great-grandfather had mental and emotional problems as well. I never thought of that as being an inherited trait or something that I had a predisposition toward.

When I was thirty-six-years-old, however, I was under tremendous pressure. The devil spoke to me and said, "You are just like your father. You look and act like him. You are going to have a nervous breakdown just like he did."

I foolishly agreed, "Yes, I'm just like my father. I'm going to have a nervous breakdown too." It was at that point that the Lord spoke to me and said, "That's right! You are just like your Father! I'm your Father, and I've never had a nervous breakdown. And neither will you!"

Jesus was bruised for my iniquities! Through the wounds and bruises He endured on the cross, the provision has been made to restore you and your family to that state of blessedness Adam and Eve once enjoyed in the Garden.

The difference between a wound and a bruise is that if you wound yourself, it will eventually scab over and heal. A bruise, however, can stay around for a long time. It may become discolored and can even go so deep as to bruise the bone. An iniquity can be compared to a bruise because it stays around and goes to the bone from generation, to generation, to generation.

The apostle Paul had a revelation of this when he wrote: "For the mystery of iniquity doth already work" (2 Thessalonians 2:7). The "mystery of iniquity" to which Paul is referring is the unseen and mysterious connection between a father's sins and the path of his children. For example, if the father is a liar and a thief, his children are prone to the same behavior, regardless of their training, social, cultural, and environmental influences.

Both sin and iniquity are spiritual terms. We don't always grasp the significance of such terms as we would for something relating to the natural. Paul wrote that the things not seen are understood by the things which are made (Romans 1:20). He was referring to the natural universe—creation—when he spoke of the things that are "made." Likewise, the spiritual can be understood by the natural.

The Law of Generation

Everything produces after its own kind. Within every seed, there is inherent ability to reproduce itself. Jesus used this law of generation in the Sermon on the Mount when He said:

> *Beware of false prophets, who come to you in sheep's clothing, but inwardly they are ravenous wolves. You will know them by their fruits. Do men gather grapes from thornbushes or figs from thistles? Even so, every good tree bears good fruit, but a bad tree bears bad fruit.*
>
> *Matthew 7:15-17 NKJV*

In the natural, we know that if the fruit is malformed or if the tree is not bearing fruit according to its stock, a mutation has taken place. The same is true in the breeding of animals. If the offspring are not true to the breed, the breeders usually "eliminate" from their pool of animals. Mutants are not wanted. They are a corruption of the line of animals being bred.

As illustrated in the creation of the earth in Genesis Chapter 1, everything reproduces after its own kind. We acknowledge this principle in buying a pedigreed animal, but we completely ignore this principle when we deal with people.

When you go to a medical doctor for a physical examination or because you have a medical problem, he will usually take a medical history before he begins his diagnosis and treatment. What you tell him of your past problems, and the problems your parents, grandparents, and siblings may have an effect on what he may look for and what tests he may order. Many diseases are genetic or inherent in a family line. These disorders may be in some or all of the offspring or may skip a generation or two and occur in the grandchildren or great-grandchildren.

Healthy couples who have healthy ancestors almost always have healthy offspring. This is the law of generation set in motion in Genesis 1: everything reproduces after its own kind. Genetic inheritance is a natural counterpart to spiritual inheritance. Understanding natural laws concerning genetic inheritance gives us a working model for the principle of spiritual inheritance.

The Bible gives examples of spiritual laws and their workings in the lives of various characters and their descendants. Noah was a man who was "perfect in his generations, and Noah walked with God" (Genesis 6:9). However, although Noah was considered "perfect," there were still some flaws in his bloodline. His son Ham was especially affected by the curse of iniquity.

When Noah became drunk in Genesis 10:20-22, he lost control of Ham. The weakness to sin caused him to give in to temptation, and the Bible says that Noah was "uncovered" in his tent. The Hebrew word for "uncovered" is used in Leviticus many times, primarily in regard to sexual sins involving incest. It is highly unlikely that it was a simple case of nudity. The curse that Noah pronounced on Canaan was too drastic for such a trivial thing as that. When we regard God's displeasure with homosexuality, we see that He judged this sin very severely. Scripture bears out this was indeed the case with Ham.

The Amorites were descendants of Canaan, who in turn descended from Ham. They were in the land of Canaan, which is the land that the Israelites were to take by force from the Amorites. These were the people who were worshiping all manner of idols and false gods, and their worship was characterized by gross sexual perversions and orgies.

The Amorites' Iniquity

In Genesis 15, we read that God gave assurance to Abram that he would inherit the land of promise because his descendants would go to a strange land for four hundred years, but after four generations they would return because "...the iniquity of the Amorites is not yet full" (Genesis 15:16).

If you recall in Genesis 13, Abram and his nephew Lot separated, and Lot chose to settle in a plain where the cities of Sodom and Gomorrah were located. The inhabitants of these cities were also Canaanites. Like the Canaanites, they practiced homosexuality, and their cities were ultimately destroyed because of it.

Abraham negotiated with God for Sodom and Gomorrah, but only righteous Lot and his family were spared. Because the rest of the inhabitants were totally corrupt, they were annihilated. At that time, the iniquity of the Sodomites and the Gomorrahites was full:

> *And Abraham drew near [to God], and said, Wilt thou also destroy the righteous with the wicked? Peradventure there be fifty righteous within the city: wilt thou also destroy and not spare the place for the fifty righteous that are therein? And the Lord said, If I find in Sodom fifty righteous within the city, then I will spare all the place for their sakes.... [And Abraham said] Peradventure ten shall be found there. And he said, I will not destroy it for ten's sake.*
>
> Genesis 18:23–24, 26, 32

The mystery of iniquity had already come to pass: the sins of the fathers had been passed to the third and fourth generations of the inhabitants of Sodom and Gomorrah. By three or four generations of successive and cumulative iniquity, the children were so crooked and perverse that there was no possibility that they would ever walk uprightly before the Lord. By four generations, their spiritual bloodline was completely corrupt and defiled. Their hearts were inclined only to evil. It was in reference to the Canaanites that God said to Israel in Deuteronomy 20:16,17: "But of the cities of these people, which the LORD thy God doth give thee for an inheritance, thou shalt save alive nothing that breatheth: but thou shalt utterly destroy them."

God's command to Israel was to kill everything that was alive—both people and animals—to kill everything that could harbor evil spirits. The New Testament gives evidence that animals can harbor spirits: "Then went the devils out of the man, and entered into the swine: and the herd ran violently down a steep place into the lake, and were choked" (Luke 8:33).

The iniquity of the Canaanites was so entrenched that they had to be completely eliminated from the face of the earth in order to destroy their bloodline. To allow them to remain would have subjected Israel to the possibility of becoming contaminated with the same iniquity, and that iniquity would no doubt have spread throughout the nation.

Israel, however, did get into serious trouble when they failed to execute God's judgments. Neglecting to eliminate the Canaanites allowed iniquity to multiply, and when the land fell to iniquity, God brought the sword and purified it. Ezekiel 8 and 9 give a vivid picture of God's having to cleanse the bloodline. In Ezekiel 8, we see the charge God had against Israel—idolatry with its attendant deterioration of moral and social disciplines. And in chapter 9, God commanded angels to slay everyone in the city who didn't have the "mark" of God on his or her forehead:

> *Go ye after him through the city, and smite: let not your eye spare, neither have ye pity: slay utterly old and young, both maids, and little children, and women: but come not near any man upon whom is the mark; and begin at my sanctuary. Then they began at the ancient men which were before the house. And he said unto them, Defile the house, and fill the courts with the slain: go ye forth. And they went forth, and slew in the city.*
>
> *Ezekiel 9:5-7*

Ezekiel recoiled in anguish at the slaughter and feared that none of the Israelites would be left. God's response to him was that He was doing what was necessary to cleanse the bloodline:

> *Then said he unto me, The iniquity of the house of Israel and Judah is exceeding great, and the land is full of blood, and the city full of perverseness: for they say, The Lord hath forsaken the earth, and the Lord seeth not. And as for me also, mine eye shall not spare, neither will I have pity, but I will recompense their way upon their head.*
>
> *Ezekiel 9:9,10*

God assured the prophet that all would be well, because in the end—after the judgments had fallen and only the righteous remained—the generations who would come from them would be righteous and serve the Lord (Ezekiel 14:22-23).

Iniquity, like sin, must be dealt with. People in both the Old and New Testaments understood this and traced their sins back to their forefathers. In Daniel 9:16, Daniel talks about the iniquity of "our fathers." In Psalm 51:5, David said, "Behold, I was shapen in iniquity; and in sin did my mother conceive me." It wasn't the sexual act that was sin, because God created the sexual union for people to reproduce and for pleasure within the bonds of marriage. David was actually saying, "I inherited the iniquity of my fathers, and through conception, their weaknesses have been passed down to me."

You've probably heard the expression: "You're just like your Aunt So-and-so." Lamentations 5:7 says, "Our fathers have sinned, and are not; and we have borne their iniquities." In other words, Aunt So-and-so may be dead, but you are carrying her iniquity or that same predisposition to sin.

As I mentioned earlier, I've seen certain behavioral characteristics in my family from time to time that I know are inherited from my parents and grandparents. I recognize them as iniquities, but I've come to realize that I don't have to live under a generational curse—and neither do you! Jesus was bruised for our iniquities, thereby making it possible for us and our children to inherit family blessings.

Chapter 5

What Brings the Curse?

Most Christians try their best to walk in the light of God's Word, and they often check on themselves to see if they're sinning against God in some way or another. But when you realize that you can come under a curse for which you are not personally responsible but which you have inherited through your ancestors, that's bad news!

God has been instructing me for a long time about blessings and curses. Some time ago, I became concerned about some of the things that have gone on in the lives of people to whom we have ministered. Terrible things were happening—asthma, cancer, obesity, alcoholism, heart conditions—and God began to show me, piece by piece, where these things really came from. These things that harass and plague us are actually *family or generational curses*—problems that began back with our ancestors and have been carried through our bloodlines until today. What's worse, they won't stop here, but can be passed on to our children and to our children's children!

The World Knows

Even the world is aware of commonalities in bloodlines. When you fill out an insurance form of any kind, it usually asks, "Is there any history of heart disease in your family? Diabetes? Cancer? Mental illness?" Why do they ask that? Because doctors understand that if such problems or diseases are in your background, you could have them too.

The mother of a woman on our staff died of an asthma-like condition. Sure enough, this woman began to suffer the same symptoms that had killed her mother. I believe that an evil spirit of disease had attacked the mother; and then when she died, that spirit waited for the next generation to attack again.

Wally and I have an adopted son, Michael. Mike was three-and-a-half when we adopted him, and he has experienced many different problems through the years. I used to wonder, *We raised him right. Why does he still experience such difficulties?* Of course, we did some things wrong; there's no question of that, and we repented of the things we did wrong. But I thought, *I never taught him to do these things, so where did they come from?*

Then I began to see that these hideous things come down from generation to generation, attacking one family member after the next. Mike didn't get those problems from Wally or me; he got them from somewhere in his biological family's history. But we're his adopted and spiritual family, and we've taken authority over the problems and have released him from the generational curse!

My Family History

I was visiting my eighty-three-year-old aunt in Sewickley, Pennsylvania. She was so healthy and doing so well that I asked her, "What is the longevity of our family?" My maiden name is Sweitzer, and she answered, "Well, the Sweitzers have a history of heart trouble. Most of them die of heart trouble." She began to tell me about their life spans. She also told me about my maternal grandmother: "Those are the ones who have the real longevity—they do not have heart problems."

I had a heart problem, but I didn't realize that it had come from my father's background. I was healed of that heart condition because I claimed that Jesus Christ came to break the curse for me! So when I heard about my father's history of heart trouble, I began to break that curse over my daughter Sarah's life. I know that Sarah is not going to have a heart problem. The devil is not going to come and attack Sarah—and Sarah's children and grandchildren aren't going to have heart problems either, because we've stopped the devil in his tracks!

Alcoholism is Not Necessarily a Sickness

Proverbs 26:2 says, "The curse causeless shall not come." If we see sin and various troubles affecting our family, that sin is always a curse. Sickness is always a part of the curse. Poverty can pass from generation to generation. God's Word tells us that these things don't just come on their own—there is a cause.

Alcohol is one of the devil's favorite tools to open the door to a hideous curse. Many people believe that social drinking is acceptable, but I tell you: *alcoholism is not so much a sickness as it is a sin*. And sin will always bring a curse.

Another woman on our staff told me that her grandfather was an alcoholic; and her father was an alcoholic; and then her brother was an alcoholic. That's a curse, and it comes down through the generations. When people get drunk, they do things they wouldn't normally do because their will is broken down. Habakkuk 2:15,16 tells us about this: "Woe unto him that giveth his neighbor drink, that puttest thy bottle to him, and makest him drunken also, that thou mayest look on their nakedness! Thou art filled with shame for glory: drink thou also...the cup of the LORD's right hand shall be turned unto thee, and shameful spewing shall be on thy glory."

Someone may get drunk in order to have some sort of sexual encounter or sin. Their will becomes broken down, and they fall into sin. People believe drinking is such a little thing, but Proverbs 20:1 says, "Wine is a mocker, strong drink is raging: and whosoever is deceived thereby is not wise."

"Well, I drink a little wine for my stomach's sake," you may say. I doubt that you do it for your stomach. I think you drink a little wine for a buzz, or you do it to be accepted socially. But God says that wine is a mocker, and it's raging. Why? Because it brings a curse.

Proverbs 31:4-6 talks about leadership: "It is not for kings, O Lemuel, it is not for kings to drink wine; nor for princes strong drink: lest they drink, and forget the law, and pervert the judgment of any of the afflicted. Give strong drink unto him that is ready to perish." Leaders shouldn't drink—not even socially—because they never know when they're going to be called upon to act in an emergency, and their actions can affect the whole nation.

There are two ways of looking at Proverbs 31:6: "Give strong drink unto him that is ready to perish." One is to say, "That man is dying.

Give him a drink to revive him. Get his heart pumping and stimulate him." I guess that's not so bad, but there are better ways to perform CPR!

The other way to understand Proverbs 31:6 is to say, "That man doesn't care much about life. Give him another drink so he'll slip into unconsciousness and eventually die. It looks like drinking has already killed his liver and his heart and his ambition, and there's not much left of him anyway. He's ready to give up and die, so let him have another drink." I pray you'll never get to that point of self-destruction that you'll drink yourself to death. Either way, alcohol is not good for the healthy man!

Proverbs 23:20 says, "Be not among winebibbers; among riotous eaters of flesh." Don't even run around with people who drink. Isaiah 5:11 says: "Woe unto them that rise up early in the morning, that they may follow strong drink; that continue until night, till wine inflame them!"

What's going to happen if you continue to drink and drink and drink? Not only will it kill you, but what's worse, you will have put a curse on your family and your descendants.

Breaking the Curse of Alcohol

Before you read any further, if you are fighting an alcohol problem that goes back generation after generation, stop right now and pray aloud this prayer:

Dear heavenly Father,
You love me! You sent Your Son to break this curse from
my past generation and from me. This alcoholic curse

is going to stop this very moment. By faith I proclaim that never again will I have this problem. I give this alcoholism to Jesus. Jesus, set me free! I have the name of Jesus, and I am under that name. That name covers me. That blood cleanses me right now, and I am free by the blood. In the name of Jesus, amen.

Now make this declaration of faith out loud:

Satan, you and your evil spirits of alcoholism have heard my prayer right now! You've had your chance, but your power is broken. Never again will I—nor anyone in my house—ever be a slave to alcohol. In Jesus' name, your curse is broken. Your interference in my life is stopped right now. I once was an alcoholic, but now I am delivered. The family curse is broken. None of my children, my grandchildren, or my great-grandchildren—no one in my family—will ever be an alcoholic because the blood of Jesus Christ has cleansed us today and for always. So, devil, get out of here!

When you've finished your confession of faith, remember to thank and praise Jesus often for His blood and His deliverance. Don't worry if the devil continues to attack you with this temptation. Remind him that Jesus has set you free from the curse of alcoholism. And if you need to, talk to your pastor or someone in your church; many churches have programs that help people overcome addictions with the Word of God.

Finally, be faithful to tell others where your "cure" from alcoholism came from: the mercy seat where the blood of Jesus was spilled out for you!

Sexual Sin Is a Curse

Another sin that can bring generational curses upon a family lineage is sexual sin. God destroyed Sodom and Gomorrah for the sin of homosexuality. From whom did the inhabitants of Sodom and Gomorrah descend? They descended from Canaan.

As we saw in the last chapter, Canaan was the first homosexual, and homosexuality was what the people of Sodom and Gomorrah were involved in. You can follow the lineage of the Canaanites all the way down through Joshua's day, and they were involved in sexual sins. They committed all sorts of perverse acts: homosexuality, lesbianism, sex with animals, sexual activity in front of idols.

There are curses that come down to attack a generation, and they have to be broken for them not to continue. You must break the family curse! You may have grandparents or parents or children who are involved in sexual sin—but you don't have to be defeated by it! The devil would like to put that family curse on you, but you can break its power over you and your family.

If you resist it, the devil may try to put it onto your children. Suddenly your children reach the age of twelve or thirteen, and you think, *What happened to this sweet little thing?* It does not have to be that way! Through the power of Jesus Christ, no generational curses need remain in our family lineage.

Chapter 6

Inherited Curses

Generational, or inherited, curses used to bother me terribly. I thought, *Now wait a minute! I don't want to have to answer for my great-grandfather's sin!* It's enough to answer for and deal with your own sins.

But there is a law in nature called the law of culpability. The word *culpability* means "responsibility for wrong or error or blameworthy." The Scripture says that all shall answer for their own sins. They will be accountable to God for their sins, but that weakness in an area of their lives—physically, mentally, or emotionally—is transmitted to the next generation and possibly the generation after that. And it happens because "...of them that hate me" (Exodus 20:5).

Deuteronomy 27-28 tell us all about the curses and the blessings Moses gave the children of Israel. As the curses were read out, everybody—the men, the women, the children, the grandmothers, and the grandfathers—heard them, and they answered, "Amen, so be it." God wanted them to know that sin brings a curse. He wasn't trying to be hard on them. He wanted to be good to them so they wouldn't bring curses on their lives.

Perhaps it seems strange to you to confess the sins of your parents. You're probably thinking, *Marilyn, I've never heard of this before.* The following Scriptures are only a few of the many that deal with this subject, but they will establish your heart in this almost forgotten biblical principle:

> *If they shall confess their iniquity, and the iniquity of their fathers, with their trespass which they trespassed against me, and that also they have walked contrary unto me...then will I remember my covenant.*
> *Leviticus 26:40,42*

> *And the seed of Israel separated themselves from all strangers, **and stood and confessed their sins, and the iniquities of their fathers.***
> *Nehemiah 9:2*

> *We acknowledge, O Lord, our wickedness, and the iniquity of our fathers: for we have sinned against thee.*
> *Jeremiah 14:20*

Proverbs 26:2 says, "The curse causeless shall not come," or to paraphrase, "When there is a curse on a generation, it didn't just happen to occur; there has to be a cause behind it." What is always the cause behind the curse? Sin. Sin is what always brings the curse. Any time there is a curse in a person's life, there is some root of sin.

Let me give you another example. When I visited with my aunt, I asked, "What was my grandfather like?"

She answered, "Let me tell you about your great-grandfather first. He would get drunk once a year, and then he would beat his animals. There were a lot of good things about him, but there was one bad thing: He was cruel to his animals."

Then she went on to say that my grandfather had that same kind of cruelty. In my family, we've seen that cruelty occur again and again. As we discussed in the last chapter, cruelty is a curse. When you are being cruel or unkind or hateful to somebody, you are operating in a curse.

Now let's look at curses which are inherited.

Droughts and Diseases

The Lord shall make the pestilence cleave unto thee, until he have consumed thee from off the land, whither thou goest to possess it. The Lord shall smite thee with a consumption, and with a fever, and with an inflammation, and with an extreme burning, and with the sword, and with blasting, and with mildew; and they shall pursue thee until thou perish.

Deuteronomy 28:21-22

Disease, and your enemy coming after you, would be a part of sin. When people sinned in the Old Testament, they broke the law, and then the curse could overtake them. Then God also talks about drought, a lack of rain:

And thy heaven that is over thy head shall be brass, and the earth that is under thee shall be iron. The Lord shall make the rain of thy land powder and dust: from heaven shall it come down upon thee, until thou be destroyed.

Deuteronomy 28:23-24

He was saying, "If you fall into idolatry and get into sin, you will cause drought and famine."

When the Israelites fell into idolatry under Ahab and Jezebel, Elijah prayed, "God, don't let it rain for three-and-a-half years." When the people repented, the fire from heaven fell. Then Elijah prayed, and he watched and waited—and the rain came. Why? When the people repented, they reversed the curse. The way to break the curse is by repentance.

Now how did Elijah stop the rain from falling in the first place? He used the Scriptures. He didn't get mad at Ahab and Jezebel and just spitefully say, "I'm going to stop it from raining." He simply prayed the Word of God: "As the LORD God of Israel liveth, before whom I stand, there shall not be dew nor rain these years, but according to my word" (1 Kings 17:1).

He said, "I've gone to the Word," and he prayed the Word, and he stopped the rain. Then he prayed the Word and broke the curse because the people repented, and the rain came again.

Hereditary Illnesses and Problems

Heredity can be defined as "the genetic transmission of characteristics from parent to offspring; the totality of characteristics and associated potentialities transmitted to an individual by heredity."

There are generations of families who suffer nothing but defeat. Wally and I know a family in which the grandfather was defeated, the father is defeated, and the two children of that family are defeated. One of the children died of cancer, and the other son is full of fear. I hate to think what will happen to the grandchildren and further on in generations to come.

There are certain family diseases:

The Lord wilt smite thee with the botch of Egypt, and with the emerods, and with the scab, and with the itch, whereof thou canst

not be healed. The Lord shall smite thee with madness, and blind-
ness, and astonishment of heart.

Deuteronomy 28:27-28

The "botch of Egypt" is boils and tumors; tumors are a form of cancer. Madness and astonishment of heart are confusion of mind and amnesia; these are mental illnesses. Blindness is glaucoma, cataracts, near-sightedness, farsightedness, and all other eye diseases. Have you ever seen a family in which every single one of them wears glasses? From the father and mother down to the littlest child, all wear glasses, usually those really thick-lensed kind. Those poor people are under a curse, and they need to be set free from it!

Then God talks about poverty:

Thou shalt not prosper in thy ways: and thou shalt be only oppressed and spoiled evermore, and no man shall save thee. Thou shalt be-troth a wife, and another man shall lie with her; thou shalt build an house, and thou shalt not dwell therein: thou shalt plant a vine-yard, and shalt not gather the grapes thereof.

Deuteronomy 28:29-30

"Well, I come from a family in which nobody knows how to handle their finances. No one ever taught me how to save money or to tithe or to be thrifty." We're talking about more than just careless habits or a lack of sound teaching—we're talking about being under a curse!

Another current example of the curse of poverty is the huge number of home repossessions and foreclosures going on in today's econ-omy. Verse 30 predicts this as well: "Thou shalt build an house, and thou shalt not dwell therein."

In many families, immorality is rampant: "Thou shalt betroth a wife, and another man shall lie with her" (v. 30). Here's what can happen: the alcoholic father takes his paycheck to the closest bar and drinks it all away. So his wife starts fooling around with the next-door neighbor because her husband is never home. Then there's a divorce; the abandoned wife is left with all the children and rarely does she get any child support. Those children grow up with their mother's having one boyfriend after another, and they hardly know who their father is.

Poverty breeds immorality, shame, carelessness, and crime. The curse starts in one generation and just grows and grows, making itself worse with each new generation. Where did that curse come from? Proverbs 26:2 tells us there is always a cause, so there must have been sin!

Breaking the Curse of Hereditary Disease

Let me give you some real-life examples of inherited curses. Several years ago I was teaching on the subject of healing at a Bible study in a home in Denver. A certain woman happened to attend this particular Bible study. During the teaching she just wouldn't sit down, and it bothered me. I thought she was antagonistic toward the Bible study.

Afterward I talked with her, and she said, "Well, you may say that healing is for today, but I don't believe it." Then she told me about two very desperate needs she had. Her father was blind. He had a hereditary eye disease that would usually strike each family member when they were in their early thirties. Their eyes would gradually get worse and worse, until by the time they were in their forties, they were completely blind.

This woman was in her mid-thirties, and she was starting to go blind. But even worse than that, her teenage daughter was beginning to go blind too. This was a generational curse!

I didn't know about generational curses at that time, but the more knowledge we get, the more we know how to attack the enemy and set people free: "My people are destroyed [perish] for lack of knowledge" (Hosea 4:6).

This woman was literally perishing, and so was her daughter. She didn't believe what we were studying, but she needed that healing desperately. And not only was she losing her sight, but I discovered that the reason she had been standing throughout the Bible study was that her hip bone had been operated on and part of the bone had been removed. She hadn't been able to sit comfortably for a very long period of time. She needed healing badly!

A well-known evangelist was coming to town, and some of the people in the Bible study invited this woman to go with them to his meetings, but she refused. But then her daughter said, "Mother, it can't hurt to go just one time." So she and her daughter went.

They were sitting in the balcony of the auditorium, and the evangelist called out for people who had problems in their hips or in their bone structure. The daughter said, "Mother, stand up! It couldn't hurt."

It certainly didn't hurt. She felt the warmth of the Lord go all over her. She knew something had happened, but she didn't know how to identify it.

That night as she was getting ready for bed, her daughter came in the bedroom and was talking with her. The daughter said, "Mother, there's an extra lump on you." The bone had been removed, so nothing showed. The daughter said, "Mother, feel for yourself. I think you have a hipbone now!"

The mother felt her hip, and she had a new hipbone! God had done a miracle! Her spirit caught on fire after that!

She came back to the Bible study and said, "I believe in healing! I believe in healing!" She told us her story, and then she said, "Now I want you to pray for my eyes."

We rebuked the devil and prayed for her eyes—and she has 20/20 vision today! And her daughter who was going blind is not blind today because the generational curse was broken!

Fighting the Strong Man

So how do you put a stop to so-called familiar spirits that visit your family with generational curses? You bind the strong man. Matthew 12:29 says: "Or else how can one enter into a strong man's house, and spoil his goods, except he first bind the strong man? and then he will spoil his house."

In this scripture, the word *house* can mean generation. (See Matthew10:6.) In order to break the curse of the generations before us—their habits, their sins, their physical weaknesses—we must go in and bind the strong man who has brought that curse down to us from past generations.

So who is this "strong man"? It is Satan, of course.

What do we have to do to him? We must bind him.

Then we take the *house*—or that generation—away from him!

We say, "Hey, devil, wait a minute! My generation doesn't belong to you because I bind you in the name of Jesus!"

We break that curse in the name of Jesus.

When awful things start to occur, we say, "I'm not going to have heart problems. I'm not going to have diabetes. I'm not going to be an alcoholic. I'm not going to have a weakness for immorality because my mother was involved in that. I'm not going to abuse my kids because I was beaten, or there was incest, or I was molested! That curse is not going to come on me. I'm not going to do it to my children, and my children are never going to do it to their children! I break that curse, and I bind that strong man. The curse of my generations is broken!"

But if you think you're going to tell the devil to "get lost" just once, you're wrong! He'll come back and attack you again and again. You've got to get serious.

This is an important lesson for young people. When the devil comes to you with immorality, that is a curse. Girls, when some guy wants something from you that you shouldn't be giving him, that's a curse. And, guys, when some girl tries to tempt you, that's a curse. If you get into immorality, you will bring a curse on yourself and on your children and on your children's children. Don't do it. Don't get involved. Be smart.

"Seven Other Spirits"

Matthew 12:43-45 tells us:

When the unclean spirit is gone out of a man, he walketh through dry places, seeking rest, and findeth none. Then he saith, I will return into my house from whence I came out; and when he is come, he findeth it empty, swept, and garnished. Then goeth he, and taketh with himself seven other spirits more wicked than himself, and they enter in and dwell there: and the last state of that man is worse than the first. Even so shall it be also unto this wicked generation.

When we defeat the devil the first time, we can be sure he's going to try again! Just as the Scripture says: "When the unclean spirit is gone out of a man, he walketh through dry places, seeking rest, and findeth none" (v. 43). So we see that the devil had been cast out. "Then he saith, I will return into my house...." The devil thinks that *your house*—your generation, your seed, your children—belongs to him!

That makes me so angry! The devil has the audacity to think that my house is his house! But my house does not belong to the devil. My house—my generation, my family, my children, my grandchildren—belongs to the Lord!

But what happens when the devil returns? When he comes in, he finds the house empty, swept, and garnished. You see, my house has been all cleaned up by Jesus. The Holy Spirit came in and threw out all the old junk and completely redecorated the whole place.

But what does the devil do then? He takes "seven other spirits more wicked than himself, and they enter in and dwell there: and the last state of that man is worse than the first. Even so shall it be also unto this wicked generation" (v. 45). We're talking about generations, about families. The devil will come in and attack your children with the old weaknesses and the old sins that you had...or your grandmother had... or your great-grandmother had. He'll go after your kids, and they'll be worse than you were—unless you bind the strong man in Jesus' name.

Why is this generation so bad? Sin is the worst we've ever seen it because the evil spirits have come with seven times more to attack. Whenever there has been a cleansing, they come after the kids to make them seven times worse.

You'd better believe it: *the devil is after your children.* But he doesn't get them because *your house is not his house.* Don't you dare let him take your children! Don't let your kids get into alcohol or drugs or immorality or any of that other garbage. Jesus came to set us free and to keep us free, and our houses belong to the Lord!

Familiar Spirits

Now, your generation may have been cleansed, but your children have got to walk in cleansing too! The curse has to be broken from them, too, or they will inherit the weaknesses from you which came from your father, your grandfather, and your great-grandfather.

What does the devil do? He watches for those new generations so he can attack them too. The Old Testament talks about "familiar spirits":

> *Regard not them that have familiar spirits...to be defiled by them: I am the Lord your God.*
>
> *Leviticus 19:31*

> *And the soul that turneth after such as have familiar spirits...I will even set my face against that soul, and will cut him off from among his people.*
>
> *Leviticus 20:6*

What are familiar spirits? They are fallen evil spirits that become familiar with a family. They follow that family with its weaknesses—physical, mental, emotional sin—all the way down each generation, attacking and tempting each member in that way because they already know that they have a weakness for it.

If your father was an alcoholic, those evil spirits will watch you. They know that you probably already inherited a weakness for alcohol, and they'll try to drive you crazy with that addiction. If you have children, they'll watch for the next generation to attack them too. They are familiar with your family from generation to generation, and they try to get each generation into sin so they can carry the curse on from there.

Saul and the Witch of Endor

An example of familiar spirits is given in the account of the witch of Endor (1 Samuel 28). Saul went to this witch because he had totally blown it with God. He had sinned, and he had not repented. He could have reversed his curse if he had admitted his sins to God.

God could have turned Saul's situation around just as He could have with Cain, and with Esau, Jacob's brother who gave away his birthright for a meal. (See Genesis 29:29-34.) But they didn't repent of their sins; it was always somebody else's fault. With Saul it was David's fault. With Esau it was Jacob's fault. With Cain it was Abel's fault. They didn't get their cleansings because they were too busy making their cop-outs!

And when Saul saw the host of the Philistines, he was afraid, and his heart greatly trembled. And when Saul inquired of the Lord, the Lord answered him not, neither by dreams, nor by Urim, nor by prophets. Then said Saul unto his servants, Seek me a woman that hath a familiar spirit, that I may go to her, and inquire of her. And his servants said to him, Behold, there is a woman that hath a familiar spirit at Endor. And Saul disguised himself, and put on other raiment, and he went, and two men with him, and they came to the woman by night: and he said, I pray thee, divine unto me by the familiar spirit, and bring me him up, whom I shall name unto thee.

Then said the woman, Whom shall I bring up unto thee? And he said, Bring me up Samuel. And when the woman saw Samuel, she cried with a loud voice... And the king said unto her, Be not afraid: for what sawest thou? And the woman said unto Saul I saw gods ascending out of the earth. And he said unto her, What form is he of? And she said, An old man cometh up; and he is covered with a mantle. And Saul perceived that it was Samuel... And Samuel said to Saul, Why hast thou disquieted me, to bring me up?

And Saul answered, I am sore distressed; for the Philistines make war against me, and God is departed from me.... Then said Samuel, Wherefore then dost thou ask of me...? Because thou obeyedst not the voice of the Lord, nor executedst his fierce wrath upon Amalek, therefore hath the Lord done this thing unto thee this day. Moreover the Lord will also deliver Israel with thee into the hand of the Philistines: and tomorrow shalt thou and thy sons be with me: the Lord also shall deliver the host of Israel into the hand of the Philistines.

1 Samuel 28:5-8, 11-16, 18-19

Saul couldn't face the truth, and he was deceived. If you refuse the truth, you will believe a lie. He went to see the witch at Endor to find out if he was going to win the battle or not. The witch called up a spirit, but I do not believe that it was Samuel. It looked like Samuel, it talked like Samuel, it had a mantle like Samuel's. It said, "Why did you cause me unrest? I was very much at peace. I'm going to tell you what's going to happen to you. Tomorrow you and your household are going to be killed."

Witches don't call us out of graves. Jesus does. He called Lazarus back from the grave (John 11). He brings the resurrection. But the evil spirit who had the appearance of Samuel was a familiar spirit.

"How could that evil spirit emulate Samuel so well?" you may ask. Because it was familiar with Samuel and his family.

There are all sorts of occult practices going on today. There are people who find somebody who is grieving over a lost loved one, and they will say, "Come in, and we will call that loved one." They knock on tables and do all kinds of strange things. Then some evil spirit enters and says, "I'm Uncle Joe. How are you doing? I miss you too." Well, it's not Uncle Joe. Those people cannot bring up the spirits of dead people. So what is that spirit? It is an evil spirit that is familiar with Uncle Joe.

If you're doing this sort of thing—playing with Ouija boards and such—then you're involved with a dangerous thing. Flee from anything like that. You do not need to be around familiar spirits or evil spirits. You need to be around the Holy Spirit constantly. And you need to warn your children about it. They should not have any part with it either.

Chapter 7

The Believer's Covenant: Redeemed from the Curse

S in is never fair, but it is predictable. Sins that are repeatedly committed are like weeds planted in the heart. You can mow them down, but until they are understood and dealt with, they will crop back up. Iniquities are like the seeds of weeds—they may die, as your forefathers have, but they will return. Whether the seeds are planted by you, your parents, or your forefathers, the result is a crop of inherited weaknesses or family iniquities:

> *As the bird by wandering, as the swallow by flying, so the curse causeless shall not come.*
>
> *Proverbs 26:2*

> *Thou shalt not bow down thyself to them, nor serve them: for I the Lord thy God am a jealous God, visiting the iniquity of the fathers upon the children unto the third and fourth generation of them that hate me.*
>
> *Exodus 20:5*

Remember, the law of iniquity states that the sins of the fathers will continue to the third and fourth generation for those who hate God. But what about those of us who love God? For us, God has made a provision to reverse the curse of iniquities. Just as iniquities are passed through the bloodline, your exemption from the law of iniquity is through blood, the blood sacrifice of your covenant with God.

In the old covenant, that blood sacrifice was of bulls and goats, but in the new covenant the perfect, precious blood of Jesus cleanses you from sin and iniquity. You no longer have to live bound by iniquities and generational curses, being defeated by sin, because Jesus became both your "sin offering" and the "scapegoat" for your iniquities. His physical body was sacrificed and His perfect blood was offered to God for your sins and iniquities. He took your iniquities and buried them in the sea of forgetfulness. You have something better than the "types" and "shadows" of the Old Testament; you have a better covenant in Jesus:

> *In the same way, after the supper he took the cup, saying, "This cup is the new covenant in my blood, which is poured out for you."*
> *Luke 22:20 NIV*

Jesus took on Himself the curse of your iniquity. He became cursed that you could be set free and blessed:

> *Christ hath redeemed us from the curse of the law, being made a curse for us: for it is written, Cursed is every one that hangeth on a tree.*
> *Galatians 3:13*

Your Emancipation Proclamation

Your "emancipation proclamation," the document of your freedom and deliverance from generational curses and iniquities, is found in Isaiah 53:5, 11:

*But he was wounded for our transgressions, **he was bruised for our iniquities:** the chastisement of our peace was upon him; and with his stripes we are healed. He [God] shall see the travail of his soul, and shall be satisfied: by his knowledge shall my righteous servant [Jesus] justify many; **for he shall bear their iniquities.***

Why was Jesus "bruised" for our iniquities? Because our iniquities, our inherent weaknesses, are like bruises. As we've already seen, natural bruises leave a discoloration. They usually hurt the most when you first get them, then they become discolored. Bruises can go very deep, even to the bone.

Bruises of the heart—iniquities—can begin with a crisis such as death, abuse, or trauma that may begin a pattern of sin which is passed on to the next generation. Unlike broken bones that can be set or a wound that can be sewn up, bruises can't be treated. A medical doctor will tell you to live with the bruise and it will eventually go away. What the doctor means is that your body will repair itself. Your blood provides nourishment to the body's cells and takes away the waste.

Just as your natural blood brings health to areas that are bruised and moves waste, the blood of Jesus is required to heal your heart bruises and carry away your iniquities. Bruises of the heart don't heal by themselves and go away; you must apply the blood of Christ for complete recovery.

Maybe a better example is what happens to a piece of fruit that gets bruised. If you drop an apple, it bruises. In fact, when an apple is bruised, it discolors, it begins to rot, and eventually the entire apple spoils. Without the help of Jesus, the bruises you receive from your iniquities, if not dealt with, will cause your heart to rot and will affect your entire life. Jesus, however, bore your bruises—your iniquities:

The Spirit of the Lord is upon me, because he hath anointed me to preach the gospel to the poor; he hath sent me to heal the brokenhearted, to preach deliverance to the captives, and recovering of sight to the blind, to set at liberty them that are bruised.

Luke 4:18

Physical Afflictions and Generational Iniquities

Doctors are aware that physical afflictions can be a result of a generational iniquity. When you show signs of certain diseases, they want to know if you have a family history of that disease. Maybe arthritis, diabetes, or heart problems run in your family. I was only twenty-three years old when the doctor told me: "You have an enlarged heart; there's nothing you can do about it."

The doctor's words tore away at my faith. Immediately, the devil reminded me that my father had had a heart attack and now the same thing was going to happen to me. I'm sure that the devil held his breath as he waited to see how I would respond to his lie.

I was a young Christian at that time, but I knew enough of God's Word to stand in faith for physical healing. While it is true that my dad did have a heart attack, I knew that Jesus had come to replace family iniquities with blessings and to set me free from every life-threatening sickness. My husband prayed with me, and we stood on the promises found in Isaiah 53:5 and Psalm 103:3-4:

The chastisement of our peace was upon him; and with his stripes we are healed.

Isaiah 53:5

[Bless the Lord,] who forgiveth all thine iniquities; who healeth all thy diseases.

Psalm 103:3-4

That same year, I was miraculously healed of an enlarged heart! Just recently I had my yearly checkup; the doctor said, "Your heart is excellent." God reversed the curse that Satan tried to pass down to me from my father. I have a "fixed" heart. You don't have to live under physical curses because Christ has redeemed you from the curse.

Roots of Iniquity

The roots of iniquity are pulled up through the blood of Jesus. Isaiah 53 says that Jesus bore our sin; He was wounded for our trespasses and bruised for our iniquities. The blood of Jesus is all sufficient, powerful, and devastating to family iniquities in your bloodline. To be effective, however, the blood of Jesus must be applied to your situation. Positive thinking, psychological counseling—even doing "religious" things like singing in the choir—while good, will not solve the problem. They may provide temporary relief, but only the blood of Jesus is the permanent answer, transforming your curse into a blessing.

The blood of Jesus has purchased your freedom from iniquity, and the witness of the Holy Spirit applies the anointing that breaks the yoke—freeing you of the shackles of your family iniquities: "And it shall come to pass in that day, that his burden shall be taken away from off thy shoulder, and his yoke from off thy neck, and the yoke shall be destroyed because of the anointing" (Isaiah 10:27).

Types and Shadows

The Old Testament is full of types and shadows of things to come. To really understand the provisions of the new covenant, we need to understand what God provided for Old Testament believers. He has made a way for His people to have freedom from generational iniquities.

The Jewish ceremony of the Day of Atonement gives us a picture of redemption. Through this ceremony you can see how Jesus purchased your freedom from iniquities. When this ceremony was reenacted in heaven on your behalf, Jesus became your High Priest and blood sacrifice.

Picture with me the most important day of the Jewish year, the tenth day of the seventh month, Tishri—the Day of Atonement. On that day the sins, trespasses, and iniquities of the people were cleansed. On the eve of the Day of Atonement, the people fasted and humbled themselves and repented. The next morning they gathered before the gates of the outer court in solemn assembly.

While the hushed crowd waited outside the temple grounds, inside the high priest, having already selected two goats, seven rams, and a bull, began the ceremony by washing (purifying) himself and dressing in the holy, linen robes of his office. All but one of the animals, a goat, would be sacrificed. The high priest offered blood sacrifices for the atonement, which means "reconciliation" of the guilt by divine sacrifice, for the sanctuary, tabernacle, brazen altar, and his fellow priests.

Then he killed the goat of the sin offering for the sins, trespasses, and iniquities of all the people of Israel. The blood from the goat chosen to be the sin offering was sprinkled on the mercy seat for the sins the people. (The mercy seat was the place where the presence of God dwelled—the golden center area on the lid of the ark of the covenant cased between the two cherubim.)

The high priest placed both hands upon the head of the remaining goat, the scapegoat, and confessed over it all the sins, transgressions, and iniquities of the people. Then the scapegoat was released into the wilderness. God had accepted the blood of the goat sacrifice as a sin offering, cleansed them of all their sins, and removed their iniquities.

Likewise, the blood of Jesus has cleansed you and your family tree of generational iniquities: "And the goat shall bear upon him all their iniquities unto a land not inhabited: and he shall let go the goat in the wilderness" (Leviticus 16:22).

A Heroine of the Old Covenant

I believe on one such Day of Atonement that waiting for cleansing from iniquities with the others was a young woman named Jehosheba. She was the bride of a young priest, and the daughter and grand-daughter of two of the most evil and wicked women in the Bible—Jezebel and Athalia.

Jehosheba had possibly the worst family tree of anyone in the Bible; yet God, even in Old Testament times, redeemed her from the iniquities of her family. The book of 1 Kings tells her family history.

Omri, Jehosheba's great-grandfather, was a "bad" king of the Northern Kingdom called Israel. He was a shrewd politician and sought to make peace with the nation of Zidon by marrying his son to Jezebel, who became the wife of Ahab. Jezebel introduced the nation of Israel to the worship of Baal—the most despicable, demonic religion of that day.

The prophet Elijah opposed Ahab and Jezebel and pronounced that there would be a drought in the land. After three years, Elijah faced down the prophets of Baal by calling down fire to consume his sacrifice to God. He then called upon the Lord to end the drought. Elijah also prophesied a curse upon Ahab and Jezebel and their descendants. He told them their family would be extinguished. That was only the beginning of the bad news for Jehosheba.

In an attempt to bring peace between the Northern and Southern kingdoms, the "good" king of Judah, Jehoshaphat, accepted a marriage between his son and the daughter of Jezebel, Athalia.

Like her mother, Athalia introduced the worship of Baal to her husband and the Southern Kingdom of Judah. After her husband died in battle, his son, Ahaziah, became king. After a few years, he was killed. Athalia saw her son's death as an opportunity to take the throne of Judah and sent assassins to murder her grandchildren.

She believed that she could gain the throne of Judah by eliminating all her son's heirs. What a grandmother! She became the only woman to reign in both the Northern and Southern kingdoms. Had she succeeded in killing all of her grandchildren, the seed of David would have ended and there would have been no Messiah because Jesus had to come through the seed of David.

When Jehosheba heard what her mother was doing, she slipped into the nursery and saved the youngest child from the assassin's blade. She and her husband guarded the child until he was seven years old. Then her husband brought him to the temple to be crowned king, and Athalia was killed.

Jehosheba became one of the little-known heroines of the Bible, despite her family tree. God doesn't care how rotten your family tree is. When you receive His cleansing, your family iniquities are broken! If God could deliver Jehosheba under the old covenant, just think what He can do through a new and better covenant for you, your children, and the next generation.

If you are concerned about your family because, unlike Jehosheba, your mate isn't a priest or even a believer yet, and you see family iniquities wreaking havoc in your home, then take heart. Remember, it takes only one believing mate to sanctify a house. If you are that one believing person in your home, it's enough. You can end the generational curse and establish the blessing for your family tree, as we already read in 1 Corinthians 7:14.

The Curse Reversed

Before I was saved and Spirit-filled, I attended a Sunday school class, and everything the teacher said, I challenged. It's rather embarrassing now to recall some of the ridiculous things I said back then. I certainly never mentioned them to my daughter, Sarah.

When Sarah was a junior at Oral Roberts University, she spent a summer in Germany at a university. When she returned to the United States, she told me that she wasn't sure that she believed in Jesus. My heart went down to my feet as I listened to her say some of the very things I had said so long ago in that Sunday school class.

Sarah was raised in a Spirit-filled home, brought up on the Word of God, and had received the Lord at an early age. The Lord spoke to me and said, "Don't fall apart—be cool!"

So I told Sarah, "The enemy is trying to steal your faith, but Jesus will make Himself real to you." Needless to say, my husband, Wally, and I prayed.

After returning to ORU, Sarah called me one night. She had recommitted her life to the Lord. When I asked her how it happened, she told me about a young man at school with whom she was studying. He had experienced a similar loss of faith while studying at Harvard. His father insisted that he attend ORU for a year; and, consequently, he regained the truth of his salvation. This young man, who just returned to the Lord himself, led her back to the truth.

Coincidence? No, God had reversed the curse and had begun the blessing, and He will do the same thing in your life and for your next generation!

Chapter 8

Responding to God

Sometimes in some areas of our lives, we think, *Why is my faith not working? What is wrong?* We raise children to serve the Lord, and then—bang!—they go haywire at a certain age. Then we ask, "What is this? God, I've got to have some answers!"

He that is spiritual judgeth [understands] all things.

1 Corinthians 2:15

They that seek the Lord understand all things.

Proverbs 28:5

Many times we have to wait on the Lord, and He gives us the answer eventually. As you wait on God, as you are in the Spirit, then He opens your understanding to see what the problem is and how to get rid of it. God never just identifies a problem and then leaves you to deal with it alone. He always gives you the solution to the problem and often the miracle that can turn it around.

Setting Our Generations Free

Deuteronomy 28:46 is an unusual verse: "And they shall be upon thee for a sign and for a wonder, and upon thy seed for ever."

Unlike the signs and wonders in the New Testament, this Scripture refers to bad types of signs and wonders. It says that these curses which come from generation to generation will be signs and wonders of the demonic power of sin and the power of the devil to keep curses perpetuating on throughout a family's history.

Now we know the way to change things for the better! We have been bound for years by the devil, but now not only can we be set free, but also we can set our generations free! We can overcome those nasty familiar spirits and set ourselves free and our children free and our children's children free to a thousand generations, Deuteronomy 7:9 tells us.

We know that we can spoil the devil's stronghold in our households by binding him in the name of Jesus, by telling him that he can't do those awful things to our house or to our generation or to the generations that follow us. Those evil spirits that are familiar with your family for generations know that you are already born with a weakness. When it's time, they make their attack on you. But you bind the devil, and you're not going to be a diabetic! You bind him, and you're not going to get into sexual sin! You bind him, and you're not going to live in poverty!

But remember: once you are cleansed, the devil is going to come back and try to take your children. If he gets them, he's going to make them seven times worse! But we don't have to let it happen to our children: We can set them free too! We don't have to put up with it any more.

Releasing Bitterness

Did you know that God wants you to be free? Did you know that the Word always brings freedom? 2 Corinthians 3:17 says: "Where the Spirit of the Lord is, there is liberty." God wants to set you free in every area of your life. He wants you to go kick the devil in the teeth:

> *Looking diligently lest any man fail of the grace of God; lest any root of bitterness springing up trouble you, and thereby many be defiled.*
>
> *Hebrews 12:15*

With all that we've learned, it's pretty easy for us to read this verse and say, "Yes, that's right. Bitterness is definitely a cause of family curses. People who are bitter because of something bad that happened to their father or their great-grandfather are probably not going to get very far with family blessings. They've got to get rid of that bitterness."

Well, that's very true. But the cure for bitterness is forgiveness, and that's one attribute most people have a problem with: true, deep, from-the-heart, long-lasting forgiveness—the kind that also forgets:

> *I, even I, am he that blotteth out thy transgressions for mine own sake, and will not remember thy sins.*
>
> *Isaiah 43:25*

> *Whereby are given unto us exceeding great and precious promises: that by these ye might be partakers of the divine nature, having escaped the corruption that is in the world through lust.*
>
> *2 Peter 1:4*

Forgiveness is a divine attribute. But we now have the nature of God in us, and that makes us partakers of all His divine attributes, including genuine forgiveness.

Esau Again

And the boys grew: and Esau was a cunning hunter, a man of the field; and Jacob was a plain man, dwelling in tents.

Genesis 25:27

Looking diligently lest any man fail of the grace of God; lest any root of bitterness springing up trouble you, and thereby many be defiled; lest there be any fornicator, or profane person, as Esau, who for one morsel of meat sold his birthright. For ye know how that afterward, when he would have inherited the blessing, he was rejected: for he found no place of repentance, though he sought it carefully with tears.

Hebrews 12:15-17

There is more that we can learn from the life of Esau. Scripture says he was a profane man. When I read that phrase, I thought, What's profane? Does that mean he used profanity—that he cursed a lot?

The Bible says, "Esau was a cunning hunter, a man of the field." From that, I think of Esau as being a "macho man"—one of those guys who likes to hunt, fish, and wrestle with the boys. "Jacob was a plain man, dwelling in tents." Jacob sounds like a mild-mannered type, more likely to engage in intellectual conversation. The two brothers—who were twins—couldn't have been more different!

But here, profane doesn't necessarily refer to Esau's language. It means that he was worldly, that he was very earth-conscious. He was an earthy person. When he woke up in the morning, he thought, *What's for breakfast? What am I going to eat all day?* His whole concern was for his physical body. He was proud of his hairy chest and his strong arms that could pull a bow. He was proud of his ability to run fast and wrestle everything down. His physical prowess made his father proud of him too. But Rebekah favored the gentle Jacob.

However, Esau's preoccupation with his physique and with his ego led him to be a fornicator. Fornication can either involve sexual sin, or there can be spiritual fornication. Esau went after idols—his own ego included—rather than after the living God. He treated spiritual things very lightly.

One day he came in from a hard day of hunting, horseback riding, and other "macho man" activities, and he was hungry. There was his brother Jacob, stirring a pot of stew. Now remember that Esau was always thinking of his stomach, always thinking of his physical comforts. He said to Jacob, "I would like what you're cooking."

Jacob answered, "Well, I would like your birthright, so let's just swap." Frankly, that wasn't very nice of Jacob to suggest such a thing, to respond to Esau's insignificant moment of hunger by countering with one of the powerful things of God. That goes to show that the devil is always on the prowl, "seeking whom he may devour" (1 Peter 5:8), just waiting for us to mistreat the holy things of God in a moment of jesting or lightheartedness, because then he can pervert God's plan for our lives. We have to be on guard, to bring "into captivity every thought to the obedience of Christ" (2 Corinthians 10:5); and "whatsoever ye do in word or deed, do all in the name of the Lord Jesus" (Colossians 3:17).

When Jacob answered Esau with "I want your birthright," he was about to change the course of history forever! Esau sold his birthright for a piece of meat. After he did that—after he ate all the stew and was lying around with a comfortably full belly—then he felt bad about it. But he didn't repent to God. He didn't say, "Dear God, You've given me so much! How could I have treated the gift that You gave me so lightly?" He just felt sorry that he had missed out on a bargain.

We can be sorry that we get caught in sin but not sorry that we sinned and hurt God or even hurt other people. We're just sorry for the consequences. That is not godly repentance. It does not bring forth the faithful or beautiful fruits of righteousness.

The Curse of Depression

Do you know what most depression is? Earthly sorrow. You are in sin when you're depressed. Please know not all depression is sin. In some cases, it may be a spiritual attack and you do have authority to stand against every attack of the devil. In other cases, depression can be the result of a chemical imbalance. But thank God, He can heal you and deliver you from it. If you need to, talk to your pastor or someone at your church—or your doctor may even be able to help.

Often people want to be petted when they're depressed. "Oh, be nice to me, treat me sweetly because I'm depressed." They are really on one of those "Woe is me! Pity me!" kicks. But the Lord is not going to sympathize with you because depression is unbelief, and unbelief is a sin!

Often, depression is unconfessed sin. You didn't deal with it yourself, thinking somebody else has treated you wrongly. But the root of depression can be giving in to sin, and that's a curse. It can lead to mental and emotional breakdown. It can lead to serious psychotic disorders. It can even lead to insanity. And it can be passed from one generation to the next.

Esau lost his birthright, and he also lost his blessing. Jacob just sailed in and grabbed the blessing. Jacob was wrong in the way he did it, and so was Rebekah. But their opportunity was created because of Esau's sin.

Esau lost his birthright, he lost his blessing, and then he ran into Isaac's tent and cried. He said, "Oh, Daddy, I've lost my birthright!" Whose fault was it? It was Esau's own fault, but he didn't say that. "Oh, Daddy, I've lost my blessing! Please, please! I feel so sorry about this!" This is earthly sorrow. "Please, don't you have another blessing?"

Esau was trying to get his father to relent and give him a blessing. But he never got it. He got just a little of the leftover blessing. "He sought it with tears," but he never got it. Esau did not show godly sorrow; he showed earthly sorrow. If he had shown godly sorrow, he would have said, "God, how I failed, and how I blew it!" Instead he said, "God, how Jacob failed, and how he blew it! And look at my mother; she's not even for me! They failed me!"

Esau became bitter in his heart against his brother and against his mother—although the Word says, "Honour thy father and thy mother" (Deuteronomy 5:16)—and probably a little against God too. Esau never used the godly repentance which would have cleansed him and set him free. He became defiled by his bitterness when he could have reversed the curse by repenting of his part in it.

That's the difference. We want everybody else to repent, but we think we don't need to because we're so sweet. "Why should I have to repent? I didn't do anything that bad."

Esau sold the birthright, so he obviously didn't think that the blessing was too important. Later, he wanted to murder Jacob for what he had done. "It's Jacob's fault! It's Mama's fault!" He was so wrapped up in his self-pity that he never realized that godly repentance would remove his fault and change the situation!

As long as you cop out, you will experience depression, and you will experience bitterness. When you are bitter, you defile yourself, and you may defile others as well. Esau defiled his generations, which is a tragedy.

Bitter Fathers—Bitter Children

Bitterness is a luxury you cannot afford. It's too expensive. It will defile you, and it will defile those around you just as Jeremiah 31:29 says: "The fathers have eaten a sour grape, and the children's teeth are set on edge."

That's exactly what happened to Esau. When Esau became bitter against Jacob and Jacob's descendants, his children became bitter against Jacob's descendants too:

And Moses sent messengers from Kadesh unto the king of Edom, Thus saith thy brother Israel, Thou knowest all the travail that hath befallen us: How our fathers went down into Egypt, and we have dwelt in Egypt a long time; and the Egyptians vexed us, and our fathers: and when we cried unto the Lord, he heard our voice, and sent an angel, and hath brought us forth out of Egypt: and, behold, we are in Kadesh, a city in the uttermost of thy border: let us pass, I pray thee, through thy country: we will not pass through the fields, or through the vineyards, neither will we drink of the water of the wells: we will go by the king's high way, we will not turn to the right hand nor to the left, until we have passed thy borders.

And Edom said unto him, Thou shalt not pass by me, lest I come out against thee with the sword. And the children of Israel said unto

him, We will go by the high way: and if I and my raffle drink of thy
water; then I will pay for it: I will only, without doing any thing
else, go through on my feet. And he said, Thou shalt not go through.

And Edom came out against him with much people, and with a
strong hand. Thus Edom refused to give Israel passage through his
border: wherefore Israel turned away from him.

Numbers 20:14-21

Edom was the country that belonged to Esau and his descendants. When the Israelites came out of Egypt, they said, "We need to pass through Edom on our way to the Promised Land. If you will let us pass through, we will pay for the water that our animals drink and that we drink. We will pay for the grass that they eat. We will pay for everything."

But the Edomites said, "No! We hate the descendants of Jacob. You can't come through here." What did the descendants of Jacob themselves ever do to the Edomites? Nothing! This was over four hundred years after Jacob got Esau's blessing! But the Edomites were bitter. Their "teeth were set on edge" because of Esau's bitterness against Jacob.

You may be bitter against someone. It may go back into your childhood, when some teacher yelled at you in school—or when the factory closed down and your father lost his job, and you had to get an after-school job to contribute to the family's income. Maybe your husband is all wrapped up in his job, and you're becoming bitter because it looks like he cares more about his work than he does about you.

If you are bitter against someone, you can't afford it! It's going to cost you your blessing. And it can cost your children's blessing too.

You had better repent. You are wrong to be bitter, and you're going to live in depression and defeat until you do.

This bitterness followed Esau all the way down through his descendants. Saul had a problem with Esau's descendants. David had a problem with the Edomites. Practically every king of Judah and some of the kings of the Northern Kingdom had trouble with Esau's seed. They were always interfering with Jacob's descendants and giving them a hard time. Why? Because their father "ate sour grapes," and all the generations' teeth were set on edge.

In the New Testament, the Idumeans were descendants of the Edomites as well. The four Herods were Idumean, which means they were Edomites too. Did they say, "Oh, here comes Jesus! We just love Jesus. We want to serve Jesus!" They never said that. Herod the Great said, "Where is He? I want to worship Him," (Matthew 2:8)—but he didn't want to worship Jesus; he wanted to kill Him! So Herod had all the male Jewish babies under two years of age murdered. Why? Because he had bitterness toward any of God's seed. It began with Esau, and hundreds of years later, Herod's teeth were still set on edge. Herod could have repented. He had heard the Word from the wise men, and he knew of the miraculous star. The instant he would have repented, that generational curse could have been broken!

The instant you repent of your sins, the curse is broken. But as long as you cop out, as long as you dump the blame on everybody else and what you think they've done to you, then the curse will not be broken in your life. You will continue to be depressed. You will continue to be bitter. And you will sow sourness in the lives of others. It's not worth it.

Each of the four Herods in the Bible had his chance to repent and break that long-standing curse. Each one of them heard God's

Word—and a couple of them were "almost persuaded"—but they ended up turning their backs on God instead. They committed some horrible crimes—including murdering several thousand babies—thus fulfilling their part in the family curse.

After four generations of trying to save the Herodian family from their cursed Canaanite heritage, God said, "Enough." And the last Herod died. There are no more Herods around today either!

If you are almost persuaded to repent of your sins, your "almost" is not enough, and you will be a failure. You stand to lose everything—your entire family may die out!—if you don't stop those generational curses right now.

You must say, "I repent of everything. I'm not going to hold bitterness in my heart." And then when you repent, you are free, and the generational curse is broken. You can free the next generation so that something seven times worse won't come upon them. Don't be like Esau who ate sour grapes and defiled all of his generations.

The Right Way

Now let me tell you something not to do at this point: don't go up to somebody at church and say, "I've been bitter against you for months; please forgive me," if that person didn't even know you had felt that way! He will think, *My, my! What did I do?* Then you walk away all forgiven, and the person becomes heartsick. If someone doesn't know he's offended you, then be quiet about it and go to God with it instead of creating another problem.

But if the person does know about your offense, especially if you've been ugly with him, then it doesn't matter what he's done—you get free before God, and you get free before him! Job got free with both God and man, and then his captivity was turned.

The Best Attitude

To the hungry soul every bitter thing is sweet.

Proverbs 27:7

If you are hungry for God, then you will not become bitter. You will make the bitter things sweet. If you're hungry for God and somebody is mean to you, you'll say, "Well, God, here's Your opportunity to make my friend at peace with me, because "When a man's ways please the Lord, he maketh even his enemies to be at peace with him" (Proverbs 16:7).

"You're calling him a friend?" someone else might say. Yes, that "enemy" is a friend "to the hungry soul," to the man or woman who is hungry after God. Do you know what happens to the hungry soul when trouble comes? He thinks that God is getting ready to give him a bigger miracle!

Are you in a financial crisis? Then praise God—and don't become bitter—because you're about to get a miracle! You make the choice. You decide what is going to happen to you, whether you're going to allow this attack on your finances to continue. Maybe it's a generational curse trying to latch onto you, but you have the choice to stop the devil in his tracks.

Turn Curses into Blessings

The biggest miracles in my life didn't come when everything was going smoothly. People weren't saying, "That Marilyn Hickey, isn't she just great!" No, they were saying, "What is she doing? She must be crazy!" Why? Because during the greatest financial crisis our ministry has ever faced, God opened the door for us to go on daily television.

When the financial pressure was on, the devil was hitting us with strife and everything under the sun, and I thought, *God, where is the nearest bridge?* I'll shoot myself and just fall over backward so I can't miss. But God kept telling me, "Hang in with Me. Stay in the Spirit, and you will get a miracle!"

It was during that time that God gave us the biggest miracle we've ever had in our ministry. Why? Because "to the hungry soul every bitter thing is sweet," and God know how to reverse the curse!

The answer wasn't for me to quit. The answer was for me to say, "God, I'm so hungry for You. What miracle do You have for this situation?" Then I watched Him come on the scene and do something out of this world!

Chapter 9

Beginning Your Heritage of Blessings

I n this chapter we will examine some very specific things you can do to begin your heritage of blessings. Yes, *you* can directly impact the spiritual growth of your family and cause it to grow in good soil with a strong, healthy root system that will produce life and not death. If you have already followed the steps to cleanse your family tree through personal and national repentance, forgiveness, and the shed blood of Jesus, then you have begun a process that will reap eternal benefits.

I like to use the analogy of a plant that is dying because it is planted in poor soil. Similarly, once a family tree is cleansed of its iniquities, it, too, must be repotted from the "bad," unfruitful soil of the past to the new, fertile soil of Jesus Christ. Once you've completed this process, you can begin to focus on establishing blessings for this and the next generation, maintaining these blessings, and nurturing a mature family tree.

The Good Soil

In nature, to grow a healthy, mature tree, the tree must be planted in good, fertile soil. The same is true for your family tree. To begin a heritage of blessings, you must plant the seed of God's Word in your own heart as well as in the hearts of your family members. The spiritual seed that you plant must be planted in "good" ground, which in God's kingdom is symbolized by the heart.

It is in the heart that the Word of God is planted, and it is in the heart that the Word of God bears much, little, or no fruit. Jesus likened the heart to the types of soil that the Word is planted in:

"A farmer went out to sow his seed. As he was scattering the seed, some fell along the path [the wayside]; it was trampled on, and the birds of the air ate it up. Some fell on rock [rocky ground], and when it came up, the plants withered because they had no moisture. Other seed fell among thorns, which grew up with it and choked the plants. Still other seed fell on good soil and came up and yielded a crop, a hundred times more than was sown."

Luke 8:5–8 NIV

"This is the meaning of the parable: The seed is the word of God. Those along the path are the ones who hear, and then the devil comes and takes away the word from their hearts, so that they may not believe and be saved. Those on the rock are the ones who receive the word with joy when they hear it, but they have no root. They believe for a while, but in the time of testing they fall away. The seed that fell among thorns stands for those who hear, but as they go on their way they are choked by life's worries, riches and pleasures,

and they do not mature. But the seed on good soil stands for those with a noble and good heart, who hear the word, retain it, and by persevering produce a crop."

Luke 8:11-15 NIV

The "path" or "wayside" is the first type of soil Jesus mentions. It represents a person whose understanding of the Word is in his head only and not in his heart. He mentally assents that the Word of God is true but lacks spiritual depth and understanding. Consequently, the devil has little or no difficulty stealing the Word that was sown in this person's heart.

The rocky ground is symbolic of the person who joyfully receives the Word as truth but has a superficial understanding of it. When the pressures of life and temptations come to challenge his level of commitment to be a doer of the Word he has received, he becomes faint-hearted and falls away. The seed that is sown in this type of ground soon withers and dies.

The thorny ground is the third type of soil. Like the Word sown in the rocky ground, the Word of truth will also be received by the person whose heart is thorny. However, the cares, riches, and pleasures of this world choke the Word in this person and cause it to become unfruitful.

Seed sown into the good ground, according to this Scripture, yields a crop one hundred times more than what was sown. This person's heart is ripe for the Word—it is pure and holy before the Father. The King James Version of Luke 8:15 says that the heart of this person is honest and good; having heard the Word, he keeps or does it and bears fruit with patience.

I once heard a well-known speaker say, "A good marriage takes work, and a bad marriage takes even more work." This same principle is true when it comes to establishing a godly family tree. Even when the seed is sown in good soil, there are things that must be done to cultivate a good crop or harvest. As is true in nature, the soil must be cultivated before the seed you sow will reap a bountiful harvest. If you sow seed on hard, barren ground, you can expect to receive little, if any, results. As a matter of fact, one of the purposes of praise and worship in our church services is to usher in God's presence and to prepare the congregation's hearts to receive the Word of God. Although the Word can be delivered without this cultivating process, you will find that the congregation is less receptive because they are still consumed with the thoughts and events of the day as opposed to focusing on the things of God.

Cultivating your family tree is a very simple process. All you have to do is make a quality decision and commitment to apply the Word of God to every area of your life. In doing this, you are uprooting any weeds of iniquity that might be present and tilling your heart and your family's hearts to receive the Word.

As a seed does in nature, the seed of the Word undergoes a process; you must allow time for it to germinate, sprout, and grow before it produces the desired fruit. The more skillful you become at cultivating your heart and your family's hearts, the more fertile your hearts will become and the more fruit you will produce as you receive the good seed—God's Word.

Feeding the Tree

As newborn babes, desire the sincere milk of the word, that ye may grow thereby.

1 Peter 2:2

*Whom shall he teach knowledge? and whom shall he make to un-
derstand doctrine? them that are weaned from the milk, and drawn
from the breasts.*

Isaiah 28:9

Feeding your family tree is a process that takes place over a period of time; it is not just a one-time thing. After you have sown the seed for a good family tree, you must care for and nurture it. To nurture means "to feed and protect; to nurture one's offspring; to support and encourage as during the period of training or development; to bring up; train."

One of the basic ways you nurture your tree is to feed it (your family) the Word of God. This can be done through regular family devotions and Scripture memorization. You will also need to block out a certain time of day in which you discuss the Word with your family. Perhaps the best time for your family to do this is the first thing in the morning or around dinnertime. The choice is up to you, but there needs to be an emphasis on the Word in your home in addition to what your family learns at church.

You're probably thinking, *Marilyn, this is so simple! It's elementary.* That's true, but I've discovered that some of the most profound revelations I've ever received have been simple. The Word is what will cause your family to overcome its inherited family iniquities: "And they overcame him by the blood of the Lamb, and by *the word* of their testimony" (Revelation 12:11). If you are going to feed your family spiritually, then you need to start with the Word of God.

Watering the Tree

In order for a tree to grow, it must be watered on a consistent basis. "How," you might ask, "do you water a family tree?" With the washing

of the water by the Word—the sanctifying work of the Holy Spirit—
who is symbolized in the Scriptures as rivers of living water:

> *Jesus stood and cried, saying, If any man thirst, let him come unto*
> *me, and drink. He that believeth on me, as the scripture hath said,*
> *out of his belly shall flow rivers of living water.*
>
> *John 7:37-38*

The rivers of living water in John 7 refer to the Holy Spirit, who re-
sides in every born-again believer. (See also 1 Corinthians 3:16; 6:19.)
Because He dwells in you, you have access to the very throne room of
God:

> *"But the Counselor, the Holy Spirit, whom the Father will send in*
> *my name, will teach you all things and will remind you of every-*
> *thing I have said [the Word you plant in your heart] to you."*
>
> *John 14:26 NIV*

> *"But when he, the Spirit of truth, comes, he will guide you into all*
> *truth. He will not speak on his own; he will speak only what he*
> *hears, and he will tell you what is yet to come. He will bring glory*
> *to me by taking from what is mine and making it known to you. All*
> *that belongs to the Father is mine. That is why I said the Spirit will*
> *take from what is mine and make it known to you."*
>
> *John 16:13-15 NIV*

One of the many roles or functions of the Holy Spirit according
to John 14:26 is to "teach you all things, and bring all things to your
remembrance" (NIV). As you and your family study the Word of God,
the Holy Spirit will give you an understanding of the truths being
presented to you and will remind you of what you have deposited in
your heart so you can apply the Word to your daily life.

This is the watering process. The Holy Spirit will water or give life and meaning to the Word as you and your family apply the Word to your daily lives. The fruit that you will bear from being watered by Him will give you insight and revelation into the mysteries of God and divine direction for your family. As you and your family plant the Word in your hearts, the Holy Spirit will water the good seed that you are planting, and it will overtake and choke out the weeds from the seeds planted by your forefathers generations ago.

In conjunction with the Holy Spirit, you and your family also have a role in the watering process. The part you and your family play can be found in James 1:22: "But be ye doers of the word, and not hearers only." In other words, as you and your family follow the leading of the Holy Spirit, you will enable Him to water the seeds that will sprout up into a good, healthy, mature family tree.

Pruning

The pruning of a family tree is just as important as feeding and watering it. When a plant or tree is pruned, all of the dead leaves and limbs are cut off. Anger, laziness, sickness, and a bad attitude are just some examples of dead weights that the Holy Spirit will prune from your family tree.

The purpose of this pruning process is to remove everything that would hinder the natural growth process of that tree. John 15:4,16 promise that as you and your family abide in God and His Word abides in you, you will produce much fruit and your fruit shall remain. Additionally we read:

> I am the True Vine and My Father is the Vinedresser. Any branch
> in Me that does not bear fruit—that stops bearing—He cuts away
> (trims off, takes away). And He cleanses and repeatedly prunes

every branch that continues to bear fruit, to make it bear more and richer and more excellent fruit.

John 15:1-2 AMP

We know from nature that whenever you plant something, such as a flower garden, both the good and the bad seed—the weeds—come up together. I've spent many a summer afternoon weeding my garden, but thank God for the Holy Spirit who does the separating and pruning of our spiritual family trees:

> *"The kingdom of heaven is like a man who sowed good seed in his field. But while everyone was sleeping, his enemy came and sowed weeds among the wheat, and went away. When the wheat sprouted and formed heads, then the weeds also appeared. The owner's servants came to him and said, 'Sir, didn't you sow good seed in your field? Where then did the weeds come from?'*
>
> *'An enemy did this,' he replied.... 'Let both grow together until the harvest. At that time I will tell the harvesters: First collect the weeds and tie them in bundles to be burned; then gather the wheat and bring it into my barn.'"*

Matthew 13:24-28, 30 NIV

As you plant the seed of God's Word in the hearts of you and your family and allow the Holy Spirit to water it, bad seed or family iniquities may surface from time to time. Be assured, however, that a time of separation will come, and the iniquities of the past will be consumed by the Word of God, thus enabling your family to inherit and pass on generational blessings.

I was a schoolteacher when I became Spirit-filled. I was teaching a literature class, and I read two or three books a week. I loved to read, but the Lord told me to quit reading fiction and to use that time to read the Bible instead. I was obedient and began memorizing one book of the Bible a year.

Although I was unaware of it at the time, God was pruning me during this period of my life. My husband and I didn't know we were called into the ministry. We were newlyweds, but God was getting us ready for the time when He would use us in the ministry.

I can look back now and see the pruning times in my life. God said I had some attitudes that I had to get rid of because they would hinder the call of God on my life. I knew I either had to let Him prune me, or my vines would wither and be fruitless.

Nurturing the Tree for Future Generations

David had a very fruitful family tree. He fed, watered, and pruned it. Although he committed adultery and murder, his repentance turned a family iniquity into a generational blessing.

Psalm 32 was written after David's sin with Bathsheba and his transgression against Uriah the Hittite were revealed. David dealt with three kinds of sin in this psalm: the sin of "missing the mark" when he had Uriah killed; the sin of transgression when he and Bathsheba committed adultery; and the sin of iniquity when he attempted to cover his sin and not confess it:

> *Blessed is he whose transgression is forgiven, whose sin is covered.*
> *Blessed is the man unto whom the Lord imputeth not iniquity,*
> *and in whose spirit there is no guile. When I kept silence, my bones*
> *waxed old through my groaning all the day long. For day and*
> *night thy hand was heavy upon me: my moisture is turned into the*
> *drought of summer.... I acknowledged my sin unto thee, and mine*

iniquity have I not hid. I said, I will confess my transgressions unto
the Lord; and thou forgavest the iniquity of my sin.

Psalm 32:1-5

David, as well as the other Old Testament saints, seemed to have had a better understanding of sin, transgression, and iniquity than the body of Christ has today. He probably knew that sexual sin was a weakness or iniquity passed from generation to generation in his family tree. As you follow his descendants, you'll see this iniquity in his sons: Amnon, who raped his half-sister, Tamar; Solomon, who had seven hundred wives and three hundred concubines; and Solomon's son, Rehoboam, who also had many wives and concubines.

When David said, "Blessed is the man whose transgression is forgiven," he was admitting his guilt, repenting to God, and asking for His forgiveness. His confession was part of the pruning of his family tree. We know from reading the Scriptures that David loved God and His Word and received revelation from the Holy Spirit. Even so, he was subject to a family iniquity of sexual sin that eventually led to murder. Although it would have been very easy, he did not give up on himself or his family. He allowed God to prune him.

Had David not confessed, a generational curse of iniquity would have continued in his bloodline and his seed would have had to be destroyed. However, because David confessed and repented, many of his descendants walked in generational blessings instead of the curse.

Once David allowed the pruning process to take place and was cleansed of sexual sin, God's promise of posterity and blessing was inherited by the next generation:

Now the days of David drew nigh that he should die; and he charged
Solomon his son, saying...keep the charge of the Lord thy God, to

walk in his ways, to keep his statutes, and his commandments, and his judgments, and his testimonies, as it is written in the law of Moses, that thou mayest prosper in all that thou doest, and whithersoever thou turnest thyself: that the Lord may continue his word which he spake concerning me, saying, If thy children take heed to their way, to walk before me in truth with all their heart and with all their soul, there shall not fail thee (said he) a man on the throne of Israel.

1 Kings 2:1, 3-4

Although David committed adultery and had a man murdered, his sins were covered by the blood of sacrifice. God saw David as righteous and blessed his family tree. He said the house of David would never end. And it won't. Jesus came from the seed of David, and we are joint heirs with Him.

The Maturation Process

The maturation process of your family tree is guaranteed as long as you continue to feed your family the Word of God and allow the Holy Spirit to water and prune it. Maturity is a process that should take place in every Christian's life. Once you have planted a good family tree, there are some very practical things you and your family should do to aid in your spiritual growth and the godly inheritance of the next generation. These things include being water baptized, regular church attendance, daily prayer and Bible reading, and being baptized in the Holy Spirit.

Water Baptism

Being water baptized is more than being immersed in cold water. Water baptism is a picture or symbol of the old nature of a person and his family iniquities passing away and the new nature of Christ being born in him, thus making him an heir to abundant and eternal life. It is symbolic of Jesus' death, burial and resurrection.

I was twenty-three years old when I was water baptized. I had been sprinkled as a baby, but I needed to obey the Scriptures and repent and be baptized: "Then they that gladly received his word were baptized" (Acts 2:41).

Church Attendance

One of the ways you and your family will grow spiritually is through regular church attendance. There is a corporate anointing or strength that comes from fellowshipping on a regular basis with other believers, and the Holy Spirit will also water the seed of the Word that you and your family have sown in your hearts during your personal times of devotion. God's Word commands you to become a part of a local body: "Not forsaking the assembling of ourselves together; as the manner of some is" (Hebrews 10:25).

Daily Prayer

Daily prayer is essential to the success of every Christian and Christian family. Prayer is not only a direct line of communication to your heavenly Father, but it is what helps you to "abide in the vine" as you are admonished to do in John 15. Paul exhorts you to "pray without ceasing" (1 Thessalonians 5:17).

Before she got married, my daughter Sarah met a young man at a secular university she was attending. She said that she liked him and was seeing him on occasion. She also told me he was not saved, and it burdened me. You know how we parents are: we're very watchful of our children. I don't know why I was so troubled about this young man, but I prayed for him. I didn't think it was good for Sarah to be friendly with him, but try to tell that to a twenty-four year-old!

She told me one day, "Well, Mother, he's only a friend." The Lord gave me a scripture to give to Sarah from James that says not to make friends with the world (James 4:4).

The next day I said, "The Lord gave me something I want to share with you." I gave her the scripture and explained to her that I didn't believe she was even supposed to be friends with this man. Well, she was not happy with me or with God. She sought God in prayer and said, "Why did You tell my mother this; why couldn't You have told me Yourself?"

When she and I were talking about it, I said, "If I told you first, you wouldn't have listened, but if I prayed about it first, I knew God would be able to deal with it."

Needless to say, Sarah quit seeing the young man. Daily prayer for you and your family can bring you to a place of trust and fellowship with God. It also can keep the lines of communication open so that God can speak to you and your family and give you the answers to the challenges you will face in life. A daily prayer life can give you the strength to overcome your family's iniquities and is a must for the maturation process of you and your family tree.

Daily Bible Reading

If you want to break the curse and establish the blessings in your family tree, then daily Bible reading is a must in your life. It is the Word that the Holy Spirit will water as you and your family mature in the things of God. Second Timothy 2:15 says: "Study to shew thyself approved unto God, a workman that needeth not to be ashamed, rightly dividing the word of truth."

It is very important that Christians feed themselves on the Word of God. People will tell me, "I'm just not fed at my church."

My response to them is, "Do you have a Bible?"

They respond, "Yes."

I'll say, "Can you read?"

Their answer of course is, "Yes."

Then I will ask, "Then why don't you feed yourself?"

Depending on your church to feed you and your family is not enough. You have to feed on the Word daily yourself. As a matter of fact, you and your family should make it a habit of reading through the Bible every year. If you read two Old Testament chapters and one New Testament chapter six days a week, and three Old Testament and two New Testament chapters on the seventh day of the week, you will have read through the Bible in one year!

Reading through the Bible on a daily basis will keep you and your family clean of generational iniquities, encouraged about the things of God, and walking in His promises. Nothing can beat it!

The Baptism of the Holy Spirit

When you become born again, you are born of the Spirit. However, to enhance the power of your prayers as well as your understanding of the Word, you and your children and your children's children can be baptized in the Holy Spirit and be filled with the power of God as written in the books of Acts:

But ye shall receive power, after that the Holy Ghost is come upon you.

Acts 1:8

For the promise is unto you, and to your children, and to all that are afar off, even as many as the Lord our God shall call.

Acts 2:39

The Holy Spirit in your life is your well of living water that Jesus spoke about in John 7:38. He said, "He that believeth in me, as the scripture hath said, out of his belly shall flow rivers of living water." The Holy Spirit wants to be a river of living water to your innermost being. He wants to refresh you spiritually:

But whosoever drinketh of the water that I shall give him shall never thirst; but the water that I shall give him shall be in him a well of water springing up to everlasting life.

John 4:14

You are not "less saved" if you aren't baptized in the Holy Spirit; neither are you "more saved" if you are. God wants you to be baptized with the Holy Spirit so that He can empower you spiritually, just as Jesus was empowered spiritually. You were already given the Holy Spirit when you were born again. Now you just have to receive His baptism. By doing so you are receiving His fullness into every area of your life, into every "room" of your being.

It is God's will for you to be born again, water baptized, and filled with the Holy Spirit, but it's up to you! The baptism of the Holy Spirit is God's miracle to bring His character and power into your life so that you can be a bold witness for Him as the Scripture says in Ephesians 3:16: "[I pray] that he would grant you, according to the riches of his glory, to be strengthened with might by his Spirit in the inner man."

The Fruit of the Spirit

The purpose of a heritage of blessings in your family tree is that you and your descendants benefit from the good fruit or blessings promised by God in His Word. Both individually and as a family, the indwelling of the Holy Spirit enables you to uproot the family iniquities at work in your lives and bear spiritual fruit that will remain:

But the fruit of the Spirit is love, joy, peace, longsuffering, gentleness, goodness, faith, meekness, temperance: against such there is no law.
Galatians 5:22-23

All fruit has seed in it. Our fruit of the Spirit leaves seed for the next generation. Praise God that you can pass on good seed and fruit for your family to inherit. Although weeds from the evil tree may still come up from time to time, they will eventually be choked out by your spiritual fruit because the Word of God guarantees that "against such [the things of the Spirit] there is no law" (Galatians 5:23).

Part Three

Prayer

Chapter 10

Prayer—it's quite possibly the number one thing the enemy will try to keep you from doing. Effective prayer is action and it causes things to change for God's glory and our victory—no wonder the devil is against it. Have you ever noticed that when you are ready to pray, things seem to just come up—the phone rings, you remember you need to do the laundry, or take the garbage out, write a letter, even pay the bills?

Marilyn had challenges with prayer just like all of us, but she found a solution to the chaos that seems to surround our prayer time. She explains, "When I heard Larry Lee teach 'Could You Not Tarry with Me One Hour,' that helped me to start a prayer pattern, which got me into prayer."

Marilyn also credits serving on the board of the Yoido Full Gospel Church in Seoul, Korea, the largest church in the world, with improving her prayer life. Pastor David Paul Yonggi Cho has been a great influence on Marilyn. She says of Pastor Cho, "He prays four hours a day. You get around people who pray and it is contagious. They don't think anything about it."

With a worldwide ministry, Marilyn spends a great deal of time studying the Scripture and in prayer. She has learned valuable keys to praying effectively and many of those are captured in the pages to follow.

Why Pray?

As economic uncertainty, violence, divorce, natural disasters, disease, and other calamities have become part of everyday life, people are desperately crying out for help. And there is only one answer—prayer.

Jesus tells us in Luke 18:1 to pray and not give up. When you feel as if there is no hope, prayer is the key to strengthen you. It will give wings to your faith to believe God for His intervention and to bring peace to your inner man knowing He hears you and is willing to move on your behalf.

Prayer has a purpose. It's not just a feeling or desperate words uttered to God when all else fails. Prayer is powerful. It is intimate fellowship with God through His Son, Jesus Christ. Prayer brings results; it gets down to the core of things and it is vital in the times in which we live.

In my travels throughout the country, I've noticed many Christians feel very defeated in their walk with God. Some have even backslidden and are angry at God because they feel He failed them when they needed Him most. But Hebrews 13:5 says God will never leave you or forsake you. God did not abandon them, but perhaps they were not praying according to God's will for them in that situation.

Unless your life is built upon more than casual communication with God, you may struggle when the storms of life blow. God's answers may be different than what you expect. But don't lose hope—God is waiting and wanting to fellowship with you. As you draw near to Him, He will shed light on your situation.

Prayer is intimate communication with your heavenly Father. It can be as personal as talking to a friend and closer than any relationship you have here on earth. Proverbs 18:24 says, "There is a friend who sticks closer than a brother" (NKJV). Jesus is that kind of a friend. In John 15:14-15, Jesus says, "You are My friends… No longer do I call you servants…I have called you friends, for all things that I heard from My Father I have made known to you" (NKJV).

Friends share things with one another that they don't communicate to the general public. God desires that kind of fellowship with you. He created you to commune with Him on a regular basis.

Prayer is so powerful. It's not just a way for you to talk to God; it's also God's way to communicate back to you. It's a two-way communication system. I believe all of us are in God's kingdom because someone prayed for us. God communicated to someone to pray for you and when they did, you came into His kingdom. It's amazing to have a relationship with God that changes hearts and lives.

Many new Christians (and some who have been Christians for years) don't know how to pray, so they pattern their prayers after the prayers of others. But prayer is an expression of your individuality. On one day it may help you release stress—the anxiety of a hectic lifestyle—and receive the peace of God. At other times, prayer may be an avenue to find solutions to problems, to rescue a loved one from the grips of hell, to be refreshed in God's presence, or even to just stay in touch with God.

In Matthew 21:22 Jesus tells us, "And all things, whatsoever ye shall ask in prayer, believing, ye shall receive." You don't receive things from God because you want them, hope you'll get them, or talk about them. You get things from God because you pray for them. This passage says you should come before God, ask in prayer, and believe that you'll receive that very thing. (See also Mark 11:24.)

You can pick up your phone, send a text message, or fly on a plane to visit someone, but there is no faster communication system than prayer. God hears you instantly. You never have to leave Him a message and His battery never runs down. Find some time to put prayer in your day.

Pray God's Way

The best way to receive answers to your prayers is to pray the way God tells you. All prayer should be directed to the Father in Jesus' name. Jesus shares this in John 14:13-14, "And whatsoever ye shall ask in my name, that will I do, that the Father may be glorified in the Son. If ye shall ask any thing in my name, I will do it."

Once my husband Wally and I purchased a lamp for our daughter's room. I didn't want to read the instructions; I just wanted to look at the picture on the box and put the lamp together. Needless to say, I was unable to assemble the lamp without referring to the directions. Prayer works in much the same way. The more you follow the directions, the more results you're going to have. Since we want results when we pray, we need to pray to the Father in the name of His Son, Jesus.

Another principle to remember is found in Romans 8:26-28. This passage tells us how the three members of the Trinity (the Father,

Jesus the Son, and the Holy Spirit) work together to help us pray. It encourages us to follow the Holy Spirit's leading:

In the same way the Spirit also helps our weakness; for we do not know how to pray as we should, but the Spirit Himself intercedes for us with groanings too deep for words; and He who searches the hearts knows what the mind of the Spirit is, because He intercedes for the saints according to the will of God. And we know that God causes all things to work together for good to those who love God, to those who are called according to His purpose. (NASB)

Not only does the Holy Spirit pray the will of God through you, but you also have Jesus praying for you, too. Hebrews 7:25 also shows Jesus is praying for you: "Therefore He is able also to save forever those who draw near to God through Him, since He always lives to make intercession for them."

The Bible says that in the mouth of two or three witnesses, every word is established (Matthew 18:16). When you pray to the Father according to His Word (which is always His will), the Holy Spirit prays in agreement with you because He prays God's Word, too. Since Jesus ever lives to make intercession for you (Hebrews 7:25), He's praying for you also. How many are praying God's will? Three. And in the mouth of two or three witnesses, your prayer is established. Then Father God honors His Word and answers your prayer.

The Court of Heaven

When you pray according to God's instructions, all of heaven is fighting for you. When the devil comes to accuse you before God, Jesus, your Attorney, is seated at the right hand of the Father, your Judge. Everything is stacked against the devil when he enters the courtroom—God, your Father is the Judge and Jesus, your Intercessor and your Redeemer is your Attorney.

Romans 8:31 says, "If God be for us, who can be against us?" God has stacked prayer together to work in your favor and to bring to pass His will in your life and in the lives of those for whom you are praying. You have three witnesses when you pray and no force in hell can defeat you—so pray in faith, believing the Word can and will work for you.

Faith in God

Once you've grasped the importance of prayer, it will become very difficult for the devil to defeat you. You will have the assurance in your spirit regardless of what comes, you can pray and God will move on your behalf. That's faith! Unlike prayer attitudes of the past, you will pray expecting results.

Faith—believing the Word of God is true and that it will work for you—is one of the major components of effective praying. The Bible says faith can move both God and mountains (Mark 11:22-23, Hebrews 11:6). The eloquence of your prayers, the abundance of your tears, or the amount of time you spend screaming at the top of your voice will not cause God to move on your behalf, but faith will.

Hebrews 11:6 says, "Without faith it is impossible to please him: for he that cometh to God must believe that he is, and that he is a rewarder of them that diligently seek him." Whenever I think of diligence in prayer, I think of Abraham. The Scripture says Abraham believed the promises (Word) of God and it was attributed to him as having right standing with God (Romans 4:1-3). Abraham is known as the "father of faith" and is listed in Hebrews 11 in what is known as the "faith hall of fame." His prayer life and walk with God was such that he knew he could approach God in prayer and God would move on his behalf.

In Genesis 18, the intimacy of God's relationship with Abraham is seen. God is preparing the destroy the city of Sodom because of their sin, but He talks it over with Abraham knowing that Abraham has relatives there. Abraham petitions (or intercedes) for his nephew Lot, knowing that he is at least one righteous man. God listens to Abraham and answers his prayer. He sends angels to rescue Lot and his family.

Five Points to Develop Your Prayer Life

Is it possible to develop the kind of relationship that Abraham had with God? Yes—absolutely. God loves you and created you for fellowship. I've outlined five fundamental Biblical truths to follow that can help you develop your faith, your prayer life, and your relationship with your heavenly Father.

1. Draw Near

You are made nigh (near) God through the blood of Jesus shed when He died at Calvary. It is your right and privilege as a child of God to seek Him in prayer and expect Him to hear and answer you as shown in Ephesians 2:12-13: "You were at that time separate from Christ, excluded from the commonwealth of Israel, and strangers to the covenants of promise, having no hope and without God in the world. But now in Christ Jesus you who formerly were far off have been brought near by the blood of Christ" (NASB).

2. The Name of Jesus

God has given you the right to use the name of Jesus, which has authority over everything in the heavens and earth and beneath the earth: "That at the name of Jesus every knee should bow, of things in heaven, and things in earth, and things under the earth; And that every tongue should confess that Jesus Christ is Lord" (Philippians 2:10-11 NASB).

3. The Holy Spirit

You have the Holy Spirit guiding you. Listen for His leading in your heart: "Howbeit when he, the Spirit of truth, is come, he will guide you into all truth: for he shall not speak of himself; but whatsoever he shall hear, that shall he speak: and he will shew you things to come" (John 16:13).

4. Be Thankful

Enter into God's presence with thanksgiving: "Come before Him with joyful singing...Enter His gates with thanksgiving, and His courts with praise. Give thanks to Him, bless His name" (Psalm 100:2, 4 NASB).

5. Pray the Promises of God in His Word

Declaring the promises of God back to Him instead of telling Him the problem guarantees results and brings the provision you need. God already knows the problem, but He needs you to release your faith that His Word is true for you. You can state the problem, but you also need to pray His Word.

Here's an example: *"Father, I'm in need of finances. You say in Philippians 4:19 that You supply all my need according to Your riches in glory by Christ Jesus. Based on Your Word, I give You thanks that this need is met, in Jesus' name. Amen."*

The Scripture for this principle is found in 1 John 5:14-15: "And this is the confidence that we have in him, that, if we ask any thing according to his will, he heareth us: And if we know that he hear us, whatsoever we ask, we know that we have the petitions that we desired of him." You can be assured you are praying God's will when you pray His Word.

Five points may sound intimidating, but remember it's the Holy Spirit that provides the guidance and the power to bring to pass what you pray. Ephesians 3:20 says the power of the Holy Spirit works through you when you pray: "Now unto him that is able to do exceeding abundantly above all that we ask or think, according to the power that worketh in us." He does the supernatural part. Your part is easy—pray and have faith in God.

Chapter 11

"I exhort therefore, that, first of all, supplications, prayers, intercessions, and giving of thanks, be made for all men."

—1 Timothy 2:1

One of the main reasons for unanswered prayer is that we lump all prayer in the same big package, not realizing there are different types of prayer for different types of needs. When a child, for example, wants a piece of candy, his request is different than it would be if he had fallen and broken his leg.

It's important to follow God's directions for prayer if you expect to get results. Different recipes call for different ingredients. If you're going to make a pound cake you don't add cottage cheese and pepper, nor do you boil an egg by putting it in a skillet. So it is with prayer. If you want an effective prayer life, follow God's prayer manual—the Bible.

The Apostle Paul had a good understanding of the different types of prayer. In 1 Timothy 2:1, he mentions supplications, prayers (which indicates prayers other than the ones listed), intercessions, and thanksgiving. Jesus also demonstrated different types of prayer during His earthly ministry. In the garden of Garden of Gethsemane, He prayed a prayer of committal; at Lazarus' tomb, He prayed a prayer of thanksgiving; and in Matthew 18, He taught His disciples the prayer of binding and loosing and the prayer of agreement. Let's review each of these types of prayer.

Prayer of Agreement

"If two of you shall agree on earth as touching any thing that they shall ask, it shall be done for them of my Father which is in heaven. For where two or three are gathered together in my name, there am I in the midst of them."

Matthew 18:19-20

The prayer of agreement is a prayer in which two or more people set themselves in agreement with God's Word, one another, and Jesus who, according to this Scripture, is in the midst of them.

Harmony, however, is important. If you or the person(s) you're agreeing with in prayer are out of fellowship with the Lord or one another, or there is unforgiveness or strife in your life, it will bind the hands of God, hinder your prayers, and leave a door open for Satan to come in and steal, kill, or destroy (Mark 11:25-26, James 3:14-16, John 10:10).

Prayer of Binding and Loosing

"Whatsoever ye shall bind on earth shall be bound in heaven: and whatsoever ye shall loose on earth shall be loosed in heaven."

Matthew 18:18

The extent to which God is free to move in the earth and in your prayer life depends on you. The prayer of binding and loosing can stop Satan in his tracks. This is "cause and effect" praying (i.e., you bind poverty and loose finances). Because you have the name of Jesus, which has authority over the very thing that is named (cancer, lack, rebellion, etc.), you can hinder Satan's ability on earth to interfere with the will of God. So what things you bind on earth, God will break or destroy in heaven.

Prayer of Petition and Supplication

"Be careful for nothing; but in every thing by prayer and supplication with thanksgiving let your requests be made known unto God. And the peace of God, which passeth all understanding, shall keep your hearts and minds through Christ Jesus"

Philippians 4:6-7

The Amplified Bible says, "Do not fret or have any anxiety about anything, but in every circumstance and in everything, by prayer and petition (definite requests), with thanksgiving, continue to make your wants known to God. And God's peace [shall be yours....]"

The only requirements for the prayer of petition and supplication are that you know what your request is before you approach God in prayer and that your request is based on God's Word. It is so encouraging to know that you don't have to be nervous, worried, or uptight about anything. You can simply petition God and He will keep your heart and mind at peace.

United Prayer

"And being let go, they went to their own company, and reported all that the chief priests and elders had said unto them. And when they heard that, they lifted up their voice to God with one accord...And when they had prayed, the place was shaken where they were assembled together; and they were all filled with the Holy Ghost, and they spake the word of God with boldness."

Acts 4:23-24, 31

The believers in the New Testament Church knew the power of united prayer. Acts 12 describes a prayer meeting of a group of believers who were praying for the release of Peter who had been imprisoned for preaching the gospel. Verse 5 says, "Prayer was made without ceasing of the *church* unto God for him." The power of their united prayer was so great that God dispatched an angel to rescue Peter out of King Herod's clutches and an iron gate opened of its own accord. There is power when the Body of Christ comes together to pray, which is why believers are admonished to fellowship and attend church on a regular basis. (See Hebrews 10:25.)

Thanksgiving and Praise

"Enter into his gates with thanksgiving, and into his courts with praise: be thankful unto him, and bless his name."

Psalm 100:4

Have you ever noticed how ineffective your prayers are and how burdened you feel when you do nothing but complain to God during your prayer time? When you enter into His courts with thanksgiving to present your petitions, like yeast causes dough to rise, thanksgiving makes your prayer requests rise into the presence of the Father, and it lifts you above the heaviness or hopelessness of your situation.

Prayer of Commitment

"Then cometh Jesus with them unto a place called Gethsemane, and saith unto the disciples, Sit ye here, while I go and pray yonder. And he went a little farther, and fell on his face, and prayed, saying, O my Father, if it be possible, let this cup pass from me: nevertheless not as I will, but as thou wilt."

Matthew 26:36, 39

From Genesis to Revelation, the Bible is clear about what is and is not God's will. In Matthew 26, Jesus is praying a prayer of commitment. It took three times for Him to totally submit to the will of God. He said, "Oh Lord, I don't want to drink this cup…If You will, let it pass from me." And finally, "Nevertheless, Your will be done." Jesus agonized in prayer over this until He submitted to the will of His Father. (See verses 36-44.) The prayer of commitment is the only time you should pray, "If it be Thy will." Otherwise, you should find a scripture to support your need and pray,

"Your Word says…."

Praying in the Spirit

"Now unto him that is able to do exceeding abundantly above all that we ask or think, according to the power that worketh in us."

Ephesians 3:20

Praying in the Spirit releases the power of God to bring your prayers to pass. The Greek word for power in this Scripture is *dunamis* and it means "miracle-working power." When you are endued with miracle-working power you can go forth in prayer and attack the enemy for Jesus Christ because of the power at work within you.

Romans 8:26-28 says you do not know how to pray for things as you ought, but the Holy Spirit prays through you with groanings and utterances that cannot be thought out. Because the Holy Spirit searches the hearts of the people who are going to be involved in your situation, He makes intercession according to God's will. When you pray in the Spirit, God makes everything (including the hearts of men) come together according to His will.

Praying God's Word

"But he answered and said, It is written, Man shall not live by bread alone, but by every word that proceedeth out of the mouth of God."

Matthew 4:4

Jesus beat the devil with the Word. You also must pray God's Word to defeat Satan. For every problem, you should pray a promise because it's the promise (the Word) that works or as Isaiah 55:11 says, "it shall not return unto me void." Praying God's Word accomplishes three things—it reminds God of His Word, it reminds the devil he is defeated, and it increases your faith because "...faith cometh by hearing, and hearing by the word of God" (Romans 10:17). Praying the Word brings the provision that you need.

Prayer of Intercession

Therefore I exhort first of all that supplications, prayers, intercessions, and giving of thanks be made for all men, for kings and all who are in authority, that we may lead a quiet and peaceable life in all godliness and reverence. For this is good and acceptable in the

*sight of God our Savior, who desires all men to be saved and to come
to the knowledge of the truth.*

1 Timothy 2:1-4

When it comes to intercessory prayer, all too often we miss the reward God has for us because we lack stick-to-it-iveness in prayer. I have often taught we should "play" until we win. Well, we should also "pray" until we win.

Exodus 32-34 gives a beautiful example of someone who prayed until he won with God, a person used by God as a powerful intercessor—Moses. When the children of Israel sinned against God by creating and worshipping a golden calf, Moses was there to intercede for them or they would have been destroyed completely. An intercessor is one who acts in behalf of someone in difficulty or trouble. He pleads or petitions someone on their behalf, or attempts to reconcile differences between two people or groups—a mediator.

Intercession is the will of God. In 1 Timothy 2:1-3, the apostle Paul lists three groups of people for whom we should intercede. He begins by being very general saying we should intercede for all men, and then narrows it to kings (political leaders), an for all who are in authority (pastors, policepersons, employers, parents, teachers, and others.)

There are two benefits of intercession according to the Scripture: it will enable us to live godly and honest lives in peace and quiet, free from a society of stress, crime, violence, and fear; and men will surrender their hearts to God and come to the knowledge of His saving grace.

There is tremendous power in intercessory prayer. Although you may not intercede for others as a lifestyle, 1 Timothy 2 commands all born-again believers to pray the prayer of intercession in much the same way you would pray a prayer of thanksgiving, or of petition and supplication.

Intercessory prayer is imperative in the times in which we live. If you are willing to intercede or mediate between God and man, then through your intercession you can change the heart of God and save a soul, a city, a state, and who knows, maybe a nation.

The Lord's Prayer

"After this manner therefore pray ye: Our Father which art in heaven, Hallowed be thy name. Thy kingdom come, Thy will be done in earth, as it is in heaven. Give us this day our daily bread. And forgive us our debts, as we forgive our debtors. And lead us not into temptation, but deliver us from evil: For thine is the kingdom, and the power, and the glory, for ever. Amen."

Mathew 6:9-13

Now that we have examined types of prayer, we need to go a little further and look at a "prayer pattern" that Jesus gave His disciples to follow. I'm sure many of you have recited this prayer at least once in your life, and even today some congregations sing it as one of their Sunday morning hymns. It is known as "The Lord's Prayer."

Sometimes you can figure out what something is by knowing what it is not. Jesus wanted to make sure His disciples knew the correct prayer method and had direction and purpose for what they wanted to accomplish in prayer...*before they prayed.*

In Matthew 6:7, He instructed His disciples *not* to pattern their prayers after the heathen because they did not know how or what to pray. They babbled the same thing over and over again, hoping they would say something that would move God. Then Jesus told them *how* to pray, "After this manner therefore pray ye…" (v. 9).

Temples of the Holy Ghost

"Know ye not that your body is the temple of the Holy Ghost which is in you, which ye have of God, and ye are not your own?"

1 Corinthians 6:19

Throughout the Old Testament we see examples of God manifesting His presence in temples made by man. For instance, in 2 Chronicles 5:13-14 at the dedication of the temple, the children of Israel are praising and worshiping God. His presence fills the temple as a cloud so thick, the priests could not see. But upon Jesus' death and resurrection, God transferred the indwelling of His presence from man-made temples into earthen vessels—you and I. First Corinthians 6:19 says that you, as a New Testament believer, are the temple of God and that the Holy Ghost (God's presence) dwells in you.

Matthew 21:12-16 draws an interesting parallel to this. In this account, Jesus went into the temple and threw out the people who were peddling their wares, declaring the temple to be a house of prayer: "And Jesus went into the temple of God, and cast out all them that sold and bought in the temple, and overthrew the tables of the moneychangers, and the seats of them that sold doves. And said unto them, It is written, My house shall be called the house of prayer" (v. 12-13).

There is an interesting progression that takes place in this passage of Scripture. If you'll notice, the first thing Jesus did was to cleanse the temple, and then He identified its purpose. The temple's purpose was not for sin or unrighteousness—Jesus referred to it as a house of prayer. Once its purpose was identified and the cleansing took place,

Jesus began healing the sick, the lame, and the blind, and then the children began to sing praises to Him (v. 14-15).

As the temple was a house or prayer during the Old Testament times, so is every New Testament born-again believer. As Jesus cleansed the temple in Matthew 21, He also wants to cleanse you of anything that could hinder the effectiveness of your prayers. The benefit to you when this process takes place is that God's power will begin to flow through you and you will begin to heal the lame, the sick, and the blind. You will become a house of praise (v. 16).

The prayer pattern outlined by Jesus in Matthew 6 will purify you and cause you to become a house of prayer and perfected praise. Jesus gave His disciples this prayer pattern so they could reap all the benefits of prayer. Each verse, or demarcation (a marker used to designate an athlete's arrival at a certain point in a marathon or related sport) of this Scripture will lead you into a different level of prayer. As you go through each point of demarcation, the Holy Spirit will show you how and what to pray.

The Lord's Prayer Pattern

"Our Father which art in heaven, Hallowed be thy name"(Matt. 6:9).

This is the first point of demarcation. At this point, you allow the Holy Spirit to unfold to you what He wants you to pray. When I pray this prayer, I get in tune with the Holy Spirit by saying, "Father, thank You that You are the God who is more than enough. You are El Shaddai. Thank You for the name of Jesus. It's because of that name, the most hallowed name I know, that my sins have been forgiven. So I am cleansed with His blood. Because of His name, I have the Holy Spirit to lead me into truth. I don't have to live in depression, be deceived, or make mistakes. The Holy Spirit will lead me into all truth."

I pray the promises of God back to Him, honoring His name. Some of the promises I used above are found in Ephesians 1:7, Colossians 1:14, and John 16:13. As you learn God's Word, the Holy Spirit will bring those promises back to your remembrance when you pray. If you don't know many promises yet, you can find Bible promise books in just about any bookstore or I have a little book called *Speak the Word* that is full of God's promises.

Next, wait on God. If you are sick, the Holy Spirit might lead you to pray His promises about healing. Perhaps something like, "Father, I thank You that because of Your hallowed name, I have health. Jesus himself took my infirmities and my diseases. By His stripes, I am healed" (Psalm 103:3, 1 Peter 2:24).

Depending on the needs of your life and the way the Holy Spirit is leading you that day, you may spend a long time at this demarcation, or the Holy Spirit may move you to the next point.

His Kingdom

"Thy kingdom come" (Matt. 6:10).

At this point, I begin by praying about my relationship with God. I might pray, "Father, I want to please You. If I have blown it in any area, or if there is something blocking our relationship, would You please show me by the Holy Spirit? Have I been ugly with my words? Critical? Prideful? Father, would you reveal it to me now by the Holy Spirit?"

Again, I wait on the Lord for a moment to see how He is leading me. If He doesn't lead me to pray about anything else concerning my relationship with Him, then I begin praying over my relationship with my husband, Wally, and my children, Michael and Sarah. Then I move on to the next point of demarcation.

His Will

"Thy will be done in earth, as it is in heaven" (v. 10).

God has a will for you in heaven for every relationship that you're involved in—your relationship with your heavenly Father, your mate, your children, and others. I might pray, "God, You have called me to Marilyn Hickey Ministries. You've called me to be a pastor's wife. Lord show me what I should do for You today."

Perhaps the Holy Spirit will give me wisdom for a certain decision facing me that day, or perhaps He will show me the face of someone in the church who needs prayer. I stay at this demarcation until the Holy Spirit directs me to the next point.

Daily Provision

"Give us this day our daily bread" (v. 11).

The Holy Spirit could lead you to pray for daily bread in a lot of ways. With me, for example, I might be stuck on a topic I'm going to teach, so I pray for revelation knowledge: "Father, would you give me a revelation in Your Word concerning this topic?"

Perhaps you have a financial or physical need. Or maybe the Holy Spirit will lead you to pray for someone else. I prayed for my mother for years: "Father, give my mother her daily bread. She's in her 80s and she needs daily health and strength. Meet her every need today."

Forgiveness

"And forgive us our debts, as we forgive our debtors" (v. 14).

God wants you to have good relationships. When you're rude or vindictive to others, God can't bless you the way He wants to. So each day during my prayer time I say, "Father, I make the decision to forgive today and walk in love toward others regardless of what they have done or may do to me. Please show me how to forgive according to Your Word."

Protection

"And lead us not into temptation, but deliver us from evil: For thine is the kingdom, and the power, and the glory, for ever, Amen" (v. 13).

Some Christians are tempted more than others because they don't pray. Jesus said to pray so you would not be tempted (Matthew 26:41). Just as God has a perfect will for you each day, the devil has designed a device in hell for each day of your life to hinder the will of God for you that day.

I might pray, "Father, don't lead me into temptation but deliver me from evil for Thine is the kingdom, and the power (out of my 'house of prayer' comes power), and the glory (praise) forever, Amen."

Chapter 12

Meditation

"But his delight is in the law of the LORD; and in his law doth he meditate day and night. And he shall be like a tree planted by the rivers of water, that bringeth forth his fruit in his season; his leaf also shall not wither; and whatsoever he doeth shall prosper."

—*Psalm 1:2-3*

editation can change your life! According to Psalm 1:2-3, meditating on the Word of God guarantees prosperity for every born-again believer. In the book of Joshua, God confirmed His Word with the promise that if you will meditate on the Word, keeping it in your mouth and acting on it, you will be successful in every area of your life—spiritually, physically, mentally, emotionally, and financially.

This book of the law shall not depart out of thy mouth; but thou shalt meditate therein day and night, that thou mayest observe to do according to all that is written therein: for then thou shalt make thy way prosperous, and then thou shalt have good success.

Joshua 1:8

Many people will say, "Well, that was only written for Joshua." But no matter who you are, obedience to Joshua 1:8 will put you on the path for prosperity in all things. This is a key scripture and carries a tremendous impact.

The word "meditate" has many meanings, some of which include to walk, talk, memorize, visualize, or personalize. Joshua 1:8 is God's command for His people to meditate on His Word. This command carries a promise that goes with everything in your life. God is saying, "If you will meditate on My Word day and night, speak that Word, and obey it in every area of your life, you will prosper and be successful in everything you set your heart to do."

Threefold Cord

There is a three-part action plan in Joshua 1:8 that God has given for meditating on His Word. Part one involves your *mouth:* "This book of the law shall not depart out of thy mouth." Meditation involves "talking" God's Word.

Part two is meditation itself: "...but thou shalt meditate therein *day and night.*" Meditation on God's Word is to be an all-consuming effort, not merely a pastime.

Part three brings in the action: "...that thou mayest observe to *do* according to all that is written therein." Meditation not only involves speaking—it involves walking. We are to be doers of the Word and not hearers only (James 1:22).

God did not say, "If you'll do this, *I'll* make your way prosperous." He said, "If you'll meditate, *you* will make your way prosperous and you will have good success." There is a big difference here. You alone make the decision. God will not force you to meditate upon His

Word; neither will he force prosperity upon you. But once you make the decision, He will help you and it's not as hard as you might think.

You may know people, perhaps unsaved people, who according to the world's standards are successful. But according to this scripture, there is a "good" success that comes with meditating on the Word. This success has to do with more than material possessions—it covers every aspect of your life and can be passed on to your future generations (Deuteronomy 7:9).

When God told Joshua to meditate, He was saying, "I want you to be saturated with the Word of God: keep it in your mind, your mouth, and your actions." Joshua became an example of God's living Word in action and so can you.

When I first started to meditate on the Word, I decided I needed a partner. I thought that in case I wanted to stop meditating or became discouraged, a partner would be a motivator for me. This seemed a good way to start, so I prayed, "Lord, with whom would You have me be a partner?" The Lord spoke to me, and it was not the person I wanted Him to choose! She was a person who griped constantly. If she got a hold of you, it would take 30 minutes for her to tell you her problems; and then she'd find you later because she had more to tell!

The Lord said to me, "I want her to be your meditation partner." I thought, *Oh Lord, anybody but her.* I thought she would spend the time griping and that we wouldn't get through the verses. Then I thought, *Oh, she'll say no.* So I called her and said, "For the rest of my life (to entrap myself in a commitment to the Lord), I'm going to meditate on the Word of God. I'll start in Proverbs, and I would like you to be my partner for that book."

She agreed, and I made arrangements to call her at 7 AM each day. I also told her that I wouldn't be able to talk for very long because I had to get my children ready for school.

The next morning when I called her, she immediately started griping.

"Let's go over our verses," I told her.

"No," she said, "I need to tell you this first. I am just so depressed."

"Well, I don't have time because my children have to get to school," I said. Then we went over our Bible verses. For the next two weeks, every time I called, this lady wanted to gripe, but I didn't have time for griping. We would go over the meditated scriptures and that was all.

When the third week began, something had happened. I called her and instead of griping she said, "I got the most marvelous thing out of this chapter! Did you get this?" She then shared the revelation she had received from the Word. It was so exciting! Her whole attitude turned around from that day on.

One day, some time afterward, my husband asked me, "What happened to that woman?" She used to be the most negative person I'd ever seen."

I said, "I can tell you what happened to her. The Word of God started coming out of her mouth through meditation and it *changed* her!"

Foundation for Meditation

The three basic steps to meditation are memorization, personalization, and visualization.

The first step is memorization. In John 14:26, Jesus promised to send the Holy Spirit who would bring "all things" that Jesus said to your remembrance: "But the Comforter, which is the Holy Ghost, whom the Father will send in my name, he shall teach you all things, and bring all things to your remembrance, whatsoever I have said unto you." But the Holy Spirit can't bring something to your remembrance if there is nothing there to draw from. You are to memorize God's Word so that He can make you remember.

Personalization is the next step to meditation. As you meditate, don't just say, "This is God's Word to all Christians." Instead say, "This is God's Word for me." Some people read the Bible as though it's for everybody but themselves. In the book of Acts, the apostle Peter discovered that God is no respecter of persons (10:34). And God is the same today, yesterday, and forever; He does not change (Numbers 23:19). His promises are for you! Personalize each Scripture by putting your name or the names of your loved ones in place of the words: you, he, she, they, them, etc.

The last step of meditation involves visualization. To visualize the Word means that you must see God's Word as coming to pass in your life in spite of what circumstances may look like. Visualization can be called "faith sight." You see it as yours through the eyes of faith (Romans 4:17). Visualization is first found in Genesis 22. The book of Hebrews gives you the New Testament version of what occurred:

> *By faith Abraham, when he was tried, offered up Isaac: and he that had received the promises offered up his only begotten son, of whom it was said, That in Isaac shall thy seed be called: accounting that God was able to raise him up, even from the dead; from whence also he received him in a figure.*
>
> *Hebrews 11:17-19*

When you meditate on the Word, begin saying what God says; begin to accept His Word as a reality in your life. Visualize it coming to pass for you.

Meditating on the Word is one of the most important things you can do as a Christian. When you set your priorities on meditation, every area of your life will be transformed. It worked for Joshua in the Old Testament, and it will work for you today.

Part Four

Know Your Ministry

Chapter 13

Know Your Ministry

Every born-again Christian has a desire to minister to others. Newly converted people usually have a tremendous zeal to reach the world for Christ. Then, as the newness of the born-again experience wears off, they sometimes have to take precautions not to lose that zeal.

One of the best ways to retain your zeal for ministry is to determine and operate within your place in the Body of Christ. Many times we try to operate in an area of ministry to which we have *not* been called. We try to "latch onto" or "compete with" ministries we may admire because we are uncertain of our own place in the Body. The results of this can be devastating: we become frustrated and discouraged and do a disservice to the people to whom we try to minister.

You or someone you know may have seen a ministry and decided, "I'm going to do that too." Many years ago, my husband Wally and I were assistant pastors at a church in Amarillo, Texas. Every morning at 9:00 AM several of us met to pray. One woman in particular was a true intercessor. After an hour of prayer, the rest of us were ready to stop—but she was just warming up! I respected and admired her so much that I—not God—decided I had a similar calling on my life.

One day I said to her, "God has called me to be an intercessor—just like you."

But to my surprise, she replied, "No, He hasn't. You respect me, so you're trying to latch onto my position in the Body. Marilyn, you need to pray and ask God what He has really called you to do."

At other times, we may try to compete with other Christians in the Body. Before we entered the ministry, I met a woman who was a great soul winner. She would go to a hospital to minister and end up winning 10 to 15 souls to Christ. I thought, *If she can do it, I can too! She won 15 souls to Christ so I'll win 20!* Was that desire spiritually motivated? No, really it was carnality. I was trying to compete with my sister in the Lord. But why did I do that? Because I didn't know where I belonged in the Body of Christ. In order to be effective ministers, we must know where we belong in the body.

Spiritual Gifts

Our heavenly Father is a loving and personal God, who wants us to have the best and be the best. For these very reasons, He has blessed the Body of Christ with spiritual gifts. There are three "gift" chapters in the New Testament: the gifts of the Spirit in 1 Corinthians 12:8-12, the ministry gifts in Ephesians 4:11-13, and the foundational gifts in Romans 12:4-8. God has devised a plan that, through the use of these gifts, we can live the fulfilling lives He has designed for us.

First, let's briefly outline the gifts of the Spirit:

For to one is given by the Spirit the word of wisdom; to another the word of knowledge by the same Spirit; to another faith by the same Spirit; to another the gifts of healing by the same Spirit; to another the working of miracles; to another prophecy; to another discerning of spirits; to another divers kinds of tongues; to another the interpretation of tongues: but all these worketh that one and the selfsame Spirit, dividing to every man severally as he will. For as the body is one, and hath many members, and all the members of that one body, being many, are one body: so also is Christ.

1 Corinthians 12:8-12

The gifts of the Spirit can be divided into groups of three: 1) the *spoken* gifts including divers tongues, interpretation of tongues, and prophecy; 2) the *power* gifts including the working of miracles, the gift of faith, and the gifts of healing; 3) the *revelation* gifts including the word of knowledge, the word of wisdom, and the discerning of spirits.

God always wants to minister to us in a threefold way. Using the spoken gifts, God ministers to us *spiritually;* using the power gifts, He ministers to us *physically;* and using the revelation gifts, He ministers to us *emotionally*—in our minds, emotions, and wills.

Next, let's briefly outline the ministry gifts:

And he gave some, apostles; and some, prophets; and some, evangelists; and some, pastors and teachers; for the perfecting of the saints, for the work of the ministry, for the edifying of the body of Christ.

Ephesians 4:11-12

The ministry gifts are sometimes called the "fivefold" ministry and are given to people who are called into the ministry on a full-time basis. The most efficient method to remember the components of the fivefold ministry and their responsibilities to the Body of Christ is to count them off using the fingers on one of your hands.

First, identify the apostle with your thumb. Your thumb can touch every finger on your hand, just as the apostle's ministry "touches" the other components of the fivefold ministry. The primary function of the apostle is to establish churches in new areas. The modern-day apostle is commonly known as a missionary.

Second, identify the prophet with your index or "pointing" finger. The prophet "points" to the future to bring revelation knowledge, and he "points" to the past to call others to repentance.

Third, identify your middle finger with the evangelist. Evangelists are soul winners; their words bring conviction to sinners and encouragement to believers.

Fourth, identify your ring finger with the pastor. He is "married" to the flock. He exercises authority over his church by feeding them, loving them, and when necessary, correcting them.

Fifth, identify your little finger with the teacher. Like the little finger balances your hand, the teacher's primary responsibility is to clarify truth to the Body of Christ.

Apostles, prophets, evangelists, pastors, and teachers all have been given to the Church to edify and equip the saints to help them mature in their Christian walks. It takes all five of these ministries working together to bring the Body into the perfection to which God has called it.

The focus of the upcoming chapters is on the final grouping of gifts—the foundational gifts:

For as we have many members in one body, and all members have not the same office: so we, being many, are one body in Christ, and every one members one of another. Having then gifts differing according to the grace that is given to us, whether prophecy, let us prophesy according to the proportion of faith; or ministry, let us wait on our ministering: or he that teacheth, on teaching; or he that exhorteth, on exhortation: he that giveth, let him do it with simplicity; he that ruleth, with diligence; he that sheweth mercy, with cheerfulness.

Romans 12:4-8

Unlike the ministry gifts, to which only certain people are called, each born-again believer is given a foundational gift. There seven gifts—prophecy, serving, teaching, exhortation, giving, organization, and mercy—which show us our position and others' positions within the Body of Christ.

When you identify your foundational gift, you can begin to operate in it and blossom in your ministry to the rest of the Body. As you read about and study these seven gifts, ask God to reveal the special gift He designed just for you.

The number seven in the Bible is the number of completion and the Bible says we are complete in Christ (Colossians 2:10). When you observe the seven gifts in operation throughout the Body of Christ, you see His complete ministry. As you study the foundational gifts, you will not only be able to identify your own gifts, but you will also be able to gain insight and respect for other people in the Body of Christ. You will see what motivates them, and you will clearly understand how much you need the rest of the Body. Sometimes we want to be Superman or Wonder Woman; we want to do it all! But we all need each other; and without every gift operating, we will miss the completeness of Jesus.

Use All the Ingredients

After identifying your foundational gift, you may realize that you may not be operating in it fully. For example, you may say, "Marilyn,

I know my foundational gift is teaching, but I don't teach. Why isn't God using me?"

Just as in cooking or baking, it is necessary to use all the listed ingredients to make your dish come out right. If you don't use all the ingredients, you will end up with a big mess on your hands. It is the same with foundational gifts. Identifying your gift is one of the ingredients; however, to produce an effective ministry, you must combine your gift with other godly ingredients. Romans 12:1-6 gives you the recipe to follow to use your gift effectively.

First we must be willing to give of our time and energy, understanding that the results will be wonderful. The apostle Paul writes about this lifestyle in Romans 12:1: "I beseech you therefore, brethren, by the mercies of God, that ye present your bodies a living sacrifice, holy, acceptable unto God, which is your reasonable service."

Some people say, "I can't go to church on Wednesday night! I'm just too tired after work," or, "Sunday morning is the only time I have to sleep in. Although I'm not actually in church, I'm there in spirit." But Romans 12:1 says we must be willing to give of our physical being in order to minister and fulfill God's call on our life. It may be a sacrifice, but it is a necessary ingredient to successful ministry. And the benefits are worth it in this life and eternity.

Second, we must keep our minds renewed to God's Word: "And be not conformed to this world: but be ye transformed by the renewing of your mind, that ye may prove what is that good, and acceptable, and perfect, will of God" (Romans 12:2).

Natural wisdom is earthly, sensual, and devilish (James 3:15). It stems from our carnal natures. If we trust in carnality or flesh, sin will be produced. And sin can only lead to death. We must continually renew our minds to God's Word, which will bring abundant life to those to whom we minister.

Third, we must remember that grace is the key to our gifts: "For I say, through the grace given unto me, to every man that is among you, not to think of himself more highly than he ought to think; but to think soberly, according as God hath dealt to every man the measure of faith" (Romans 12:3).

Grace means that God gave us a gift in spite of what we deserved. He doesn't give us gifts because of our looks, education, or personalities. When people say, "I have a ministry," I think, *No, you really don't have a ministry. God has the ministry, and you allow Him to flow through you.* Let's not get on an ego trip about God's grace; it is available to all.

Fourth, we must remember that our gifts are unique: "For as we have many members in one body, and all members have not the same office: so we, being many, are one body in Christ, and every one members one of another. Having then gifts differing according to the grace that is given to us" (Romans 12:4-6).

When we gain a burden for something oftentimes we want others to share that burden. You may have a very strong desire to give or to exhort, but don't get upset with your neighbor if he or she doesn't share those same desires. Perhaps the Lord has given your neighbor a desire to teach or to organize. We all have different gifts according to the measure of grace given to us. And in order for the Body of Christ to function effectively, *all* the gifts must be in operation.

Finally, you may ask, "Marilyn, is it possible for me to have more than one foundational gift?" As you study the gifts described in the following chapters, you may—and probably will—recognize that certain traits of more than one gift are operational in your life. (Most of us are used in a number of ways when we're available to Jesus.) But there will be one gift with which you identify the most closely and in which you obtain the most success. That gift—whether it be prophecy, organizing, giving, serving, exhortation, mercy, or teaching—is *your* foundational gift.

Once you have identified your gift, you will notice it flows through all your spiritual activity within the Body. For example, if you counsel others, and your foundational gift is mercy, you will be a merciful counselor. Allow the Holy Spirit to lead you and guide you in this study of foundational gifts. He will show you your perfect position within the Body of Christ.

Chapter 14

Foundational Gifts: Prophecy, Serving, Teaching, Exhortation

"Having then gifts differing according to the grace that is given to us, let us use them: if prophecy, let us prophesy in proportion to our faith; or ministry, let us use it in our ministering; he who teaches, in teaching; he who exhorts, in exhortation; he who gives, with liberality; he who leads, with diligence; he who shows mercy, with cheerfulness."

—*Romans 12:4-6 NKJV*

Every believer has a principal foundational gift and often attributes of many of the gifts. As each of the seven foundational gifts is explored in this chapter, consider the characteristics you recognize in your life. Pray this prayer and invite God to reveal His gifts and callings for you:

Dear Heavenly Father,

Thank You for giving me a unique and perfect foundational gift. I realize it is not through my own works, but through

Your grace that I have received this gift. Father, I will endeavor to be available to minister in my gift whenever You call me to do so. I will strive to keep my mind renewed to Your Word, so I will know what Your perfect will is for me. Now, Father, as I study the different gifts listed in Romans 12, I ask Your Holy Spirit to reveal to me the identity of my special and unique gift, in Jesus' precious name, Amen.

The Gift of Prophecy

"...whether prophecy, let us prophecy according to the proportion of faith."

Romans 12:6

Prophecy has been defined as a gift that never tears others down, but views everything in light of God's standards. Prophecy-motivated people have great spiritual insight into what motivates others. They "see" the motivation behind others' actions and can identify them as being evil or good. However, they should use scriptural guidelines to identify evil, not their own opinions or personal convictions. Because my strengths and weaknesses are different than yours, God may convict me of things that you feel perfectly free to do.

When I was first Spirit-filled, God convicted me about reading fiction. I was a literature teacher and, generally, read three to four books a week. But I really felt God wanted me to read the Word instead. Although the Lord has convicted me about reading fiction, I never tell others it is wrong. Why? Because it is God's personal conviction to me. It doesn't necessarily mean it is wrong for others to read fiction.

When my husband Wally and I began in the ministry, we traveled to various areas to conduct evangelistic meetings. At one particular meeting, several people came forward for salvation. We were so happy, but the pastor of the church in which we were ministering didn't appear happy at all. In fact, he was frowning!

After the meeting, Wally asked the pastor if we had done something wrong. "No," he replied, "you haven't done anything wrong. However, there is a woman in our congregation who approaches all of the new women in this church. She tells them now that they are born-again, they can no longer wear make-up or jewelry. She's practically turning people away from the church faster than we can get them in here!"

Apparently this woman felt convicted not to wear make-up or jewelry, but she was imposing her personal conviction on others and causing turmoil in her church. It is very important that people who have the foundational gift of prophecy identify evil through scriptural means.

Prophecy-motivated people are very frank and direct verbally. They are not afraid to point out weaknesses, and they are very eager to have their own weaknesses exposed as well. However, there are some people who like to tell what's wrong with everyone else, but if someone happens to point out one of their weaknesses, they become offended. If you like to point out weaknesses in others, but fall apart when one of your weaknesses is exposed, then you probably don't have a prophecy motive; you may be insecure in who you are in Christ. Get in the New Testament and study what God says about you—what He made you through Christ Jesus. Don't let a critical spirit ruin your relationships.

Next, prophecy-motivated people are extremely protective of God's program. They want to see born-again Christians living righteous lives and setting godly examples for others.

Several years ago, an extremely well known evangelist began to have trouble. He was caught drinking heavily and having extra-marital affairs. Another minister who had a prophecy motive spotted the evangelist on an airplane. The evangelist was drunk and flirting with the woman sitting next to him. This grieved the other minister and he went to the evangelist, knelt in the aisle beside him, and begged him to repent. The minister was so concerned about preserving the reputation of the ministry that he didn't care what the other people on the plane thought.

Prophecy-motivated people also want to see outward evidence of change once others have repented. Don't try to do mere lip service to prophecy-motivated people—they won't buy it!

Finally, prophecy-motivated people often use visual aids to demonstrate the truth. For example, Ezekiel often used visual aids when speaking to the Israelites. Once he even used his own hair as a visual aid!

And you, son of man, take a sharp sword, take it as a barber's razor, and pass it over your head and your beard; then take scales to weigh and divide the hair. You shall burn with fire one-third in the midst of the city, when the days of the siege are finished; then you shall take one-third and strike around it with the sword, and one-third you shall scatter in the wind: I will draw out a sword after them. You shall also take a small number of them and bind them in the edge of your garment. Then take some of them again and throw them into the midst of the fire, and burn them in the fire. From there a fire will go out into all the house of Israel.

Ezekiel 5:1-4 NKJV

What an unusual visual aid. Ezekiel cut his hair and beard, chopped up a third of the hair with a knife, threw another third into the wind, and burned the last third. This was a prophetic demonstration of what would happen to the Israelites during King Nebuchadnezzar's siege:

one-third would be killed by the sword, one-third would flee, and one-third would burn in the city.

I'm sure the Israelites did not easily forget this visual aid. And that is precisely the point: prophecy-motivated people will use extremely colorful and creative means to demonstrate their point. Visual aids not only help bring others to repentance, but they help others to remember the message given.

Guidelines for Prophecy-Motivated People

As with all foundational gifts, prophecy-motivated people must utilize their gift in conjunction with the Holy Spirit. Incorrect usage can fail to glorify God and consequently hurt the Body of Christ. Following are some guidelines that prophecy-motivated people can use to insure they minister in the Spirit:

1. Be certain to speak the truth in love.

It is vitally important that prophecy-motivated people be led by the Holy Spirit when pointing out others' weaknesses. Remember, just as Paul charged Timothy, we too, are charged to treat others gently and meekly: "In the presence of God and of Christ Jesus, who will judge the living and the dead, and in view of his appearing and his kingdom, I give you this charge: preach the word; be prepared in season and out of season; correct, rebuke and encourage—with great patience and careful instruction" (2 Timothy 4:1-2 NIV).

2. Guard against rigidity.

Prophecy-motivated people can set such high standards for righteous living that they become legalistic and hinder others' spiritual growth. For example, when a person first becomes born-again, some habits from his or her old nature—like smoking—may linger. (Only our spirits are completely renewed at the new birth; our souls are renewed by meditating on and applying God's Word to our lives.)

But a prophecy-motivated person may be inclined to go up to young Christian and say, "What's wrong with you? Don't you know it's a sin to smoke?" Remember, young Christians need time to become mature spiritually. It's important their spiritual growth is not hindered by a more mature Christian's convictions of righteousness.

John the Baptist

For a Biblical example of a man whose foundational gift was prophecy, let's look at John the Baptist.

In Luke 3:3, he calls people to repentance: "And he came into all the country about Jordan, preaching the baptism of repentance for the remission of sins." Remember, prophecy-motivated people always call others to true repentance.

He "saw" the motivation in their hearts. The Jews thought since Abraham was their father, they had no need to repent. But John the Baptist saw this motivating factor in their thinking and quickly dismissed it as a reason not to repent. On the contrary, John wanted the Jews to repent, and he wanted to see outward evidence of this inward change that had taken place in their hearts: "Bring forth therefore fruits worthy of repentance, and begin not to say within yourselves, we have Abraham to our father: for I say unto you, That God is able of these stones to raise up children unto Abraham" (Luke 3:8).

John the Baptist also used visual aids. What did he wear to his gospel services? A three-piece suit and a tie? No, his garments were made of camel's hair, and he wore a leather girdle around his waist (Matthew 3:4). And what did he eat? T-bone steaks and Caesar salad? No, he only ate locusts and wild honey. He looked and acted like a wild man—and he had a wild message. God knew that His Word, combined with John's unusual behavior and attire, would make a lasting impression on the Jews' hardened hearts and ultimately bring them to repentance.

The Gift of Serving

"Or ministry, let us wait on our ministering…"

Romans 12:7

The gift of serving is very important because it motivates those who have it to meet the practical needs in the Church. The server sees all the needs in the ministry and tries to meet them. For this reason it always pleases me to see servers called into the five-fold ministry.

You may ask, "Marilyn, how can one be called into the five-fold ministry and have serving as a foundational gift? Shouldn't a person in those ministries have prophecy or teaching for a foundational gift?" No, not really. In fact, a server who is called into full-time ministry will probably be more successful than other ministries with other foundational gifts. Let me explain why. My husband Wally and I have had a lot of staff members come and go during our 40-plus years in the ministry. Some people have left to begin their own ministries, and the ones who are really practical—who put their hands to the plow and not just behind the pulpit—are the ones who get their churches going and minister effectively to the people.

A few years ago, a young married couple on our staff felt called to move to another state and begin a ministry. Now, neither of them had a pulpit ministry when they worked for us, and when they announced their plans to begin a church, I thought, *Oh Lord, I hope they really heard from You on this!* I knew they had both performed many practical tasks in the ministry, but I was concerned that neither had any pulpit experience.

Yet, today, their ministry is flourishing. Why? Because they're practical; they see needs and they meet them. You may be the finest teacher or preacher in the world, but if you don't meet your congregation's needs, you are not doing what you've been called to do. Now I'm not saying that only servers should be in the five-fold ministry; I'm simply saying they have an advantage. Those of us in the five-fold ministry must adopt an attitude of a servant to be truly successful.

What are the characteristics of servers? They are willing to employ physical energy almost to the point of exhaustion. They will accept any challenge and stick with it to completion—even if that means forfeiting several hours in which they could be doing something else they enjoy.

And servers take on these tasks wholeheartedly. I love their attitude! They don't say, "I'm an executive. I'm too important to do a menial task!" No. Servers fashion themselves after Jesus. He wasn't an executive, was He? Jesus made no reputation of himself and took on the form of a servant (Philippians 2:7), and the Bible encourages us to do likewise: "Let this mind be in you, which was also in Christ Jesus" (Philippians 2:5).

An interesting component of a server's personality is he or she need recognition. For example, many years ago a woman who designed clothing professionally began to attend our church. She was very talented and had even designed clothing for Hollywood stars. But now, she wanted to put her talents to use for God. She approached me after church one Sunday morning and offered to design some clothes for me. I was just beginning to travel in the ministry and needed some new clothing, so I accepted her offer. She made some beautiful outfits for me including a gorgeous long coat with a fox fur collar and cuffs.

I was very appreciative, but for some reason that didn't seem to satisfy her. Whenever I came home from a trip, she would meet me at the airport and ask, "Did anyone notice your coat?"

I prayed, "Lord, why does this woman need so much reassurance?"

And the Lord answered me, "She is a server, and her service is unto Me. When people don't recognize her work, she feels she has failed Me." In other words, recognition for her work assured her that her ministry was effective!

Servers are also aware of others' preferences and remember details. For example, if you go to a server's home for coffee, they will make a mental note of whether you use cream, sugar, or whatever. And the next time you go to their home, you won't have to remind them of your preference. They'll serve your coffee exactly the way you like it.

Servers prefer to work on projects that yield immediate results. They may even appear to be intimidated by long-range projects. Why? Because servers have a tendency to try to undertake everything singlehandedly. Also, servers are not ordinarily well organized and can be overwhelmed by the prospect of organizing a long-range project.

In Philippians 4:2, Paul admonished two women, Euodias and Syntyche, to live in harmony. I wonder if these two women were servers. If so, I think I know how their difficulties may have begun.

In Biblical times women did all the cooking, and at an event, they all cooked together. Now, remember, servers are not ordinarily well organized, and both of these women may have been trying to do all the work, thus duplicating some tasks and ignoring others. Undoubtedly, they ended up arguing over who was going to perform which task.

This again shows us the importance of all the foundational gifts working together within the Body. If someone with the foundational gift of organizing had been working with Euodias and Syntyche, then everything probably would have gone very smoothly. The organizer would have said, "Syntyche, you do the salads and the vegetables, and Euodias, you do the meat and gravy." Organizers will help servers to set goals so they can minister with maximum efficiency.

Guidelines for Serving-Motivated People

Remember, anyone who ministers must do so under the anointing of the Holy Spirit. Otherwise, the results can be devastating and other people can be hurt. Following are some guidelines servers should follow to insure they remain in the Spirit:

1. Make certain God has called you to do the task you are performing.

In their enthusiasm to serve, some servers can become overly aggressive. Be careful you are not performing a task God would like another to do.

2. Do your work as unto the Lord.

Sometimes servers become offended when they aren't complimented and recognized. Remember, although people may not recognize your work, your heavenly Father is always aware of your accomplishments, and He values your willingness to serve Him.

3. Keep your priorities straight.

Sometimes servers become so motivated by the tasks they are to perform they neglect their personal relationship with God. Our relationship with God must always have first priority in our lives, and if we neglect Him, we need to reassess our priorities and put them in proper order.

4. Be careful not to interfere with God's dealings with others.

Sometimes a server will leap in to help someone whom God is trying to teach a lesson. One man in our congregation had tremendous fear about tithing and giving. He confided his fear to us, and we ministered to him by giving him scriptures on God's promises to those who give faithfully. But the man did not heed our advice and soon began to experience financial difficulties. Two other people in our church, whose foundational gifts were serving, felt led to take up an offering to help this man with his finances.

Wally and I felt strongly this was not the course of action the Lord was directing. We said, "Wait! God may be trying to teach this man a lesson and although an offering may help this man out of a particular bind, we may be interfering with God's plan to change his life."

Servers must be certain to follow God's leading. If these two servers had gone ahead with their plans to help this man financially, they may have interfered with God's plan to bring this man into obedience. And which is better? Should we be concerned with solving short-term problems or with following God's directions, which will bring eternal results?

Martha and Mary

Martha is a wonderful Biblical example of a woman who loved to serve others:

Now it came to pass, as they went, that he entered into a certain village: and a certain woman named Martha received him into

her house. And she had a sister called Mary, which also sat at Jesus'
feet, and heard his word. But Martha was cumbered about much
serving, and came to him, and said, Lord, dost thou not care that
my sister hath left me to serve alone? Bid her therefore that she help
me. And Jesus answered and said unto her, Martha, Martha, thou
art careful and troubled about many things: but one thing is need-
ful: and Mary hath chosen that good part, which shall not be taken
away from her.

Luke 10:38-42

I suspect Martha had invited many people to dinner that day. And I have a feeling a lot of people just dropped in because Jesus was there. Martha probably began to panic and said, "Oh dear, I don't have enough food for all these people! And on top of that Mary is just sitting around doing nothing!"

Martha became so involved in the task of serving that her eyes strayed from the One whom she served, Jesus Christ. Martha became impatient and tried to vent her feelings on Mary. But this account does not say that Mary didn't help; rather it says she also sat at Jesus' feet (10:39). What does this mean? She had been helping Martha, but she stopped in order to spend time with her Savior. Mary had her priorities in the proper order, whereas Martha became too involved in her task and lost perspective on what was truly important.

John 11 reveals how deeply Jesus loved and appreciated Martha:

Now a certain man was sick, named Lazarus, of Bethany, the town
of Mary and her sister Martha. (It was that Mary which anointed
the Lord with ointment, and wiped his feet with her hair, whose
brother Lazarus was sick.) Therefore his sisters sent unto him, say-
ing, Lord, behold, he whom thou lovest is sick. When Jesus heard

that, he said, This sickness is not unto death, but for the glory of God,
that the Son of God might be glorified thereby. Now Jesus loved
Martha, and her sister, and Lazarus.

John 11:1-5

Everything in the Bible has a specific purpose, and I think Jesus was showing Martha how much He truly loved and appreciated her.

When Jesus arrived at the tomb to raise Lazarus from the dead, He said, "Martha, if you will believe, you will see the glory of God" (v. 40).

Who was involved in believing with Jesus to see Lazarus brought back to life? Martha, not Mary, nor any of the mourners who were there. Jesus specifically chose Martha because He wanted her to know she was a very valuable asset to the kingdom of God.

All servers are valuable to the kingdom of God. And if your foundational gift is serving, remember, not a single task you perform goes unnoticed by your heavenly Father. You have a vital ministry in the Body of Christ.

The Gift of Teaching

"...or he that teacheth, on teaching."

Romans 12:7

People with the foundational gift of teaching receive great joy from studying the Word and doing Biblical research. And they would like to see everyone else equally turned-on to the Scriptures! Teachers are so involved in the Word that, in most cases, they enjoy studying the Word more than they like presenting their findings to others.

Teachers prefer to use Biblical examples and rarely season their lessons with stories that relate to personal experiences. Why? Because teachers' spiritual lives are motivated almost wholly by the Word; they usually prefer to use Biblical illustrations to support their teaching.

Teaching-motivated people sometimes like to test others' Biblical knowledge. Teachers are very watchful that others who may teach the Word do not deviate from the truth. For example, if during a sermon, a preacher would say, "Cleanliness is next to godliness," a teacher would think, *Don't say that! It's not scriptural!* Teachers' hearts are so burdened with establishing God's people in the truth that they don't want others to present it incorrectly, no matter how slight the deviation might be.

Another characteristic of teaching-motivated people is they like to present truth systematically. However, teachers must remember not everyone uses the same teaching methods or learns the same way. Many years ago a minister, who is now well known, conducted a series of meetings at our church. This man had just begun to travel in the ministry, and I had never before heard him preach.

Now this man does not teach the Word systematically—he just opens his mouth and talks, and I wasn't getting anything out of his teaching. In fact, I thought, *This is terrible! Why on earth did Wally agree to let him speak here?* But as I looked around at the people in our congregation, I noticed they were absolutely enthralled by his teaching. So, I prayed, "Lord, is there something wrong with me?"

The Lord answered, "Marilyn, you think you can only understand lessons that are presented in an orderly manner. Stop trying to understand the Word with your head and try listening with your spirit." God really taught me something in that service; He taught me to have "hearing ears." Today, I can listen to any teaching, and as long as it is Word-centered, I can learn from it.

God wants us to have hearing ears, and He wants us to learn in a variety of ways. We would be bored out of our minds if everyone used the same teaching methods; in fact, it would be like eating mashed potatoes and gravy for dinner every night. Now, you may like mashed potatoes and gravy, but after eating them seven days a week, 365 days a year, just looking at them would make you feel ill! God doesn't want us to become bored with His Word, so He gives us a variety of ways to learn it. That way, every time we feed on the Word, it will taste fresh and sweet.

Finally, teachers use Biblical foundations to test new truths. The Bible is not self-contradictory; it always flows together. And if a new teaching contradicts foundational Biblical truth, it is false teaching and should be ignored.

Many years ago, a woman in our congregation got into the habit of giving a word of prophecy before each service. No matter who was preaching that day—whether it was Wally, me, or a special guest speaker—she would prophesy beforehand. Her prophecies always advised against teaching the Word, because, she said, there was "a more excellent way" to learn from God.

One night a special guest speaker at our church became ill with laryngitis and was having trouble carrying on short conversations, let alone preaching for an hour! The woman prophesied that if this speaker wouldn't insist on teaching, God would heal him as there is a "more excellent way" than teaching.

Later, I asked her to show me in the Bible where it said there was a more excellent way than teaching God's Word. She answered, "Oh, Marilyn, it's not in the Bible. If you depend on the Bible alone, you will never receive new revelation from God. I have found there is even a more excellent way than the Bible to hear from God."

"Oh really?" I asked. "What is it?"

"Through personal prophecy one to another," she replied.

Is that scriptural? No, indeed it is not. In fact, three times in His Word God explicitly tells us the dangerous consequences of tampering with His Word:

For I testify unto every man that heareth the words of the prophecy of this book, If any man shall add unto these things, God shall add unto him the plagues that are written in this book: And if any man shall take away from the words of the book of this prophecy, God shall take away his part out of the book of life, and out of the holy city, and from the things which are written in this book.

Revelation 22:18-19

Ye shall not add unto the word which I command you, neither shall ye diminish ought from it, that ye may keep the commandments of the LORD your God which I command you.

Deuteronomy 4:2

Every word of God is pure: he is a shield unto them that put their trust in him. Add thou not unto his words, lest he reprove thee, and thou be found a liar.

Proverbs 30:5-6

There is not a "more excellent way" than God's Word, and everything we teach should be centered on it. That incident happened over 30 years ago, and today, that woman no longer prophesies about a "more excellent way" but instead she serves God in truth.

Guidelines for Teaching Motivated People

You can see why the foundational gift of teaching is so important to the Body of Christ. Without teachers, the Body may deviate from the Word as its source of truth and revelation knowledge from God. Following are some guidelines teachers can use to ensure they minister under the direction of the Holy Spirit.

1. Teachers should be careful to present their material in an interesting fashion.

Sometimes teachers get so involved in their material they forget about the people they are teaching. Several years ago, a man who professionally coached others in speech presentation said to me, "Marilyn, sometimes you are really boring."

Now I was quite shocked to hear that, but as sweetly as possible, I responded, "Oh, I didn't realize that. What do you think is wrong with my teaching?"

"Well," he said, "it's as if you take a cup, jam-pack it full of knowledge, and them dump it on the people you teach. You really need to watch your audience and be more tuned in to their reaction."

Now as soon as the man said this, I knew he was telling me the truth. Even my husband Wally has said to me on occasion, "Do you have to tell them everything you know? Can't you save some for next week?" Teachers must always remember to "tune into" their audience; otherwise, their audience will "tune them out" and their message—no matter how good it is—will fall on deaf ears.

2. Teachers should make sure their lessons have practical application.

You can tell people all the facts, but if they can't apply them to their everyday lives, your lesson is fruitless. People, not facts, are God's greatest concern. We are precious to Him, and He wants to meet our daily needs. Teachers should never allow facts to become more important than the people to whom they are being presented.

3. Teach with humility and compassion.

Because teachers love to spend time in the Word, they often become very knowledgeable about it. This may lead to a prideful attitude. They may know many Biblical facts, but if that knowledge doesn't help someone, the teacher is just on a head-trip. And we need teachers to be on heart-trips, not head-trips, don't we?

Teachers can also become more concerned about the material they study than the people to whom they present, as I mentioned before. It is important that teachers not only study but retain godly love and compassion toward those for whom it is meant—people.

Paul

Paul's foundational gift was teaching and he was also called into the five-fold ministry as a teacher (Acts 13:1). Paul felt teaching was the most important foundational gift and he was very involved in research and study of the Word. He even emphasized it to Timothy: "Study to shew thyself approved unto God, a workman that needeth not to be ashamed, rightly dividing the word of truth" (2 Tim. 2:15).

Paul loved to study the Word. While in Arabia, he didn't complain about being lonely as an exhorter would have. Instead, I'm sure Paul thought, *Good, there are no people here to bother me. Now I can really study.*

Paul used his time wisely—while in Arabia and while in prison—to research and study the Word. As a teacher, Paul always needed his books: "…when thou comest, bring with thee, and the books, but especially the parchments" (2 Timothy 4:13).

Following one of the true characteristics of a teaching-motivated person, Paul sometimes tested others' knowledge of the Word. While at Areopagus, Paul tested the Athenians' knowledge (Acts 17:18-34).

Paul frequently tied Old and New Testament teachings together. He presented Old Testament examples to confirm new truths:

He will swallow up death in victory; and the Lord GOD will wipe away tears from off all faces; and the rebuke of his people shall he take away from off all the earth: for the LORD hath spoken it.

Isaiah 25:8

So when this corruptible shall have put on incorruption, and this mortal shall have put on immortality, then shall be brought to pass the saying that is written, Death is swallowed up in victory. O death, where is thy sting? O grave, where is thy victory? The sting of death is sin; and the strength of sin is the law. But thanks be to God, which giveth us the victory through our Lord Jesus Christ.

1 Corinthians 15:54-57

He was very precise in writing down the truth. He had a great burden always to teach the truth because of his love for the church. His heart was burdened with grounding God's flock in the Word: "how I kept back nothing that was helpful, but proclaimed it to you, and taught you publicly and from house to house."

Acts 20:20 NKJV

The Gift of Exhortation

"Or he that exhorteth, on exhortation…"

Romans 12:8

Exhortation is the foundational gift that is very strongly life-related: it draws upon the practical applications of life's experiences to produce abundant living in others. Exhorters are very well liked and loved. They tend to have very loving, positive attitudes and desire more than anything that believers mature and grow in their relationship with God.

Exhorters like to give others "steps of activity" to follow to bring them out of their misery, trials, and tribulations. For example, many years ago, we had a pastor on staff whose foundational gift was exhortation. A young woman had come to him for counseling regarding her broken marriage: her husband had left her and was living with another woman. The pastor counseled the young woman and prayed with her. And then he asked the woman if her husband would be interested in coming in for counseling too.

"No, I don't think so," was her simple reply.

"Well," said the pastor, "let's pray about it. I would really like to see your marriage healed."

The young woman asked her husband if he was interested in counseling and to her astonishment, he agreed to go! But during the counseling session, the pastor began to give the man steps of action to take in accordance with the Scriptures. "Stop right there," protested the woman's estranged husband. "I'm agnostic, so don't tell me anything about the Bible. I don't believe in it." He then walked out of the pastor's office.

But the pastor didn't give up; instead, he prayed, "Father, give me some actions steps to reach this man for You." James 1:5 says, "If any of you lack wisdom, let him ask of God, that giveth to all men liberally, and upbraideth not; and it shall be given him."

The pastor asked for God's wisdom and He gave it to him. The Lord said, "Write this man a letter and deal with him as an American citizen. Show him his duties as an American husband and father." Now, the pastor gave the man spiritual steps of action, but he listed them under the auspices of American citizenship. Upon reading the letter, the man followed the steps of action: he came to church and received Jesus Christ as his personal Lord and Savior. The young couple's marriage was saved and today they are living in another state and are serving the Lord.

After hearing this testimony the world would say, "There's more than one way to skin a cat!" But God has called us to be fishermen for Him, and He has given us more than one kind of bait to catch those fish. Exhorters love to use all God's methods to bring people closer to Him.

Exhorters also enjoy seeing others apply Biblical truths to their lives. In 2 Kings 5, Naaman came to the prophet Elisha for healing. (Elisha was called into the fivefold ministry as a prophet, but his foundational gift was exhortation.) Instead of ministering to Naaman personally, Elisha sent a servant with instructions for Naaman to go to the Jordan River and wash himself seven times. Elisha gave Naaman steps of action to take in order to be healed. And after washing in the river seven times, Naaman was healed of leprosy.

Another time in 2 Kings, the prophets of Jericho had a terrible problem: their water was cursed and caused everything to miscarry—the animals lost their young, and trees and plants did not yield any fruit.

Elisha gave the men action steps to follow in order to make their water blessed instead of cursed: "Bring me a new cruse, and put salt therein" (2:20).

After the men followed Elisha's instructions, he poured salt from the cruse into the water and said, "Thus saith the LORD, I have healed these waters; there shall not be from thence any more death or barren land" (2:21).

It was only after the men had followed Elisha's action steps that he could perform the miracle God had prescribed to sweeten the water. That miracle happened over 2,500 years ago, and the water in Jericho is sweet to this day.

Can you think of time when Jesus gave people instructions to follow in order to receive miracles? (Jesus operated fully in all seven foundational gifts.) Jesus gave the servants steps to follow when He turned the water into wine at the wedding in Cana (John 2:9); He gave the lepers instructions to receive their healing (Luke 17:14); He gave the blind man at Siloam steps to follow to be healed (John 9:7); and Jesus instructed Peter to catch a fish to pay their taxes (Matthew 17:27).

Next, exhorters like teaching from God's Word to be applicable to everyday living. In contrast to teachers, who would explain every detail of a subject, exhorters would give you the practical application of it. Exhorters want you to relate to the subject matter and incorporate it into your daily life so that your spiritual development may reach its fullest potential.

People with the foundational gift of exhortation are very perceptive to others' reactions. When exhorters minister on a one-to-one basis, they look for signs that indicate whether or not the person to whom they are ministering is benefiting. For example, when exhorters are ministering to you, they will watch your eyes and listen to the tone of your voice to determine if you are benefiting from their ministry. If not, they feel that they have failed.

Exhorters like to relate personal examples to Biblical truths. They love to think of a personal experience and then look up a Scripture that applies to that example.

Finally, people with the foundational gift of exhortation love to cousel others. They love to give others new insight into the Word so they can practice it and see changes in their lives.

Guidelines for Exhorters

Following are some guidelines exhorters should follow to insure they minister under the direction of the Holy Spirit.

1. Be sensitive to the Lord's leading.

Sometimes exhorters over-emphasize their actions steps more than they depend on the Lord who gives them the steps. I'm sure other lepers heard about Naaman's cure and may have come to Elisha for healing. But just because one leper was healed by washing in the Jordan, didn't mean every leper who washed in the Jordan would be healed. Exhorters must be sensitive to what God wants to do in a situation. The Holy Spirit will manifest results differently in various people's lives, and we must remember that what works for one person won't necessarily work for another.

2. Have faith in God.

If the people to whom exhorters minister do not follow their advice, the exhorters sometimes feel they have failed. But we cannot always walk by what we see, can we? If you have sown the Word in love and by the power of the Holy Spirit, then you have to trust in God to bring the results.

One time as I was waiting for a friend in a large shopping mall, I noticed a woman who was obviously very distraught over something: she was extremely nervous and was chain-smoking cigarettes. I was concerned about the woman and decided to take the opportunity to witness to her. Well, to say she didn't appreciate my intentions is an understatement! She said, "Lady, if I want a sermon, I'll ask for one." In other words she told me to "bug off."

That was a time when I really had to walk by faith and not by sight. I said, "Lord, I really believe You wanted me to witness to that woman. I repent if I didn't minister to her correctly, but Father, please protect the seeds I have sown into her heart and let them bear fruit." And I left the whole situation in God's capable hands.

Recently, this woman contacted me. "I doubt you remember this," she began, "but sometime ago you tried to minister to me at a shopping mall. I became very angry and really told you off. But a friend of mine who is born again, ministered to me too, and now I am born again and Spirit-filled. I just wanted you to know your ministry to me was not in vain."

It is important to be faithful to God. If the people to whom you minister don't openly accept your efforts, then trust God to continue to work in their hearts. Remember, your labor in the Lord is never in vain.

3. Be careful not to take Scripture out of context.

Sometimes exhorters want so badly to prove their points that they twist the Scriptures to correspond to the example they are giving. Second Peter 1:20 says, "Knowing this first, that no prophecy of the scripture is of any private interpretation."

Revelation 22:18-19 fully explains the serious repercussions that those who "privately interpret" God's Word will encounter:

For I testify unto every man that heareth the words of the prophecy of this book, If any man shall add unto these things, God shall add unto him the plagues that are written in this book: And if any man shall take away from the words of the book of this prophecy, God shall take away his part out of the book of life, and out of the holy city, and from the things which are written in this book.

Exhorters must be careful not to manipulate Scriptures to coincide with their personal examples; rather, their examples should coincide with Scripture.

Barnabas

Barnabas is a beautiful example of a person with the foundational gift of exhortation. He first appeared in Acts 4:36: "And Joses, who by the apostles was surnamed Barnabas, (which is, being interpreted, The son of consolation,) a Levite, and of the country of Cyprus."

What a tremendous compliment! The apostles were so uplifted and encouraged by Joses that they changed his name to Barnabas, meaning "the son of consolation." We see how Barnabas' ministry continues to bless the Body of Christ today.

Acts 13:2 tells of Barnabas' call to the ministry: "As they ministered to the Lord, and fasted, the Holy Ghost said, Separate me Barnabas and Saul for the work whereunto I have called them."

Paul and Barnabas made an excellent ministerial team: Paul was a teacher and Barnabas was an exhorter. Their foundational gifts complimented each other very well. Another young man named John Mark accompanied these two on their first journey. Now, John Mark was called into the ministry but he wasn't quite prepared for the hardship a minister of the gospel had to endure. He became very homesick, and when the three arrived in Pamphylia, John Mark went home.

Paul and Barnabas' first journey together was a tremendous success, but trouble began to brew when Barnabas suggested that John Mark accompany them on their second trip.

"No!" said Paul. "You can't depend on him. Leave that mama's boy at home!" Granted, Paul's attitude toward John Mark was somewhat less than gracious, but don't get upset with Paul—his motivation within the Body of Christ was simply different than Barnabas' motivation.

The contention between the two ministers became so intense that they separated: Paul took Silas on his trip, and Barnabas took John Mark on his. Barnabas encouraged John Mark and helped him to develop his ministry. Later, in his second epistle to Timothy, Paul wrote: "Take Mark, and bring him with thee: for he is profitable to me for the ministry" (2 Timothy 4:11).

Why did Paul change his mind about John Mark? Because John Mark himself had changed; he had matured and become a profitable minister of the gospel. But how did this change occur? Because Barnabas, the exhorter, did not give up. He encouraged John Mark and helped him to become an efficient servant of the Lord Jesus Christ.

Paul wrote several books in the New Testament, and John Mark wrote the gospel of Mark. Did Barnabas write any books in the New

Testament? No, he did not. But without Barnabas' encouragement and patience, John Mark wouldn't have written anything either. Because of Barnabas' encouragement to John Mark, a book was written that continues to bless us today. Barnabas was just as important to the Body of Christ as Paul or John Mark. All three men held different positions and had different callings and anointings on their lives; yet all three made a decisive impact on the growth of Christianity.

Chapter 15

Foundational Gifts: Giving, Organization, Mercy

Having then gifts differing according to the grace that is given to us, let us use them: if prophecy, let us prophesy in proportion to our faith; or ministry, let us use it in our ministering; he who teaches, in teaching; he who exhorts, in exhortation; he who gives, with liberality; he who leads, with diligence; he who shows mercy, with cheerfulness.

—Romans 12:6-8 NKJV

The last three gifts found in Romans 12 are giving, organization or leading, and mercy. Perhaps your foundational gift is one of these three but even if you do not find your main gift in these areas, you may find elements that apply and will be helpful to you. The knowledge of all the foundational gifts will help you understand how to work effectively with others in the Body of Christ.

The Gift of Giving

"...he that giveth, let him do it with simplicity..."

Romans 12:8

The New Testament draws examples of giving from the Greek word *metadidmoni*, which means, "to impart, give." In other words it means to share things, spiritual gifts, finances, oneself, and the gospel. People who are motivated to give not only offer their money, but also their time and themselves to the Lord's work and, therefore, bless the kingdom of God.

Giving-motivated people feel they are a part of any ministry into which they give. This is a very scriptural attitude because Matthew 6:21 says, "For where your treasure is, there will your heart be also." Givers may not be involved with the day-to-day activities of the different ministries to which they give, but they feel they are knit together *spiritually* with those ministries.

As pastors, Wally and I are often contacted to give to various ministries either financially or through personal ministry. Although we may only be in contact with those ministries on an annual basis, we continue to pray for them and feel knit together with them. Giving-motivated people often feel this way too. No matter how many ministries they may support, their hearts are knit with them.

People who are motivated to give are often used by God to motivate others to give as well. So if someone you know continually encourages you to give, don't be offended—that's probably his or her position in the Body.

Givers are very burdened that the church's financial needs are met. Many years ago, a giving-motivated man held a position on our board of directors. The first thing he would ask at our monthly meetings was, "Are you paying your bills?" I got so tired of that question! I longed for the day when he would ask, "How many people were saved last month? How many were Spirit-filled?" Once I even asked him if he wanted to know if our congregation's spiritual needs were being met. His quizzical expression made it very obvious that he couldn't have cared less. I was so offended by him that I asked the Lord, "Doesn't that man care about anything *spiritual*?"

The Lord answered me very simply, "Giving is his spiritual desire and motivation. It's his place in the Body and I made him that way."

Then I began to compare some of the foundational gifts in the Body of Christ: an exhorter would care if people were being saved; a teacher would want to know if we were teaching the Word; a server would ask if the people's practical needs were being met; a person who was mercy-motivated would want to know if emotional wounds were being healed; and a prophecy-motivated person would ask if people were being called to repentance. That particular man on our board of directors was a giver, and it was perfectly normal for him to ask if we were spending our money wisely.

Do you see how much we need each other? If everyone had the same foundational *gift*, many needs in the church would be totally neglected. We all need each other to perfect the Body and help it mature into the Bride without "spot or wrinkle" for whom Christ will return.

Next, giving-motivated people do not like to be pressured into giving. For example, they are often offended when they receive appeal letters from ministries. Why? Because they are already *very* motivated toward giving, and they are embarrassed to think someone would feel it necessary to encourage them to give.

Givers are delighted when their offering is the answer to another's prayer. One summer our ministry was experiencing a terrible financial crisis due to mail theft at our local post office. We estimate, in a few short months, $200,000 was stolen from us. Our financial forecast was so gloomy it looked like we would have to close our doors. But God had another plan in mind, and He rescued us from our financial woes in a very unique manner: He impressed upon a man in another city to send us $50,000! This was the largest one-time gift we had ever received, and it couldn't have come at a more opportune time.

I called the man on the telephone to thank him and to let him know what a tremendous need his generous gift had met. He was delighted that he had been obedient to the Holy Spirit and that God had used him to minister to us so wonderfully.

People who are motivated to give will often rely on their mate's confirmation when they feel led to give. For example, almost 25 years ago, ministers T. L. and Daisy Osborn were conducting a meeting in Denver to raise funds for a new building in Tulsa, Oklahoma. They asked for $1,000 gifts, which was a very large sum of money in the early 1960s.

Wally and I had just started our own church and we had carefully saved $1,000 toward purchasing a new car. The car we had then was a real clunker and we knew it would not be long before it broke down completely.

When the Osborns asked the participants at the meeting to pledge $1,000, I didn't even think about giving the money we had saved so diligently. Now, I had always believed in tithing—I even tithed before I was born again—and I had experienced the glorious blessings God bestows on those who are faithful to give. But before we started our church I didn't understand abandoned giving: I just wanted to tithe 10 percent—period.

Wally felt led to give our $1,000 and he asked me if I felt the same. Before I knew what was happening I said, "Yes, I do." But as soon as I said "yes" I thought, *Why did I agree to that?* However, it was too late: Wally had already pledged our money.

After the meeting I tried to smile and be very spiritual, but really I was worried sick. I even awoke in the middle of the night and began to worry about it. The car was about to fall apart and when it did, we would not have the means to buy a new one. What would the people in our congregation think when they left church and saw us waiting at the corner for a bus? What an example of prosperity that would have been! Then I thought, *Why am I worrying by myself? Wally gave the money away, so he should worry with me.* I woke him up and told him to worry.

He said, "Marilyn, God told me to give that money. He knows our situation and when the time comes, He will provide a new car. Now go back to sleep."

Well, the time came. One of our assistant pastors wrecked our car, and we were put in the uncomfortable position of borrowing one from a friend. However, we didn't have to borrow that car very long. One night a guest speaker at our church said to Wally, "Pastor Hickey, I see the letters C-A-R over your head. Do you need a new car?"

"Well, kind of," Wally replied.

Kind of! I thought. *We're so desperate for a new car that it's pathetic.* The guest speaker took an offering from the congregation and we were able to buy a new car with the money we received. I was so glad Wally had relied on me to confirm giving that $1,000 toward the Osborn's building fund, because that experience truly helped me learn to give unquestionably when the Lord asked it of me.

Finally, giving-motivated people like to give very high quality gifts. They will give away the best items and keep the lesser quality items themselves. Missionaries have told me that at various times they have received barrels of unfashionable ties and even used tea bags from people who were trying to bless the kingdom of God in giving! These are not the characteristics of a true giver. Rather, he or she will give away new items and keep used ones.

Guidelines for Giving-Motivated People

Following are some guidelines that givers should always keep in mind to insure they are using their gift under the direction of the Holy Spirit:

1. Remember God is your source.

Sometimes people use giving as a means of manipulation—they put strings on their giving to receive something in return. For example, someone may say to me, "I'll give $5,000 toward your television ministry if you hire my daughter to work in your office." Is that spiritual giving? No, indeed, it is not. That is trying to make someone else your source instead of God. We must watch those kinds of attitudes and motivations.

2. Remember others may need encouragement to give.

Givers may become offended when ministers appeal to their congregations for money. You must keep in mind some people must be *taught* to give.

It is just as scriptural to teach others to give as it is to teach them to pray or to read the Bible. All these activities reap tremendous rewards in the believer's life, and ministers would be remiss in their duties if they did not teach their congregations how to receive all the blessings God has for them.

3. Maintain balance in your giving.

This is an important point because givers must resist the tendency to go to extremes. Some givers become so involved in their giving to churches, they become too frugal with themselves and their families. Several years ago a giving-motivated woman inherited a large sum of money from her father. She sowed the money into her church and other Christian organizations, but neglected some of her family's very basic needs. Now that's not wisdom, is it? We need to be careful not to become so overwhelmed by our giving that we totally neglect ourselves or our loved ones.

On the other hand, some givers may have a tendency to become too materialistic. They begin to think about the large homes or extravagant cars they could buy. Solomon is a good example of a godly man who became too materialistic. God had blessed and prospered Solomon, but he became consumed with his wealth and lost the vision God had given him. It is very important givers keep a godly perspective and give as the Holy Spirit directs them.

Abraham

Abraham is a prime Biblical example of a giver. Because of his faithful heart, he became a friend of God: "And the scripture was fulfilled which saith, Abraham believed God, and it was imputed unto him for righteousness: and he was called the Friend of God" (James 2:23).

Abraham was generous in giving to others and to God; therefore, God gave generously back to Abraham. Let's look at some specific examples that show Abraham's characteristics as a giver:

First, Abraham dealt generously with others. He gave his nephew Lot a vast amount of unselfish help as well as his choice in obtaining fertile land:

Is not the whole land before you? Please separate from me. If you take the left, then I will go to the right; or, if you go to the right, then I will go to the left." And Lot lifted his eyes and saw all the plain of Jordan, that it was well watered everywhere (before the Lord destroyed Sodom and Gomorrah) like the garden of the Lord, like the land of Egypt as you go toward Zoar. Then Lot chose for himself all the plain of Jordan, and Lot journeyed east. And they separated from each other.

Genesis 13:9-11

Second, Abraham tithed faithfully. He tithed even before the Law required it. Abraham considered it his responsibility to give back to God: "And blessed be the most high God, which hath delivered thine enemies into thy hand. And he gave him tithes of all" (Genesis 14:20).

Third, Abraham was willing to give anything—including his own son—to God: "And they came to the place which God had told him of; and Abraham built an altar there, and laid the wood in order, and bound Isaac his son, and laid him on the altar upon the wood. And Abraham stretched forth his hand, and took the knife to slay his son" (Gen. 22:9-10).

Fourth, Abraham was concerned about prices and values. He used wisdom to buy a burial cave for his wife Sarah: "And he communed with them, saying, If it be your mind that I should bury my dead out of my sight; hear me, and intreat for me to Ephron the son of Zohar, that he may give me the cave of Machpelah, which he hath, which is in the end of his field; for as much money as it is worth he shall give it me for a possession of a burying place amongst you" (Genesis 23:8-9).

We are all to have a giving spirit because that is what God commands, but giving-motivated people especially bless the Body of

Christ. They tirelessly give of themselves and of their resources to up-lift and enrich our lives. I thank God for each and every one of them.

The Gift of Organization

"...he that ruleth, with diligence..."

Romans 12:8

In Romans 12:3 to rule means, to be over, superintend, preside over. Other definitions include to stand in front of others. Rulers, also known as organizers, stand in front because they have the ability to lead and direct others. Through their God-given leadership ability, the facilitate tasks for the rest of the Body of Christ.

Organizers can visualize the overall picture and plan long-range goals. Organizers love new challenges, and they know what steps will be needed to meet each challenge. Once the steps are determined, organizers love to implement those steps to meet the goals.

Organizers gain tremendous satisfaction in achieving their goals and involving others in that. Now I like to set goals, but I am not par-ticularly good at assigning tasks to those who could perform them the most efficiently. However, this is where organizers really excel: they have great spiritual insight to designate tasks.

Several years ago, a man with the foundational gift of organiza-tion came to work for our ministry. He organized his department and placed people in positions that I was not quite certain they were equipped to perform.

I asked him, "Are you sure this will work?"

He answered me, "Oh, yes, I'm sure. Wait and see—they will be ex-cellent in these positions." And he was right—in fact, they performed their tasks outstandingly well and achieved many goals that I had thought unlikely.

One day, I asked the man, "How did you know that this would work so well?"

"Marilyn," he replied, "I simply had an inner witness that those people could perform those tasks."

Organizers are aware of the available resources to complete a task. Many times when cooking, I will begin a recipe without making certain I have all the necessary ingredients. An organizer would never do that; rather, he or she would make certain all the necessary ingredients were in the kitchen before beginning the recipe.

Upon completing projects, organizers are eager to move onto new challenges. For example, one of our employees became very involved during the construction of our ministry building. He was there day and night—generally 12-15 hours a day—seven days a week. And he wasn't paid overtime—he just wanted to be involved.

After the building was completed I said to him, "Now you can rest."

But he replied, "I am rested. What's the next challenge?" Organizers like to be busy all the time.

Organizers are not overly sensitive to criticism; they are concerned with achieving goals, not pleasing people. I really admire this quality in organizers and wish that more Christians would develop this attitude. We must learn very early in our Christian walks that not everyone is going to think we are the greatest thing since hot popcorn with freshly salted butter.

When God gives you a vision, you can rest assured that someone will criticize you for it. That criticism may hurt your feelings, but you will never achieve your goal if you allow negative comments to affect you. I'm not telling you to be hard and cruel to others, but I am saying that you cannot let criticism hold you back. You must pursue the vision that God has given you, regardless of others' attitudes. By nature, organizers are very good at doing this.

Guidelines for Organizers

Following are some guidelines organizers can use to ensure they always minister under the anointing of the Holy Spirit:

1. Use your talents.

Romans 12:8 says he that rules should do so diligently. "Diligence" comes from the Greek word *spoude* meaning "hastily or earnestly." People with the foundational gift of organizing will often wait until they are asked to get involved in a project. Organizers should not wait until they are asked to get involved; rather, they should make themselves available to minister to the Body.

2. Supervise your projects closely.

Some organizers have a tendency to over delegate their responsibilities. They are so busy getting everyone involved they don't oversee the project as closely as necessary and things may begin to fall apart.

3. Explain why certain tasks are necessary.

Organizers often can see the overall goal and the steps necessary to reach that goal, but they may not realize everyone else involved in the project may not be as spiritually perceptive. Organizers must be willing to explain details and spend time outlining tasks to workers.

4. Remember, people are more important than projects.

Sometimes organizers become so excited about completing a project that it may seem more important than those whom the project is designed to help. But in order to be worthwhile, projects must meet people's needs. If this isn't accomplished, we have missed our mark.

5. Remain sensitive to others.

Organizers like to complete tasks swiftly and at times, may appear to be insensitive to others' schedules and priorities. Remember that people have other demands on their time and lives and probably won't be able to devote themselves full-time to your project.

Nehemiah

The name Nehemiah means "comforter." In the Hebrew it is the same name for the Holy Spirit—*parakletos*—meaning summoned, called to one's side, called to one's aid. Other definitions include, "someone who takes you by the arm and helps you along." Nehemiah, like most organizers, worked in much the same way: he took the Israelites by the arm and helped them to complete the wall that surrounded and protected their temple.

Nehemiah had heard that the temple in Jerusalem had been rebuilt but the temple's walls were yet to be completed. The walls were very important components of a city because they acted like a policing system. The lack of sturdy walls left the city and its inhabitants virtually unprotected from enemy attacks. This grieved Nehemiah so he went to the king and asked permission to help the Israelites rebuild the wall.

Organizers always set goals and Nehemiah set a goal to complete the wall within a certain time frame:

And I said to the king, "If it pleases the king, and if your servant has found favor in your sight, I ask that you send me to Judah, to the city of my fathers' tombs, that I may rebuild it." Then the king said to me (the queen also sitting beside him), "How long will your journey be? And when will you return?" So it pleased the king to send me; and I set him a time.

Nehemiah 2:5-6 NKJV

Nehemiah took a detailed inventory of the walls' condition before beginning to rebuild them:

And I went out by night through the Valley Gate to the Serpent Well and the Refuse Gate, and viewed the walls of Jerusalem which were broken down and its gates which were burned with fire. Then I went on to the Fountain Gate and to the King's Pool, but there was no room for the animal under me to pass. So I went up in the night by the valley, and viewed the wall; then I turned back and entered by the Valley Gate, and so returned.

Nehemiah 2:13-15 NKJV

Why did Nehemiah take such a detailed inventory of the walls' condition? He was determining the steps that would be necessary to complete the task. He didn't just say to the people, "We're going to rebuild these walls," without having an organized plan in mind. No, Nehemiah set his goal and determined what would be necessary to achieve it.

Nehemiah had great spiritual discernment in assigning people to suitable tasks (Nehemiah 3). Remember, organizers facilitate assignments so they may be completed in an efficient manner. Nehemiah assigned people to do work that was in near proximity to their homes, thus, making it convenient for them to complete their tasks.

Nehemiah explained to the Israelites the overall goal and necessary steps to achieve that goal:

And the officials did not know where I had gone or what I had done;
I had not yet told the Jews, the priests, the nobles, the officials, or the
others who did the work. Then I said to them, "You see the distress
that we are in, how Jerusalem lies waste, and its gates are burned
with fire. Come and let us build the wall of Jerusalem, that we may
no longer be a reproach."

Nehemiah 2:16-17

Nehemiah faced opposition to his plan. Sanballat was an influential Samaritan who tried to thwart Nehemiah's plan to rebuild the walls (Nehemiah 2:10). He tried several methods to deter Nehemiah.

First, Sanballat ridiculed Nehemiah: "But when Sanballat the Horonite, Tobiah the Ammonite official, and Geshem the Arab heard *of it,* they laughed at us and despised us, and said, 'What *is* this thing that you are doing? Will you rebel against the king?'" (2:19 NKJV).

Second, Sanballat conspired against Nehemiah: "Now it happened, when Sanballat, Tobiah, the Arabs, the Ammonites, and the Ashdodites heard that the walls of Jerusalem were being restored and the gaps were beginning to be closed, that they became very angry, and all of them conspired together to come *and* attack Jerusalem and create confusion" (4:7-8 NKJV).

But did Nehemiah faint in the wake of adversity? No! Instead, he prayed: "Hear, O our God, for we are despised; turn their reproach on their own heads, and give them as plunder to a land of captivity! Do not cover their iniquity, and do not let their sin be blotted out from before You; for they have provoked *You* to anger before the builders" (4:4-5 NKJV).

And Nehemiah continued to work: "So we built the wall, and the entire wall was joined together up to half its *height,* for the people had a mind to work" (4:6 NKJV). Through steadfast courage, Nehemiah overcame discouragement from his friends:

> *Then Judah said, "The strength of the laborers is failing, and there is so much rubbish that we are not able to build the wall." And our adversaries said, "They will neither know nor see anything, till we come into their midst and kill them and cause the work to cease." So it was, when the Jews who dwelt near them came, that they told us ten times, "From whatever place you turn, they will be upon us." Therefore I positioned men behind the lower parts of the wall, at the openings; and I set the people according to their families, with their swords, their spears, and their bows. And I looked, and arose and said to the nobles, to the leaders, and to the rest of the people, "Do not be afraid of them. Remember the Lord, great and awesome, and fight for your brethren, your sons, your daughters, your wives, and your houses."*
>
> *Nehemiah 4:10-14 NKJV*

Although they faced terrible conditions of harassment and opposition, Nehemiah and the Israelites completed the walls within 52 days. God gave Nehemiah the vision to rebuild the walls and, with God, all things are possible. We too must remember to keep our spiritual eyes focused on Him—even when enemies and friends oppose us. God will move heaven and earth to help us achieve our goals.

The Gift of Mercy

"...he that shewth mercy, with cheerfulness"

Romans 12:8

The Greek word for mercy is *eleeo*, meaning "to be gracious, to spare, to console." Other translations define this word as the outward manifestation of pity. God is rich in mercy and extends it to all who fear Him: "And his mercy is on them that fear him from generation to generation" (Luke 1:50).

Likewise, people with the foundational gift of mercy are happy to show it. It is not a burden to them; rather, it is help given when someone is afflicted and in great need.

Mercy-motivated people like to encourage and help distressed people. It doesn't deter merciful people when it appears the person to whom they minister does not benefit. Merciful people know that the seed has been planted and, eventually, will produce fruit.

Mercy-motivated people rebuke others only when it is absolutely necessary. It is very difficult for merciful people to correct another person because they are concerned they may do more harm than good. However, when it is obvious that strong correction is in order, mercy-motivated people will rebuke others.

People with the foundational gift of mercy are very sensitive to words and actions that may hurt others. Many years ago a guest speaker addressed our congregation. Apparently he was angry over some personal problems he had experienced, and he proceeded to take his anger out on the people in our congregation. He really laid them out without flowers!

My husband Wally is definitely motivated by mercy, and while driving home in the car he announced, "That man's words hurt our people, and I will never again give him the opportunity to hurt them." And he never has—that minister has never been invited back to speak at our church.

Mercy-motivated people have an ability to discern others' true motives. In this sense, those with the foundational gift of mercy are very similar to prophecy-motivated people. Both these groups can sense the intentions of others' hearts and identify their motives.

Those with the gift of mercy prefer to minister to emotional rather than physical needs. Merciful people truly desire to remove hurt from others' lives and are swift to offer mercy to those suffering from mental or emotional anguish. Mercy-motivated people are willing to pray for those with physical illnesses; however, they prefer to minister to emotional needs.

Merciful people are sensitive to others' reactions to spiritual happenings. For example, during a church service, mercy-motivated people will sense others' responses to the message. You may say, "But Marilyn, some people are *naturally* sensitive!" Yes, that's true. However, merciful people have a unique *spiritual* sensitivity that allows them to discern if people within the congregation need to be born again or receive counseling for emotional wounds. And merciful people can also discern if the message taught really applies to the people's lives and meets their needs.

Guidelines for Mercy-motivated People

Following are guidelines that mercy-motivated people may follow to remain under the anointing of the Holy Spirit:

1. Allow God to deal with others' offenses.

Romans 12:8 specifically encourages mercy-motivated people to minister cheerfully. Why? Because they feel so deeply for others they sometimes begin to be offended for them. And it doesn't help others or minister to them in any way when we allow ourselves to pick up their offenses as our own.

Whenever I am offended, I want to tell my husband Wally. When my mother was alive, I would tell her too. They are both mercy-motivated people, and I could usually depend on them to say, "Oh, you poor thing! How could that person have done that to you?" And my mother and my husband would become offended too.

However, the Bible says if you are suffering for righteousness' sake, then you will receive a great reward (Matthew 5:10). The Lord will protect me and bless me if I have been offended unjustly; however, if I have a "pity party" and don't trust in God's Word, I will miss my blessing.

On the other hand, if I have done something wrong and it is just my pride that is causing me to be offended, I don't need others to pity me. I need them to point out my error so I may repent and allow God to deal with that area of my life.

What happens to mercy-motivated people who become offended for others? The Bible says glory rests upon the righteous (1 Peter 4:14). God's glory may rest upon those who are righteously offended, but it doesn't rest upon those who pick up others' offenses as their own. When you become offended simply because others are offended, you will lose God's glory.

2. Make decisions based on the Word of God.

Mercy-motivated people have a tendency to make decisions based on their emotions rather than on the Word. Remember, your emotions are neither reliable nor infallible. To make sound decisions, always make certain they are in agreement with God's Word.

3. Exercise caution when ministering to members of the opposite sex.

You may become too seriously involved and cause further injury or problems. I know a mercy-motivated pastor in the northwestern part of the United States, who began to counsel a young single woman with deep emotional wounds. Sometimes the woman would call the pastor at home, and he would go to her house to minister to her. His wife cautioned him, "She is beginning to rely on you rather than on the Lord. I think, perhaps, you are becoming too involved in her problems."

But the pastor replied, "She needs my help and I feel I should continue to counsel her."

Soon the pastor started going to her house, not only to counsel her, but also to repair broken appliances and to do other work. Eventually, the pastor and the single woman became sexually involved.

The pastor felt terrible about the affair. He confessed his sin to the board of directors at his church and offered to resign. Then he confessed to his wife and asked her to forgive him. The board forgave him and refused to accept his resignation; however, his wife was very hurt and wanted to leave him. The Lord said to her, "If you don't forgive him for this sin, then I cannot forgive your sins either." God helped the woman forgive her husband and today they have a very happy marriage.

Now this experience ended happily, but I know a lot of people—and I'm sure you do too—whose lives have been ruined by similar experiences. Because of their kind hearts and sensitivity, mercy-motivated people are particularly susceptible to becoming more involved in situations than they should be. Remember, God can send laborers who will not further complicate situations for those who are already experiencing pain and anguish.

4. Make an effort to fellowship with a variety of people.

Mercy-motivated people are inclined only to fellowship with others who are also mercy-motivated. You may say, "The love of Jesus doesn't flow out of people who aren't compassionate, so I don't want to be around them." But perhaps God wants you to minister compassion and mercy to those who seem to be lacking these characteristics. Or, perhaps, God wants them to minister to you in an area where you are lacking. Whatever the case may be, we must always be ready and willing to move as God leads us.

The Good Samaritan

Undoubtedly, the good Samaritan was motivated by mercy. In Luke 10, a man had been beaten by a group of thieves. They robbed him and left him to die. A priest and a Levite both passed the wounded man on the road, yet neither stopped to help him: "But a certain Samaritan, as he journeyed, came where he was: and when he saw him, he had compassion on him, and went to him, and bound up his wounds, pouring in oil and wine, and set him on his own beast, and brought him to an inn, and took care of him" (Luke 10:33-34).

The Samaritan felt great compassion and mercy for the man in need, and the Samaritan actively helped the wounded man by cleaning and dressing his wounds and by taking him to an inn: "And on the morrow when he departed, he took out two pence, and gave them to the host, and said unto him, Take care of him; and whatsoever thou spendest more, when I come again, I will repay thee" (v. 35).

The Samaritan paid the innkeeper in advance for the wounded man's lodging. This shows the Samaritan had great spiritual insight. He perceived the innkeeper was honest and would not make the wounded man leaven the inn after the Samaritan left.

Luke 10:35 also shows us the Samaritan did not want the innkeeper to approach the man about paying for additional expenses. Why?

Because the Samaritan wanted to spare the wounded man from suffering any further emotional pain or embarrassment.

Jesus, too, was a man of great mercy. Throughout the New Testament we find examples of people who came to Jesus and begged Him to have mercy on them. And Jesus extended His mercy to all who asked it of Him: He healed their physical ailments and delivered them from demons and mental distress. His ultimate act of mercy occurred when He died on the cross to atone for our sins. Each and every day, let's praise Jesus for His mercy.

Part Five

Healing

Chapter 16

Healing

This message has gone around the world bringing a simple, but profound message of the healing God has provided for His children. This concise teaching contained in Marilyn's book *God's Benefit: Healing*, is powerful for new and seasoned believers, reinforcing God's benefit of healing in our physical bodies.

God's Benefit: Healing

One of the most important things to be considered when choosing a job is the benefit package offered. Employers talk about "fringe benefits," "health benefits," "dental benefits," "maternity benefits," "travel benefits," and others. A good question to ask, whether you're applying for a job or maybe even considering an insurance policy, is, "What are the benefits?"

I like this definition for *benefit*: anything contributing to an improvement in condition. A benefit should improve our condition! That's why we like all those benefits—because they make things better for us.

Do you know that God has benefits for His children? He does! They're benefits that really improve our condition. Psalm 68:19 says, "Blessed be the Lord, who daily loadeth us with benefits...."

Two of those benefits are listed in Psalm 103:2-3: "Bless the Lord, O my soul, and forget not all his benefits: Who forgiveth all thine iniquities; who healeth all thy diseases." Aren't those two wonderful benefits? I don't know of any employer who offers benefits like those!

Would you ever work for a company and not accept their benefits? That wouldn't be very smart, would it! We'd never consider doing something like that in the natural; but I want you to know, there are many people who refuse God's benefits.

People say to me, "I don't believe it is God's will to heal everyone," or, "I don't believe this is the dispensation for healing." But if you're a child of God, one of the benefits of that relationship is healing for your physical body. "...forget not all his benefits...Who healeth all thy diseases."

Human nature is funny to me. In the days that Jesus walked upon the earth, the Pharisees didn't become upset over His healing of the sick; they became upset about His forgiveness of sins.

In our day it's just the opposite! People don't become upset when you say that Jesus forgives sins, but mention that Jesus heals sickness and they really get uptight. Actually, it's the same old enemy, fighting against the full message, the entire Good News, of what Jesus wants to do for mankind. God wants to forgive us of our sins, thus allowing Him to give us a new life and nature; and He also wants to heal our physical body. Don't forget *all* His benefits!

Psalm 103:3 is very revealing. It shows how forgiveness and healing go hand in hand: "...Who forgiveth all thine iniquities; who healeth all thy diseases." They shouldn't be separated!

In the New Testament, the Greek word *sozo* is translated "save" and "heal." In Mark 5:23, Jairus asked Jesus to lay hands on his sick daughter, "That she may be healed." And in Acts 2:47 it is recorded that "...the Lord added to the church daily such as should be saved."

Sozo is the Greek word used in both verses. It is used interchangeably to mean "save" or "heal." Since we know it is God's will to forgive sins and save, we must also accept the fact that it is His will to physically heal and make whole.

Healing is not something new. God's healing begins in the Old Testament and flows throughout the New Testament. It continues to flow today!

I always take the overall view of the Bible on any topic. Some people say that they just like to study the New Testament, and some people like to study the Old Testament. I like to study both because then I think I get the full message of what the Lord is trying to say to me.

The Healing Lamb

Healing begins to flow in the Old Testament in Exodus 12. Do you remember the account of the passover lamb? The whole family ate of the lamb, and the Bible tells us that when the destroyer came, he passed over the households where the blood of the lamb was seen on the door posts, where the people had partaken of the lamb.

The blood on the door posts saved the people from the destroyer. After eating the lamb, the Bible says the children of Israel left Egypt in great physical strength and with good health (Psalm 105:37). God took away sickness from the midst of them (Exodus 23:25).

Why did they not have any sickness? The reason, I believe, was because they were full of lamb. When you are full of the Lamb, I believe you receive strength and health. They ate of that lamb, and there was no sickness in their midst.

The Bible talks of elderly people who marched out of Egypt in great strength and divine health. Partaking of the lamb was not only for their forgiveness, it was not only to protect them from the destroyer, but it was also to give them strength and health.

Look to Jesus as your Healer, but also look to Him as your strength—physical strength. Joel 3:10 says, "...let the weak say, I am strong." And David, in Psalm 29:1, says, "The LORD will give strength unto his people...." We have begun to see the unfolding of it. God saved His people from the destroyer (the devil) and gave them physical health and strength.

Hezekiah's Healing Prayer

Second Chronicles 30 relates how Hezekiah renewed the passover. The Israelites had not been eating the passover, and when it was renewed, the king prayed for the sick, "and the LORD harkened to Hezekiah, and healed the people" (2 Chronicles 30:20). It was in the eating of the passover and in the king's praying that the nation was healed. Once again the lamb was connected with healing. The Lamb of God brings forgiveness *and* healing.

Healing for the Leper

Cleansing was provided for the leper, and the preparation for cleansing included the slaying of a lamb. Leviticus 14:25 says:

And he [the priest] shall kill the lamb of the trespass offering, and the priest shall take some of the blood of the trespass offering, and put it upon the tip of the right ear of him that is to be cleansed, and upon the thumb of his right hand, and upon the great toe of his right foot.

The lamb brought salvation to the Israelites from their Egyptian oppressors, and the lamb also brought cleansing to them when they needed healing. The lamb that brought deliverance was the same lamb that brought wholeness. When we partake of the Lamb of God, we enjoy salvation and healing. The same Lamb provides both benefits!

Healing in the Wilderness

God wants His people well, but it is up to us to make the decision to walk in health. One thing that works *against* good health is murmuring.

Numbers 16 records how the Israelites murmured against Moses and against Aaron. Verse 49 says 14,700 people died in the plague that followed the murmuring. The Bible says that a lot more were going to die, but Aaron made intercession as a priest and stopped the plague.

Jesus is our great High Priest, and He has come down to the people to stop the plague of sin and sickness. He does not want us to be sick. He wants us to be healed. He wants to improve our condition.

There was another time that the Israelites murmured. Numbers 21 tells of how "...the people spake against God, and against Moses" (v. 5). Fiery serpents came against the people and began to bite them. The people became sick and were dying. The Lord gave Moses a remedy: "Make a brass serpent, Moses. Put it high on a pole, and everyone who looks at it will be healed" (v. 8).

Jesus referred to that incident when He said, "And as Moses lifted up the serpent in the wilderness, even so must the Son of man be lifted up" (John 3:14). Everyone who looks to Jesus will be saved eternally. When we lift up Jesus as Savior, He heals people of sin; and when we lift Him up as Healer, people are healed physically, just as the Israelites were healed physically.

If people are not being healed in your church, maybe it is because Jesus is not lifted up as Healer. If those people in the wilderness hadn't looked up to the serpent, they would not have been healed. If you don't look up to Jesus to be your Healer, you will remain sick and in pain. It is very, very important that He be lifted up as Healer, as well as Savior.

Healing in the Psalms and Proverbs

"Bless the Lord, O my soul, and forget not all his benefits: Who forgiveth all thine iniquities; who healeth all thy diseases; Who redeemeth thy life from destruction who crowneth thee with lovingkindness and tender mercies; Who satisfieth thy mouth with good things; so that thy youth is renewed like the eagles."

Psalm 103:2-5

You don't have renewed youth unless you have good things in your mouth. If you murmur, you are going to be sick and cut short your life span, and you will be weak while you are alive. But if you speak good things (who Christ is, what He's done) the benefits are that He forgives your iniquities, He heals you of disease, He redeems your life, He crowns you with lovingkindness and tender mercies, He satisfies you with good things, and He renews your youth.

Those are the benefits of Jesus! Don't neglect any of them. Don't say, "Well, He forgave me of my sins—that's enough." Take them all. They're all your benefits. Step up for every one of them!

"My son, attend to my words; incline thine ear unto my sayings. Let them not depart from thine eyes; keep them in the midst of thine heart. For they are life unto those that find them, and health to all their flesh."

Proverbs 4:20-22

God has given us the Word to bring life and to bring health. We have the heavenly prescription for good health: attend to the Word by listening to it (which implies obeying it), reading it, and meditating on it. God is always wanting to improve your condition by giving you health for all your flesh.

If you are not in the Word every day, if you are not confessing the Word, I don't believe that you have that health flowing through you all the time. Jesus said, "My words are spirit and they are life" (John 6:63). If you are not using the Word, then I do not believe you have that life flowing in you all the time. I think that is one reason why Christians decay and fall apart, because they haven't kept the life principle of the Word in them *all the time.*

Have you noticed that sometimes when you get up in the morning the devil really hits you? Maybe you had a bad dream, or things were not going very well, and the enemy talks to you and says, *This day is going to be a drag. It's going to be terrible. You've got all these things to do, and everything is falling apart around you.*

When that happens, I pray and go through the Scriptures that I'm confessing that day. After I'm through confessing the Word, there is something of *life* that begins to go around inside of me. Then I think, *This isn't a bad day. This is the best day of my life!* The Word has brought *life* into the situation. That's a wonderful principle, and we need to exercise it every day.

Healing in the New Testament

Very early in His ministry, Jesus stood up in the synagogue to read. He was handed the book of Isaiah and read: "The Spirit of the Lord is upon me, because he hath anointed me to preach the gospel to the poor; he hath sent me to heal the brokenhearted, to preach deliverance to the captives, and recovering of sight to the blind, to set at liberty them that are bruised, To preach the acceptable year of the Lord" (Luke 4:18-19).

He said that He was "...To preach the *acceptable year of the Lord*." What is the acceptable year of the Lord? I believe it refers to the year of Jubilee, mentioned in Leviticus 25.

Every fiftieth year the trumpet was sounded and liberty was proclaimed throughout all the land. Everyone who owed debts and everyone who was in trouble was set free to go back and claim their own land. It was a beautiful time when everyone celebrated.

When Jesus stood up and said, "This is the acceptable year of the Lord," He was saying, "This is Jubilee! You can claim back all your possessions that Adam lost to Satan." The brokenhearted could be healed, the captives could be set free, the blind could receive their sight, and people who were bruised emotionally could be set free.

Jesus was standing up, and, in a sense, blowing a trumpet and saying, "This is Jubilee! There's Good News! Get back all your possessions that you lost in Adam. I've got them all back for you." One of those possessions is divine health. Jesus got it back for you. Claim healing as your rightful possession.

Healing's Price

You have every legal right to claim your healing, and I want to consider this carefully. In Matthew 8:17 there is a reference all the way back to Isaiah 53. Jesus had just physically "...healed all that were sick..." in that area, and the Bible says He healed them "that it might be fulfilled which was spoken by Isaiah the prophet, saying, Himself took our infirmities, and bare our sickness."

Isaiah, speaking of the suffering Savior, said, "But he was wounded for our transgressions, he was bruised for our iniquities: the chastisement of our peace was upon him; and *with his stripes we are healed*" (Isaiah 53:5). On the cross, Jesus paid the price for our transgressions. It was on the same cross and by the same suffering that Jesus paid the price for our healing. We have every legal right to forgiveness of sins because Jesus bore our sins for us. We have the same legal right to healing because Jesus bore our sickness and carried our diseases.

Do you believe it? Are you sure it's true? Healing must be believed and received, just as forgiveness of sins must be believed and received. The reason I know that is true is found in the first verse of Isaiah 53: "Who hath believed our report? And to whom is the arm of the LORD revealed?" Are you going to receive this report, or are you going to turn it down? Receive it today!

A Cause of Sickness

In the New Testament, many people were sick because they did not discern the Body of Christ (1 Corinthians 11:30). Paul, under divine inspiration, said that they were sick and weak because they were not properly discerning the Body of the Lord Jesus, and, as a result, many of them died early.

It is in the Body of Jesus Christ that we find strength and healing. It is God's will that we, as part of the Body of Christ, enjoy the life and health that is in that Body. You expect forgiveness in that Body, and if you'll discern that there is also healing in that Body, you can have it. Properly discern the Lord's Body when you take communion, and you'll enjoy life and health.

Paul gives the best description of the Last Supper of any of the writers in the Bible. The gospel writers give us some description, but

Paul gives the best—even though he wasn't there! How did he know so much? The Bible says he received it by revelation. That's revelation knowledge. God wants us to receive by revelation the knowledge that His Body has forgiveness and healing.

Healing in a Name

If we understand who Jesus is, then we will better understand His Body. Names are very important in the Bible. The compound names of Jehovah in the Old Testament correspond to Jesus in the New Testament and help us discern the Body of Christ. There are seven names:

Jehovah-Shammah: It means "the Lord is there."

Jesus said, "Lo, I am with you always, even unto the end of the world" (Matthew 28:20); therefore, Jesus is Jehovah-Shammah.

Jehovah-Shalom: God is our peace.

Shalom means "peace." Jesus said, "Peace I leave with you, my peace I give unto you" (John 14:27). Part of redemption is having the presence of the Lord.

Jehovah-Raah: "The Lord my Shepherd."

Jesus says, "I am the Good Shepherd" (John 10:11).

Jehovah-Jireh: "The God who sees ahead and provides."

"Jireh" came about as a revelation on Mt. Moriah when God provided Abraham a sacrifice instead of his son, Isaac (Genesis 22:12-14). This was a type and shadow of God's true sacrifice of his own Son, Jesus. On Mt. Calvary, Jesus offered Himself as the Lamb for the sins of the world. Jesus is the provision for redemption.

Jehovah-Nissi: It means "victory."

Paul said, "Now thanks be unto God which giveth us the victory through our Lord Jesus Christ" (1 Corinthians 15:57). Jesus is our victory.

Jehovah-Tsidkenu: It means "God our righteousness."

"God our righteousness" in the Old Testament is "Jesus our righteousness" in the New Testament. First Corinthians 1:30 says, "Jesus is made unto us wisdom, righteousness, sanctification and redemption."

Jehovah-Rapha: It means "the Lord my Healer."

Jesus took our sicknesses and our diseases. In His redemptive work, He is the Lord our Healer. The Old Testament constantly revealed God as the One who healed in many ways.

Methods of Healing

The Bible records a number of different methods used to bring about healing. We use the same methods today. Sometimes we lay hands on the sick and there is an instant miracle. Other times we lay hands on the sick and they don't appear healed—it doesn't seem that they have received an immediate miracle. Sometimes we have people lay hands on us and we get better a little at a time.

Remember the little boy in the gospels who "began to get well" (John 4:52) when Jesus spoke the Word? The mending seemed to take a period of time. Don't be discouraged if you don't see or feel something instantly. The Bible says that believers "… shall lay hands on the sick, and they shall recover" (Mark 16:18). Sometimes it seems you must stand on the Scriptures until you almost think it is taking an eternity to recover!

I remember when the Lord promised us a child. I had gone to many doctors, fertility experts, and they all said that I could never have a baby. But my husband and I never agreed with those words. We believed that God wanted us to have a child.

When we first started in the ministry, we were in Dallas, Texas, where a man named William Branham was ministering. One night I stood on the platform before him, and he looked at me and said, "You're not from here. You are from a wooded area. You are from Denver, Colorado, and you have a female condition."

All the time he was speaking I had the most unusual sensation. I saw something in my spirit (not with my physical eyes), and I felt something that went round and round. It was whirling. It was almost like I could hear the sound of it. As it became stronger and stronger, I thought, *If I step into that, I will die.* It was a fearful thing to me.

The evangelist said, "Go home and receive your baby," and that whirling (I believe it was the presence of God) went into my feet and came up into my body. A very unusual experience!

"Well, did you get your baby that year, Marilyn?"

No, we didn't get the baby until ten years later!

My husband never quit believing. He always said, "Marilyn, God is going to give us a child."

When I began my thirties, I thought, *Forget it, God. Don't listen to my husband. Listen to me.* But Wally stood in faith, and when I was thirty-six, I went to a doctor because I was having some unusual things happen in my body.

"You're not pregnant," he told me. "You're just going through 'the change.' Don't even tell your husband that you think you're pregnant."

I waited a few more months (I would have been about four-and-a-half months along by then), and I was having some more changes. I thought, *Somebody's wrong!* After a check with another doctor, I was told, "Lady, what you are feeling is life. You are pregnant." At last Sarah, our miracle baby, was born.

What am I saying to you in all of this? When you don't see it, do you quit believing? When you don't feel it, do you leave it alone? No! But you say, "Ten years!" Well, Abraham waited twenty years, and look what he got—an Isaac. There are times when it seems that you wait and wait and wait. (I didn't wait, but my husband did!) Don't cash in on your faith!

Another time I had a back ailment. Every time I picked up something heavy I would be in terrible agony. Finally I went to a doctor. He took X-rays of my back and told me, "You have the strangest spinal formation I have ever seen. As you get older, it will get worse. You can't pick up anything heavy because you won't be able to walk if you do."

Once again I didn't receive the report. After I went home and told my husband, he agreed with me in prayer that I was healed. I stood on Mark 11:24, and you know what? I got worse! I got worse almost every day. I had to get out of bed at night and sleep on the floor because of the pain. Sarah was just a baby then; I'd pick her up, and she'd be heavy, which would make my back worse.

Every day I'd say, "According to Mark 11:24 I believe I have received." I didn't say the symptoms weren't there, and I didn't say there was no pain. I just said, "I believe I have received."

At the end of six months, without anything dramatic happening (no cloud or warm glow or anything) I just stood up one morning, and I was all right. I stood on that Scripture for a long time, and God brought it to pass; however, there have been other times when I've had prayer and instantly been healed.

When my husband and I started our church, I had a tiny growth on my finger, and it was the ugliest thing! I went to church one day and showed it to one of the ladies in the church. "Oh dear," she said. "I had a friend who had some of those come on her fingers, and it was cancer, and she died."

Thanks a lot! That was a great help to my faith! But in a service one night I said, "God, I'm not going to have that anymore." The growth began to turn dark on my finger during the service, and when I got home, it fell off. Whether it is an instant miracle or a recovery, God still wants to heal!

Health and Old Age

Some people will look for any excuse to be sick! They will say, "Well, you know, your body just wears out when you get older, and you're bound to be sick." Really? Let's read what the Bible says:

The days of our years are three score and ten.

Psalm 90:10

O my God, take me not away in the midst of my days.

Psalm 102:24

Why shouldest thou die before thy time?

Ecclesiastes 7:17

"Well, Marilyn, if people never get sick, how are they going to die? They can't live forever." The Word says, "Thou takest away their breath, they die, and return to their dust" (Psalm 104:29). God can take away your breath and you just go, and that's it! The Old Testament doesn't talk about the patriarchs dying in agony with a big cancer on each side of their head. It says they gathered up their feet and were gathered up to their people. That was it. They seemed to know when they were going to die.

Paul, in the New Testament, said that he would far rather die and go on to be with Christ, but he made a choice to stay because the Church needed him. Paul believed he had authority over his life span. And I do too! I'm just that radical. I believe that there is a life span that we can have, and when it is time, we can say, "Okay, Lord, I believe that I've fulfilled what You told me to do. I'm willing to go on now." At that time I believe He can take our breath, and we'll be gone.

I don't believe that we are to die in defeat. It bothers me when I see Christians suffering, and I don't believe that you should wait until you are seventy years old to start claiming strength for your old age. I think that every day you should thank God for the "law of the spirit of life in Christ Jesus" that sets you free from the law of sin and death.

Start planning and planting right now for your older years to be strong and healthy. Don't wait. That doesn't mean that you can break all of the health rules either. People who do not brush their teeth are going to get cavities. You can't say, "I just gave up that old devil toothbrush." I think you should take care of your body, feed it properly, and give it rest. I also believe that we should thank God every day for the divine health that flows through us. We should still be at our best at the time the Lord calls us home. We can say, "Okay, Lord. I've completed Your plan for me. Take me home. I'm ready to go." Don't go sick—go in health!

Healing and Thorns

There's another favorite excuse people like to use to justify staying sick—Paul's thorn in the flesh. I want to discuss Paul's thorn, but most of all I want to tell you, "Don't look for excuses!"

When you are believing for healing and people come to you with negative reports, don't receive them into your spirit. I don't think you have to slap the person down and say, "Shut up! I don't want to hear you." But I think you can say in your own spirit, "I just don't receive this. This isn't mine. I'm not going to take this into my spirit. I'm standing on the Word, and I believe I have received."

When you begin to walk in faith in the area of healing, the devil will test you and test you. Sometimes people will bring certain Scriptures to you, and they'll say, "See, it isn't always God's will to heal!" One thing they will always bring up is Paul's thorn in the flesh. I'm going to expose the devil right now so that he can't use Paul's thorn to create doubt in your mind and cause you to not believe God for your healing.

The first thing we need to do is read the Bible instead of listening to what other people say about Paul's thorn. Carefully read 2 Corinthians 12:7-10:

And lest I should be exalted above measure through the abundance of the revelations, there was given to me a thorn in the flesh, the messenger of Satan to buffet me, lest I should be exalted above measure. For this thing I besought the Lord thrice, that it might depart from me. And he said unto me, My grace is sufficient for thee: for my strength is made perfect in weakness. Most gladly therefore will

I rather glory in my infirmities, that the power of Christ may rest upon me. Therefore I take pleasure in infirmities, in reproaches, in necessities, in persecutions, in distresses for Christ's sake: for when I am weak, then am I strong.

Now, people will say, "See, Marilyn, he was sick! And God didn't remove his sickness because His grace was sufficient. And sometimes more glory is given to God for people to be sick and endure it and be sweet before the Lord than if they got healed."

Have you ever heard that story? Maybe you told it in the past! I know that I have visited with some in the past, and they have said, "Well, I'm a real blessing being sick like this because people come here and I can comfort and strengthen them."

Sometimes people say, "I went to pray for Sister Jones, and she was so sick. But, when I left, she had ministered to me. I just wonder if her sickness wasn't in the will of God so that she could show how she endured illness in Jesus."

Those are all suppositions. When you begin to rationalize, you find yourself in trouble with the Word of God. You can end up rationalizing away God's promises! I know because I have done it. It happens like this. You think, *Well, if Paul had a thorn in the flesh, and he's more spiritual than I am, then I suppose sickness is my thorn, too.*

Don't rationalize the Word. Don't "suppose" yourself into being sick! Before you go confessing something about sickness, you had better know what the Word really says! The best way to understand the Bible is to let the Bible interpret the Bible. Doesn't that make sense?

The Bible tells us very plainly what Paul's thorn was. Paul knew the Old Testament intimately. He had memorized great portions of it. Old Testament examples and quotes and expressions are abundant in his writings. In 2 Corinthians 12, Paul uses an Old Testament expression to describe what it was that was given to him.

Read Numbers 33:55: "But if ye will not drive out the inhabitants of the land from before you; then it shall come to pass, that those which ye let remain of them shall be pricks in your eyes, and *thorns in your sides*, and shall vex you in the land wherein ye dwell."

Joshua 23:13 says: "Know for a certainty that the LORD your God will no more drive out any of these nations from before you; but they shall be snares and traps unto you, and scourges in your sides, and *thorns in your eyes*, until ye perish from off this good land which the LORD your God hath given you."

And Judges 2:3: "Wherefore I also said, I will not drive them out from before you; but they shall be as *thorns in your sides*, and their gods shall be a snare unto you."

What, according to the Bible, are thorns? Sickness? No! Thorns are people. Now go back to 2 Corinthians. What are thorns? They are simply people. Did you ever have some people who were thorns to you? Maybe a nasty relative! Scripturally speaking, thorns are people, not sickness.

Paul describes what the thorn was doing. "It was the messenger of Satan to buffet me." Buffet means "to hit." And messenger here means "an angel of Satan." A fallen angel was coming along and beating on him.

Ananias prophesied when he met Paul. He said, "Paul, you're going to suffer many things for the name of Jesus. You're going to be persecuted." And sure enough, every place that Paul went he was persecuted. They physically hit him, they stoned him, and they beat him.

Who was inciting all those things? Satan. Paul saw behind the people and knew that Satan was behind the persecutions.

The Bible does say that Paul was sick at the beginning of his ministry (Galatians 4:13), but the Bible also says that at the end of his life he said, "I labored more than all of them." That doesn't sound like a very sick man, does it? It sounds like he was healed and went on to labor for the Lord.

Some say that Paul had an eye disease and that he had running pus coming from his eyes. But the Bible doesn't say that! The Bible says in Acts that people took aprons from Paul's body and put them on the sick and they were healed. Paul had divine health flowing through him!

Paul says he most gladly will glory in his infirmities (2 Corinthians 12:10). Was Paul speaking of sickness there? According to Vine's Expository Dictionary, infirmities means "want of strength, weakness, indicating inability to produce results." Paul was rejoicing in his own inability to do anything for the Lord: "...for when I am weak, then am I strong" (12:10).

Paul listed his infirmities in 2 Corinthians 11:23-30 and never once listed sickness! We need to know these things so that the devil has no ground to put sickness on us!

No matter how much you talk to some people, they'll still fight to keep their sickness. Even if you convince them from the Scriptures Paul's thorn was not sickness, they'll still say, "Well, I just don't think that it's God's will to heal everyone." I want to let you read what the Bible says about that. The Word is very clear regarding God's will to heal all. Jesus is God's will in action (John 5:19). What did Jesus do when confronted with sickness?

And Jesus went about all the cities and villages, teaching in their synagogues, and preaching the gospel of the kingdom, and healing every sickness and every disease among the people.

Matthew 9:35

I want you to have so much Scripture, and so much faith in the Word, that you would be ashamed to be sick anymore. Does that scripture say He healed *some* sickness? No, He healed *every* sickness and *every* disease.

And when he had called unto him his twelve disciples, he gave them power against unclean spirits, to cast them out and to heal all manner of sickness and all manner of disease.

Matthew 10:1

But when Jesus knew it he withdrew himself from there; and great multitudes followed him, and he healed them all.

Matthew 12:15

Is it His will to heal part of the people? To heal how many? *All!*

And Jesus went forth, and saw a great multitude, and was moved with compassion toward them, and he healed their sick.

Matthew 14:14

It doesn't say He just healed part of them. It says, "...he healed their sick."

And when the men of that place had knowledge of him, they sent out into all that country round about, and brought unto him all that were diseased, And besought him that they might only touch the hem of his garment; and as many as touched were made perfectly whole.

Matthew 14:35-36

It is His will to heal all. Everyone who touches Him is made perfectly whole.

And he came down with them, and stood in the plain, and the company of his disciples, and a great multitude of people, out of all Judea and Jerusalem, and from the seacoast of Tyre and Sidon, who came to hear him and to be healed of their diseases, And they that were vexed with unclean spirits; and they were healed. And the whole multitude sought to touch him; for there went virtue out of him, and He healed them all.

Luke 6:17–19

Virtue means "miracle-working power." The same word is used when you are filled with the Holy Spirit. You are filled with power. Did you know that you are filled with miracle-working power? That's why Jesus said to lay hands on people—so that the miracle-working power could come out of you. It wasn't given just to be in you. It is to flow through you. "And he healed them all."

In His hometown Jesus didn't heal many people, but that was because of their unbelief (Mark 6:6). God's benefit package includes healing for your physical body. Will you believe it and receive it?

"Who hath believed our report?" (Isaiah 53:1). Will you say, "I do!" If you'll believe, the arm of the Lord shall be revealed to you!

Part Six

Winning Over Weight

Chapter 17

Winning Over Weight

Marilyn holds healing meetings all over the world and teaches physical, emotional, and spiritual healing through Jesus Christ, but she is also an advocate of good health through sensible eating and exercise. The message contained in her book *Winning Over Weight*, has been very popular over the years and helped thousands keep their weight in check.

Winning Over Weight

Always and forever, the Bible is practical. It's not just "pie in the sky," or fantasy, or something that collects dust on your coffee table. The Bible is a book you can live by! It works. It deals with where you live and is concerned with what concerns you! Therefore, the Bible is concerned with your eating habits. It has much to say that will help you in the area of your eating.

The Trouble with Food

You are not the first person to have had trouble with food. What was the first thing Adam and Eve got into trouble over? Food. What did they eat? Forbidden fruit.

What did Esau get into trouble for? Eating beans. He loved lentils. It's not wrong to eat beans, but he sold his birthright for a bowl of beans. Food became his downfall.

Do you remember Belshazzar? The night Babylon fell, he threw a big feast that turned into a drunken brawl. He drank from holy vessels. Food contributed to his fall from power.

There is another man in the Bible who *literally* fell because of overeating. He even passed on his bad eating habits to his sons. His name is Eli, and he was fatter than a forty-pound robin! He loved that fat meat. The Bible tells us this in 1 Samuel 1-4.

Eli's sons began to love fat too, and they would steal it from the sacrifices. God told Eli, "You get those sons under control or I'm going to take away your ministry." God warned Eli twice, but he liked to eat rather than obey.

Eli's situation is sad because he really did love God. But he could not give up his eating habits or discipline his sons. He was so overweight that when he heard that the Ark of the Covenant had been stolen, he lost his balance and fell backwards off a stool, breaking his neck!

Wrong eating habits produce all kinds of bad things, but be encouraged, God has the way out of these bad habits.

The Lusting for Food

All of us have a desire for food—that's only natural. Our bodies require food to sustain them. But when we get into the area of "lusting" after food, we're in trouble! When we talk about lusting, we usually think of it in the sexual realm. There is, however, an area of food lusts. If we can discover the cause for these, I think it will help you.

Once in a while I get a craving for a chocolate bar with almonds. It's not very often (thank goodness!), but when I do, I'm constantly thinking, *Chocolate with almonds. Chocolate with almonds!* One chocolate bar won't do much damage, but if I continue to eat chocolate bars with almonds, it could prove disastrous.

One time I tried to analyze *when* I especially found myself craving chocolate bars. I believe I found the answer to it in Proverbs, that good *practical* book on wisdom: "Slothfulness casteth into a deep sleep; and an idle soul shall suffer hunger" (Proverbs.19:15).

Idle people are hungry people! Have you ever noticed that when you don't have much to do and you don't have your mind on anything, that is the easiest time to run past the refrigerator and help yourself? Have you ever noticed that when you're not really busy, you tend to think more about food?

When we are not engaged in some meaningful activity, we can easily get hung up on food. It's good to keep busy. It will help you to become thin and stay thin.

It's good to keep your body busy, and it's good to keep your mind busy. Proverbs 27:7 says, "The full soul loatheth an honeycomb; but to the hungry soul every bitter thing is sweet." The soul is composed of the mind and the emotions. Notice that this verse speaks of a full soul: a mind that is full, complete; a mind that is constantly thinking about worthwhile things, worthwhile plans. People with full souls are not thinking about sweets all the time—they are too busy filling their minds with thoughts of achievement.

On the other hand, the hungry soul, or the person whose mind is idle and undisciplined, thinks that everything tastes good. Even bitter things taste good to this person! Keep your body busy, and keep your mind busy and full of the Word—that will cause your eating habits to be pleasing to the Lord.

Another key to eating properly is found in Proverbs 13:25: "The righteous eateth to the satisfying of his soul: but the belly of the wicked shall want." The important word to see here is *satisfying*. You can eat to the satisfying of your soul or you can go beyond that amount and stuff yourself. Most of the time we go beyond being satisfied because the food tastes *so* good. Proverbs says the righteous don't go beyond being satisfied; they stay within that limit.

We all like pastries, don't we? They are marvelous! One time my husband and I were in Finland to minister. I have never seen so many pastries in my life. Practically every other shop on every street had pastries in the windows. We thought we had to sample one of everything that was different. It got to be dangerous to go out of our hotel.

Scripture has some interesting things to say about pastries—it calls them "deceitful dainties." Proverbs 23:3 says, "Be not desirous of his dainties: for they are deceitful meat." Overindulgence in sweets can hurt you. They look good, but looks can be deceiving!

Here is a verse that might surprise you: Proverbs 25:27, "It is not good to eat much honey." That has to do with sweets. It is better to eat natural sweets like fruit. Honey is good, but too much of any good thing is dangerous—unless it is the Word!

We've covered the dangers in eating sweets; now let's look at the dangers in eating too much meat. I can remember several years ago when eating meat was supposed to pick you up if you were tired. There were bumper stickers that said, *Eat beef*; then the lamb people came out with something about eating lamb.

Soon scientists began to say that Americans had too much protein in their diets. Solomon knew thousands of years ago that consuming foods with too much protein was undesirable. He said in Proverbs 23:20, "Be not among winebibbers; among riotous eaters of flesh." We are a nation of meat eaters. Every restaurant serves meat—steak, steak, steak. Too much meat is not good, just like too many sweets are not good!

The Eating of Food

Eating got Adam and Eve into trouble; it also got Esau, Eli and his sons, and Belshazzar into trouble. Eating too many sweets is not good and eating too much meat is not good. None of us wants to overindulge and get into trouble with our eating. We want to be healthy people. The next question would naturally be, "What can I do to change my eating habits?"

The Bible tells us how to handle our craving for too much food. First, of course, it is good to confess the Word about your health. But I don't think it is good to confess the Word and then do everything wrong! Someone once told me he had so much faith that he threw his toothbrush away. That's not faith, that's bad breath! The Bible gives us certain guidelines and as much as we can, we need to obey those suggestions.

The first scripture we need to consider in changing our eating habits is 1 Corinthians 10:31: "Whether therefore ye eat, or drink, or whatsoever ye do, do all to the glory of God."

Ask yourself if your eating habits glorify God. And remember, you can be *skinny* and still not glorify God in your eating. If, on the other hand, you look like a blimp, will people see God in you? If you have tried this and your body still doesn't seem to get in line, I will give you something a little stronger.

Proverbs 23:2 says, "And put a knife to thy throat, if thou be a man given to appetite." That is pretty serious! Get strong with yourself and say, "I have taken this lust for food to the cross, and I reckon myself dead to this sin and alive unto God." Saying this is a little better than actually putting a knife to your throat, but the idea of putting a knife to our throats shows how serious we need to be when it comes to wrong eating habits.

Somebody always says, "But what if I starve to death?" I have a good answer for that! Proverbs 10:3 says, "The LORD will not suffer the soul of the righteous to famish: but he casteth away the substance of the wicked." God will not allow you to starve; don't let the devil feed you a lie.

When I am traveling, there is sometimes little opportunity to eat at a convenient time. I will hold a meeting and then have to catch an early plane to the next meeting. Normally I don't like to eat before a service because my mind doesn't have the recall it should. I am not as spiritually alive if I eat a big meal before a meeting.

Each of us has to evaluate what eating habits work best for us, but for me I don't usually eat breakfast, so that by three or four o'clock I'm really hungry. That's when I eat a big meal. After the evening meetings I'm hungry again, but by then it's late and I don't want to eat right before going to bed. It's not good for your sleep or for your body!

But my mind will say, "You'll starve if you don't eat something now. You'll really get sick if you don't eat more food." Isn't that ridiculous! I wouldn't get sick on one *good* meal a day. I could make it very well. I have to cast down the lie of the enemy and discipline myself to stick to correct eating habits.

One of the best ways to handle a bad eating habit is to pray in the Spirit. Romans 8:26 says: "Likewise the Spirit also helpeth our infirmities: for we know not what we should pray for as we ought: but the Spirit itself maketh intercession for us with groanings which cannot be uttered."

What is an *infirmity?* It is a weakness. The Spirit helps you when you are not firm, when you are not strong or disciplined.

Are you firm in the area of proper eating? If not, pray in the Spirit before you sit down to eat. The Spirit will help you when you are weak. Pray for ten minutes before you begin to eat. Pray in the Spirit before you pass the refrigerator. Praying in the Spirit will help you in your area of weakness and turn it into one of your areas of strength.

How to Eat

We have looked at the dangers involved in eating, what *not* to eat, and some ways of breaking bad eating habits. Now, let's be positive and examine *how* to eat. Proverbs 18:20 says, "A man's belly shall be satisfied with the fruit of his mouth; and with the increase of his lips shall he be filled."

Speak right things about your food before you eat it. Speak a positive word over your meals. It may not look like something from the Hilton, but it will taste a lot better if you speak well of it, rather than complaining about it.

When our children, Mike and Sarah, were growing up, if they said, "I don't like that!" my husband would say, "We like everything at *this* house; we like it *all*." Mike and Sarah would have to take a little of everything on their plate, whether they liked it or not. Guess what happened over a period of time? You're right. They began to like everything.

Mike told me once that he was just amazed at how many kids his age were picky eaters. He said, "It's just disgusting that so many of my friends don't like this and don't like that. I like everything!"

I asked him, "What do you think made you like that?"

"Dad!" That was all he said.

Speak right things before you eat. If you make a face or say something bad about your food before you eat, you set up your body to reject what you are eating, and you will lose out on the nutrition your body needs.

Many people are in trouble over food because they eat when they are depressed. Proverbs has something to say about this too: "All the days of the afflicted are evil: but he that is of a merry heart hath a continual feast" (Proverbs 15:15).

Eat when you are happy, and it will be a feast to you. It could be crackers and milk, but you'll be happy. It will taste good to you. Whatever you eat when you are happy will be a continual feast. You will receive more strength from your food if you eat it with joy. Nehemiah says this in chapter 8, verse 10: "Eat the fat, and drink the sweet, and send portions unto them for whom nothing is prepared...for the joy of the LORD is your strength."

If you are depressed, stay away from food. If your emotions are bad, your food will knot up in your stomach. The Bible puts it this way in Proverbs 15:17: "Better is the dinner of herbs where love is, than a stalled ox and hatred therewith."

Don't eat when you are uptight. Eating at times like these can cause physical illness. How do you think people get ulcers? They get them by eating when they are nervous, when there is unforgiveness in their spirit, or when they are full of hatred. Correct your attitude first, then eat with joy and you will have a continual feast.

The Bible goes on to tell us to eat with temperance: "Hast thou found honey? Eat so much as is sufficient for thee, lest thou be filled therewith, and vomit it" (Proverbs 25:16). Isn't the Bible right on our level? Keep yourself in balance. Eat only what you know you can handle—only what is sufficient.

Do you like chocolate chip cookies? My, couldn't you just eat a dozen of them before you know it? That's over-sufficiency! Your body knows what is sufficient. If you overdo it, this verse says that you will vomit. No one should come to that place!

Ask the Lord to help you in this area of temperance. Before you sit down to eat, tell yourself that you will eat only that which is sufficient for you.

One Scripture I have loved for years is Proverbs 30:8. I have taken it in a spiritual way and also in a natural way: "Remove far from me vanity and lies: give me neither poverty nor riches; feed me with food convenient for me."

We need to get our eyes off physical food and be fed with what is really necessary for our growth. We need to feed ourselves a balanced diet of physical and spiritual food.

Ask the Lord to give you what is convenient for you at this time. It may be that you need to be encouraged from the Word in a particular situation so that your eating habits get in line with the guidelines we have been studying.

The Sanctifying of Food

One of the most important aspects of eating and something that will help you to keep a right attitude in your eating is found in 1 Timothy 4:3-5:

Forbidding to marry, and commanding to abstain from meats, which God hath created to be received with thanksgiving of them which believe and know the truth. For every creature of God is good, and nothing to be refused, if it be received with thanksgiving: for it is sanctified by the word of God and prayer.

These verses tell us that we do not have to be vegetarians. Every creature is good for food. Remember, though, that we are not to be *riotous eaters of flesh.*

Pray Over Your Food

Did you know that what you pray over, giving thanks, is set apart by the Lord for your well being? I believe if nutrition is lacking in what you have to eat, God can make it up to you if you will give thanks for it and pray over it.

However, that doesn't mean you can neglect good meal planning. But sometimes you may be in a position where you can't eat correctly. I fly quite often and I know that the food on planes or in airports isn't always the most nutritious. I like to claim Deuteronomy 7:13-15 over my food. It says that the Lord will bless my meat and drink and take away all sickness.

And he will love thee, and bless thee, and multiply thee: he will also bless the fruit of thy womb, and the fruit of thy land, thy corn, and thy wine, and thine oil, the increase of thy kine, and the flocks of thy sheep, in the land which he sware unto thy fathers to give thee. Thou shalt be blessed above all people: there shall not be male or female barren among you, or among your cattle. And the Lord will take away from thee all sickness, and will put none of the evil diseases of Egypt, which thou knowest, upon thee; but will lay them upon all them that hate thee.

If you believe everything you hear or read about food, you will become frustrated. One report says coffee causes cancer and the next says it's good for you. If you followed it all, you wouldn't know what to eat! Ask God to bless and sanctify your food, and He will take away sickness from you. You can't always be extremely selective about what you eat, but you can pray the right thing over your food before you eat it.

I believe that sometimes God has protected our ministry team because of the right confessions of our mouths. Let me share one experience that occurred while we were in Mexico.

We went to a little village way out in the country. After church, we were asked to stay and eat. The people were warm and friendly, and we couldn't refuse. To this day I am not sure what was in the meal we ate! It was a *very* poor town, and I didn't see many dogs around—seriously! Could the meat that was served have been dog?

The people said we were eating mole'. I've had mole' before—chicken and turkey—and I like it. But I thought at the time, *If this is dog mole', I'm going to eat it and like it! Lord, I'm receiving this with thanksgiving and prayer.* I ate it all and didn't get sick.

Some people go to Mexico and come home sick, but we didn't! I was speaking the right thing. That food was "set apart" for me through thanksgiving and prayer.

The Choosing of Food

The Bible gives us an idea of what we *should* eat: "When he (Paul) therefore was come up again, and had broken bread, and eaten, and talked a long while, even till break of day, so he departed" (Acts 20:11). Paul had a habit of eating bread with believers. They did it for fellowship. Something goes on in eating with others that brings a unity.

Paul ate with a great expectation: he expected to be healthy from his eating. He expected something out of the bread that many others didn't understand. A good example of this is seen in Acts 27. Paul warned the owners of a ship not to sail because of impending danger. They refused to listen to him and sailed anyway. A tremendous storm arose, and it looked like they were all going to die.

Paul fasted and prayed and urged the others to do the same. Surprisingly, the unsaved members of the crew of that ship fasted with Paul. After fourteen days, Paul received a visit from an angel telling him that no one would die.

"Wherefore, Paul said, I pray you to take some *meat*: for this is for your health" (Acts 27:34). God is practical! He knew those men needed some meat for their health.

"And when he had thus spoken, he took bread, and gave thanks to God in presence of them all: and when he had broken it, he began to eat" (v. 35). Then notice verse 36: "Then were they all of good cheer, and they also took some meat."

Pay careful attention to what Paul ate and what the crew ate. They did not eat the same thing. The unsaved crew ate meat, while Paul ate bread. If meat was good for the crew, why wasn't it good for Paul? I believe the Lord has given me the correct answer.

When the early Christians met together, they often had a communion service. They broke bread and drank together as they celebrated the death and resurrection of Jesus. The bread they ate was leavened bread, which is most significant.

Throughout the Old Testament, in most instances, the bread that was used in the religious feasts was unleavened bread because leaven was a type of sin. But in 1 Corinthians 11:23-24, Paul says that Jesus "took bread: and when he had given thanks, he brake it, and said, Take, eat."

The bread mentioned in the above Scripture is leavened bread, or raised bread. In Acts 27 it says that Paul ate *raised bread* (the Greek word *artos* used in both verses signifies a raised bread) and the crew ate meat.

Why did Paul eat raised bread in Acts 27, and why did the early Christians eat raised bread? Because the raised bread represented the raised body of Jesus! The raised bread symbolized resurrection power to them!

When we partake of communion, we should expect resurrection power to operate in our bodies. We should expect all sickness to be taken away from us! But we must eat the right kind of food! If you are tempted to eat a blueberry pie or a piece of cake, think of eating "raised bread." Think of partaking of resurrection power—the power you need to overcome all those bad eating habits. The more resurrection power you feed to your mind and body, the easier it will become to say, "No!" to bad eating habits.

The Kingdom of Food

By way of review, the following points have been covered to help you maintain a proper diet and stay in shape physically, so that your body will look the way God intends for it to. We have looked at all the troubles food can bring to people and have seen how to deal with food lusts, how to eat different kinds of food, how to "set apart" our food and have it produce strength and good health in our bodies. Last of all, we have learned to choose the most important food of all—the "raised bread" that brings resurrection power into our eating habits.

The last point is without doubt the most important one. Paul said in Romans 14:17: "For the kingdom of God is not meat and drink: but righteousness, and peace, and joy in the Holy Ghost."

We are not to major on the "kingdom of food," but we are to major on the *Kingdom of God*.

Do not dwell on your eating habits, whether you are too fat or too skinny. Today, take your eyes off the problem and put your eyes on the Kingdom of God. Pray in the Spirit and begin to devour the "raised bread" that will supply all the power you need to overcome bad eating habits.

Here are some practical steps to change your eating habits and see your figure improve:

1. Keep your mind active—think on right things. (Proverbs 19:15; 27:7.)
2. Don't eat to stuff yourself, but to satisfy yourself. (Proverbs 13:25.)
3. Watch your intake of sweets and meats. (Proverbs 23:3, 20.)
4. When you eat, do it to glorify God. (1 Corinthians 10:31.)

5. Take your bad eating habits to the cross and reckon them dead. (Proverbs 23:2.)

6. Pray in the Spirit for ten minutes before you sit down to eat. (Romans 8:26-27.)

7. Speak right words about your food before you eat. (Proverbs 18:20.)

8. Don't eat when you are depressed. (Proverbs 15:15.)

9. Pray God's Word over your food. (1 Timothy 4:4-5; Deuteronomy 7:13-15.)

Now that you have this information, *act* on God's Word. It will work for you and help you *win over weight*!

Part Seven

End Times

Chapter 18

The House of Revelation

The last book of the Bible—Revelation—is packed with end-time truths that are so important to these final days in which we live. As we look ahead in Revelation, the mysteries surrounding the second coming of the Lord are revealed and we realize God's provision for the future of His children is great. To make God's miracle plan easier to understand, I'm going to present an overview of Revelation in this chapter.

Revelation can be best understood by dividing it into sections. To help people grasp the message, I like to use the illustration of a seven-room house. Moving from room one to room seven, the advancement of this "house" represents the progression through the Revelation timeline. The seven rooms are described as the following:

First Room: Christ, Chapter 1

Second Room: The Churches, Chapters 2-3

Third Room: Heaven, Chapters 4-11

Fourth Room: Earth, Chapters 12-16

Fifth Room: Satan's False Church, Chapters 17-18

Sixth Room: The Kingdom of God, Chapters 19-20

Seventh Room: The Holy City, Chapters 21-22

The third, fourth, and fifth rooms are separated because they take place simultaneously in Revelation's timeline. You might think of them as the upstairs, ground floor, and basement.

First Room: Christ, Chapter 1

The first section of Revelation presents a powerful fourfold description of Jesus Christ, our Redeemer. It is a beautiful and highly symbolic picture of Jesus as Prophet, Priest, Judge, and King. These four aspects of our Savior reappear throughout the remainder of the book. We can see Jesus is well qualified to be the Savior of the world.

From this room there is only one door leading to the second room.

Second Room: The Churches, Chapters 2-3

The second section of Revelation, which refers primarily to the Church and Church history, reveals God's instructions to the Body of Christ from the Day of Pentecost through the Rapture.

As the body of Christ in the earth, the Church is God's agent in redemption. I personally believe the local churches pictured (Ephesus, Smyrna, Pergamum, Thyatira, Sardis, Philadelphia, and Laodicea) represent churches that actually existed at the time—and in a broader sense, illustrate seven ages of church history.

This second room offers three doors through which to pass to the events of rooms three, four, and five. Events in these three rooms occur simultaneously, and cover the period from the Rapture to the Return of Christ. Although they cover the same time span, the three rooms present three different viewpoints: Heaven, Earth, and Satan's False Church.

The third room portrays the events chronologically from heaven's point of view. The fourth room describes events in topical order from the perspective of the earth. The fifth room shows the same period of time from Satan's position.

Third Room: Heaven, Chapters 4-11

In the third room, which reveals events from heaven's point of view, the Church Ages are over and we see the activities immediately after the Rapture in heaven and on earth.

This section contains John's vision of God's throne, the seven-sealed book, and the seven trumpet judgments. The saints are organized to administer God's judgments contained in the seven-sealed book. Keep in mind that this section covers the time from the Rapture until Christ's return with the saints to destroy the wicked kings of the earth at Armageddon.

From the third room, there is a door leading into the sixth room, The Kingdom of God. But first, we must consider the fourth and fifth rooms since they are happening simultaneously.

Fourth Room: Earth, Chapters 12-16

Another door from the second room (The Churches) opens into the fourth room, Earth. Like the third, this fourth room begins with the Rapture and ends with the return of Christ. It pictures events on earth, showing the persecution of the tribulation saints by the Antichrist and the preparation for Armageddon. This fourth section is comprised of Revelation, Chapters 12-16, which provide a second witness to Chapters 4-11. The fifth room, Satan's False Church (Chapters 17 and 18), comprise a third witness.

Symbolic language is used extensively in these chapters. From the fourth room, Earth, we look down on earth and witness the activities resulting from the happenings in heaven. Later, the point of view changes, and we are on the earth to witness the man-child caught up to heaven. Then we see the persecution of the Antichrist and the conflict of the armies of the world against the Lord.

As the third room opened to room six, so does the fourth room. But first, we need to look at the fifth room.

Fifth Room: Satan's False Church, Chapters 17-18

The last of the three doors in the second room (The Churches) opens downward to the fifth room. This room follows the activities of the false church of Satan, pictured as the harlot of Revelation in Chapter 17 including Satan's kingdom and prosperity. (See also Revelation 2:20-24.) The harlot is the counterfeit of the true Church that is represented by the woman in Chapter 12. The true Church enters New Jerusalem and makes it home for all eternity, while the false church of Satan goes into perdition.

This fifth room provides additional details to the events of rooms three and four, Heaven and Earth. Here we see the mystery of evil and its final destruction. There is no outlet from this room because everything that cannot be redeemed will be destroyed.

Sixth Room: The Kingdom of God, Chapters 19-20

The sixth room describes the Kingdom age. After seven years of tribulation, Jesus is crowned King of kings and Lord of lords, followed by the great wedding in heaven, the marriage supper of the Lamb. We are united as the bride of Christ and reign with Him during the Millennium and forever.

The Millennium, during which Satan is bound in chains, is a time of preparation for the earth to be turned over to God. At the end of this thousand-year period, Satan prepares for a final battle. In this battle, fire from heaven devours Satan's followers and ultimately, Satan himself is cast into the lake of fire. (See Revelation 20:10.)

From this room, only one door leads us to the final room.

Seventh Room: The Holy City, Chapters 21–22

The seventh room ushers us into the very presence of God, the eternal home of the saints. This is the final room and the end of time that is written of in the Bible, but we know God has great things for us even beyond this age. As the apostle Paul said, "…Eye hath not seen, not ear heard, neither have entered into the heart of man" all the wonderful things God has for us (1 Corinthians 2:9).

Chapter 19

Who Is the Antichrist?

One of the most popular downloads from the website for Marilyn Hickey Ministries, www.marilynandsarah.org, is the outline, "Who is the Antichrist?" Marilyn presents the topic with great insight and understanding and as end-time believers, it's important for us to be able to inform others about the age we live in. In the following chapter, Marilyn discusses in detail the prophecies throughout the Bible that paint the picture of what kind of person the Antichrist will be.

Who Is the Antichrist?

For centuries, people have wondered about the identity of the Antichrist. Some have even guessed he was an infamous world ruler. Names such as Napoleon, Hitler, and Mussolini have been tossed into the hat for possible Antichrist candidates. But I am not going to try to name him. I prefer to look at the Scriptures surrounding the identity and take our cue from their wisdom.

We first encounter the Antichrist in the book of Genesis and continue reading about him through Revelation. We must be aware of these Scriptures in order to know about his rise to power because he is a key personality who has a significant role in the end times.

From the first three chapters of Revelation, we know that we are currently living in the last segment of the Church Age. I believe that because we are living in the end of the age when Jesus returns, the Antichrist could be alive today.

Let me emphasize that there is no reason to fear the Antichrist any more than there is a reason to fear the devil. According to the Word, he is a defeated foe. The only fear we are supposed to have is the fear, or reverence, of God. When you know who His Son Jesus is and what He's done for you, it just comes naturally. Proverbs 9:10 tells us the fear of God is the beginning of wisdom—the wisdom that is essential for living in the last days and for a fulfilling Christian life. It is the wisdom to educate ourselves on the details the Scriptures provide about the Antichrist so that we are not ignorant of Satan's devices. Understanding the Antichrist's role in the dramatic events of the last days is an important part of our mandate to watch and pray.

One passage that describes the Antichrist is 1 John 2:18 and 22:

Little children, it is the last time: and ye have heard that antichrist shall come, even now are there many antichrists; whereby we know that it is the last time.

Who is a liar but he that denieth that Jesus is the Christ? He is antichrist, that denieth the Father and the Son.

Notice verse 18 warns us not only of the Antichrist, but also of many antichrists to come. This is one of the main ways Christians will recognize the end is near.

Ruling Systems

While there is only one Antichrist who will fulfill John's vision in Revelation, there are many antichrists of lesser significance (but who are still treacherous and misleading) in today's society who are examples of the spirit of antichrist working in the world.

For instance, there are ruling systems against Christ, such as Communism. This theory and system of social and political organization was a major force in world politics during much of the twentieth century and still has some single-party communist countries in existence today.

Communistic governments eliminate the freedom of religion and Christianity from its people. Any government system that is against Christ can be considered antichrist.

People/Movements

Throughout history, various individuals and movements have reflected the spirit of antichrist. Secular humanism and New Age movements promote life without dependence on God. These movements teach that humankind is supreme in ourselves, without the need for any outside creator or divine being. This antichrist spirit works today to infiltrate the minds of individuals.

Other infamous people in history exemplified the spirit of antichrist. Hitler provides us with a strong example of this. His hatred for God's people, the Jews, marked one of the cruelest atrocities in history.

While the spirit of the antichrist is seen in various realms of influence today, there is still only one Antichrist. The Bible refers to the

Antichrist by many names. We just saw in 1 John 2:18 and 22 he is identified by the first name—Antichrist.

I want to talk about some of the other names of Antichrist because it will help develop his character for you and give you a profile of him (what he will be like, what he'll do, his personality), although I won't try to say specifically who he is. Some of these names are symbolic references to him. God often uses symbols in His Word to paint a visual picture of divine concepts. This kind of biblical symbolism helps us to comprehend and hold on to the principles of God.

First Name—"Antichrist"

What does the term *Antichrist* mean? Dividing the word, we see two parts: anti and Christ. Simply put, *anti* means opposed to: AGAINST. *Christ* means "Messiah." Basically, the name *Antichrist* means "against Christ." So, according to the meaning of his name, he is against Jesus Christ. And he will live up to his name.

When the Antichrist arrives on the public scene, he will attempt to emulate Christ by eventually seeking to position himself in Jesus' place.

Second Name—"Little Horn"

I considered the horns, and, behold, there came up among them another little horn, before whom there were three of the first horns plucked up by the roots: and, behold, in this horn were eyes like the eyes of man, and a mouth speaking great things.

Daniel 7:8

And out of one of them came forth a little horn, which waxed exceeding great, toward the south, and toward the east, and toward the pleasant land.

Daniel 8:9

The second name the Bible gives the Antichrist is "little horn." We see this name in the book of Daniel during two of Daniel's visions, both of which reveal end-time events. I believe Daniel called the Antichrist "little horn" because the Antichrist will exalt himself.[2]

Daniel gives a wonderful description of what is going to happen with nations and world empires in the end time. His visions even provide a good idea of the general location from where the Antichrist could come.

In Daniel's vision, he predicted the rise of ten kingdoms. Out of those kingdoms, one kingdom (belonging to Antichrist) will rise and conquer three of the others because the Antichrist will have great power to make war. Then the other seven kingdoms will say to him, "Don't fight with us! We will just come along with you!" What does he do really well to make people follow him? He knows how to make war.

Before we look at the third name of the Antichrist, let's look at a dream that the Babylonian ruler King Nebuchadnezzar had. Understanding this king's dream will help us to understand the meaning of Daniel's vision and things to come in the last days.

Nebuchadnezzar's Dream

During the Jewish captivity in Babylon (which is present-day Iraq), the ruling King Nebuchadnezzar received a dream that troubled his spirit (Daniel 2:1). Unfortunately, he could not remember his dream when he awoke. Frustrated and angry, he demanded that the wise men of Babylon recall and explain his dream or suffer a vicious death.

When Daniel learned of this plan, he went in to see the king and asked him to give him a little time, and he would tell the king his dream and what it meant. Then Daniel went home and petitioned God to reveal the dream to him. In a vision, God revealed Nebuchadnezzar's dream and the interpretation to Daniel, thus sparing the lives of all the wise men. Daniel praised God's sovereignty and wisdom exclaiming:

> *Blessed be the name of God for ever and ever: for wisdom and might are his: and he changeth the times and seasons: he removeth kings, and setteth up kings: he giveth wisdom unto the wise, and knowledge to them that know understanding: He revealeth the deep and secret things: he knoweth what is in the darkness, and the light dwelleth with him. I thank thee, and praise thee, O thou God of my fathers, who hast given me wisdom and might, and hast made known unto me now what we desired of thee: for thou hast now made known unto us the king's matter.*
>
> *Daniel 2:20-24*

After asking mercy for the wise men, Daniel was brought to the king, and he told the king the dream and interpreted it. In his dream, Nebuchadnezzar saw a four-part creature (vv. 31-45). The head was gold, the arms were silver, the belly was brass, the legs were iron, and the feet were a mix of iron and clay. Daniel's interpretation of this dream illustrated the major world empires predicted for the future. Daniel explained that the golden head represented Babylon. Babylon was to be the first world empire.[3]

Notice in this example, gold is the most precious metal. The first empire in Nebuchadnezzar's dream is gold and each empire decreases in metallic worth as we look down the creature's body. The silver arms represent the Medes and Persians—a two-part empire. The stomach of brass represents Greece. The two legs of iron are the Roman Empire.

Finally, you could say that the creature's two legs extend down into the end times, and we see ten toes. The ten toes are made of clay and iron.

I believe that these ten toes represent the ten kingdoms that spring forth from the Roman Empire.[4] These kingdoms are the revived Roman Empire during the end times. You may wonder where the Roman Empire is located. It is in Europe, parts of the Middle East, and parts of Africa.

The revived Roman Empire will encompass the area around the Mediterranean Sea. According to Bible prophecy, the ten kingdoms that are going to rise out of the Roman Empire will be from this area.

The Crushing Stone

Suddenly there is a turning point in the king's dream. A stone smashes the feet of the creature and brings down the entire structure.

Thou sawest till that a stone was cut out without hands, which smote the image upon his feet that were of iron, clay, and brake them to pieces.

Then was the iron, the clay, the brass, the silver, and the gold, broken to pieces together, and became like the chaff of the summer threshing

floors; the wind carried them away, that no place was found for
them: and the stone that smote the image became a great mountain,
and filled the whole earth.

Daniel 2:34–35

The stone represents Jesus Christ and His kingdom. As one Bible commentary describes it, "In its relation to Israel it is a 'stone of stumbling' (Isaiah 8:14) on which both houses of Israel are 'broken,' not destroyed, as Antichrist and his faction shall be (Matthew 21:42, 44). In its relation to the Church, the same stone which destroys the image is the foundation of the Church (Ephesians 2:20). In its relation to the Gentile world-power [the Antichrist], the stone is its destroyer."[5]

Notice that the stone did not just crush the toes; the whole statue fell. In history, we know that each empire fell. Babylon fell to the Medes and Persians. The Medes and Persians fell to Greece. The Greek Empire fell to the Romans.

However, when we see the ten toes, the stone crushes the entire statue. Many agree on what this symbolizes—that the ten nations that used to be part of the old Roman Empire (including historical Babylon, Medes and Persia, Greece, and Rome) are going to rise again in Europe. This area of the world is going to become very strong in end-time politics, geography, and war.

It is from one of those ten nations that the "little horn," or leader, will arise. The leader will be very skillful at making war, and he will fight. His skills of warfare will attract people to follow him. This will begin his reign of deception.

The number one tool the Antichrist will use is deception.

We do not see this little horn mentioned in the above reference of King Nebuchadnezzar's dream. You may be wondering where that little horn's tie to the ten kingdoms comes from. It is taken from two other visions that Daniel experienced.

In these visions, the Lord expounded on King Nebuchadnezzar's dream of the four empires. (See Daniel 7:1-28 and 8:2-27.) I'm not going to go into much detail here except to say that the little horn will surface from these empires. As we have seen, he will be strong and powerful, and he will lead by deception. He will end up conquering three of the little kingdoms and then will begin to grow in popularity and power.

Eventually, he will become greater than the country he came from and will desire imperial power. This will cause him to conquer the ten kingdoms from that part of the Mediterranean world. (Remember, this little horn represents the Antichrist and corresponds to the message portrayed in King Nebuchadnezzar's dream.)

After the little horn, or Antichrist, arises from the ten kingdoms, a crushing stone will take him down and that stone represents the kingdom of Jesus Christ.

Third Name—"Vile Person"

The third name the Bible gives the Antichrist is "vile person." Daniel spoke about this "vile person" during one of his visions:

And in his estate shall stand up a vile person, to whom they shall not give the honour of the kingdom: but he shall come in peaceably, and obtain the kingdom by flatteries.

Daniel 11:21

This verse is describing something that happened in the life of Antiochus IV Epiphanes, who represents the Antichrist. He persecuted the Jews and desecrated the temple, foreshadowing the offenses that the Antichrist will commit against the Jewish people.[6]

In this Scripture, Daniel warned that the Antichrist, or vile person, will utilize flattery to overcome nations. The Hebrew word in this passage for *vile person* makes an interesting point. The word is *bazah* which, according to *The Theological Wordbook of the Old Testament* is a title given to a person who "despises the Lord [and] is devious in his ways." This undoubtedly portrays the Antichrist as someone who will outwardly despise anything having to do with God and His people. This will be evident in his actions towards the people of God during the Tribulation.

Also significant is the fact that although the Antichrist is described by the Bible as being a vile person, he is able to use peaceable methods to build his empire. Notice in verse 21, the Bible says he uses flatteries. This again proves his method of operation is deceit.

The unsuspecting kingdoms will be given over to the Antichrist. They will not realize they are giving control to a vile person. The Antichrist will use deception to manipulate and gain control. It is only in the latter part of the Tribulation that his true colors will be revealed.

Fourth Name—"Assyrian"

And the Lord shall cause his glorious voice to be heard, and shall shew the lighting down of his arm, with the indignation of his anger, and with the flame of a devouring fire, with scattering, and tempest, and hailstones. For through the voice of the Lord shall the Assyrian be beaten down, which smote with a rod.

Isaiah 30:30-31

O Assyrian, the rod of mine anger, and the staff in their hand is mine indignation. I will send him against an hypocritical nation, and against the people of my wrath will I give him a charge, to take the spoil, and to take the prey, and to tread them down like the mire of the streets. Howbeit he meaneth not so, neither doth his heart think so; but it is in his heart to destroy and cut off nations not a few.

Isaiah 10:5-7

The term "Assyrian" in these passages is generally considered to be a symbolic representation of the Antichrist. In calling him the "Assyrian," Isaiah gives some indication of where he will emerge, but opinions vary on this. He could be a Jew born somewhere within the borders of the old Assyrian empire, although it is doubtful. It is more likely that he will come from one of the European countries that was once part of the Old Roman Empire. No one knows for sure.

Fifth Name—"Gog and Magog"

And the word of the Lord came unto me saying, Son of man, set thy face against Gog, the land of Magog, the chief prince of Meshech and Tubal, and prophesy against him, and say, Thus saith the Lord God: Behold, I am against thee, O Gog, the chief prince of Meshech and Tubal: and I will turn thee back, and put hooks into thy jaws, and I will bring thee forth, and all thine army, horses and horsemen, all of them clothed with all sorts of armour, even a great company with bucklers and shields, all of them handling swords.

Ezekiel 38:1-4

Here we see Ezekiel describing Antichrist as the chief prince of the countries of Meshech and Tubal. Originally, Meshech and Tubal weren't countries; they were grandsons of Noah who settled near the Black and Caspian seas, which are currently bounded by Syria, Turkey, Romania, the Ukraine, Iran, Iraq, and others.

Many people think that "Gog" and "Magog" are the names of Russia, but I don't think that at all. Some Bible scholars believe they refer to the Antichrist in the sense that Gog and Magog represent all those who oppose Jesus, that they symbolize the anti-Christian forces on the earth.[7]

I agree Gog and Magog have to do with Satan and his power through Antichrist in the sense that "Gog" has to do with Satan and "Magog" has to do with Antichrist who comes out of Satan warring and fighting.

Sixth Name—"Man of Sin"

Now we beseech you, brethren, by the coming of our Lord Jesus Christ, and by our gathering together unto him, that ye be not soon shaken in mind, or be troubled, neither by spirit, nor by word, nor by letter as from us, as that day of the Christ is at hand. Let no man deceive you by any means: for that day shall not come, except there come a falling away first, and that man of sin be revealed, the son of perdition; who opposes and exalteth himself above all that is called God, or that is worshipped; so that he as God sitteth in the temple of God, shewing himself that he is God. Remember ye not, that, when I was yet with you, I told you these things?

2 Thessalonians 2:1–5

The apostle Paul in his letter to the Thessalonians mentioned the name, "man of sin," to them. Paul was directly answering misunderstandings concerning the timing of the events of the end times. He told the Thessalonians not to listen to rumors and reports that the day of the Lord had already begun because a number of events must occur before Christ returns. For one thing, there will be a great rebellion against God led by the man of sin (or lawlessness), the Antichrist. And God will remove all the restraints on evil before He brings judgment on the rebels.

The Antichrist is referred to as the "man of sin" because everything he will work to accomplish on earth will be opposite of God. He will conduct affairs lawlessly and without restraint. The Antichrist is a true picture of sin incarnate.

Seventh Name—"Beast"

In Revelation 13, the Bible describes the Antichrist as a "beast."

> *And I stood upon the sand of the sea, and saw a beast rise up out of the sea, having seven heads and ten horns, and upon his horns ten crowns, and upon his heads the name of blasphemy.*
>
> *Revelation 13:1*

The beast in Chapter 13 actually refers to two key end-time personalities represented by a first and second beast. The first is the Antichrist, the future political ruler who will oppose God and all of His followers; the second is the false prophet, the future religious ruler who will force the world to worship the Antichrist (the first beast.) This next passage gives a very clear picture of what the Antichrist as both will seek to accomplish.

And they worshipped the dragon which gave power unto the beast:
and they worshipped the beast, saying, Who is like unto the beast?
who is able to make war with him? And there was given unto him
a mouth speaking great things and blasphemies; and power was
given unto him to continue forty and two months. And he opened
his mouth in blasphemy against God, to blaspheme his name, and
his tabernacle, and them that dwell in heaven. And it was given
unto him to make war with the saints, and to overcome them: and
power was given him over all kindreds, and tongues, and nations.
And all that dwell upon the earth shall worship him, whose names
are not written in the book of life of the Lamb slain from the foun-
dation of the world.

Revelation 13:4–8

In verse 11-15, we read about the beast again. This second reference (of Antichrist as the beast) refers to the false prophet, the religious ruler who will force the world to worship the Antichrist as the first beast mentioned in this passage.

And I beheld another beast coming up out of the earth; and he had
two horns like a lamb, and he spake as a dragon. And he exerciseth
all the power of the first beast before him, and causeth the earth and
them which dwell therein to worship the first beast, whose deadly
wound was healed. And he doeth great wonders, so that he maketh
fire come down from heaven on the earth in the sight of men, and
deceiveth them that dwell on the earth by the means of those mira-
cles which he had power to do in the sight of the beast; saying to
them that dwell on the earth, that they should make an image to the
beast, which had the wound by a sword, and did live. And he had
power to give life unto the image of the beast, that the image of the

beast should both speak, and cause that as many as would not wor-
ship the image of the beast should be killed.

Revelation 13:11-15

The Antichrist is also called "beast" in Revelation 17:3. John wrote, "So he carried me away in the spirit into the wilderness: and I saw a woman sit upon a scarlet coloured beast, full of names of blasphemy, having seven heads and ten horns."

Notice John was in the Spirit when he saw the beast. There is great significance in the fact that John received the vision of Revelation from the Holy Spirit. How did John recognize the beast? He was able to identify him from the guidance of the Holy Spirit.

The Antichrist is always the opposite of Jesus. We know that Jesus is the Lamb; therefore, is it any surprise that the Antichrist is the beast?

Eighth Name—"Of Tyre"

The Antichrist will be a great builder of cities. He will even rebuild Tyre and Babylon. Tyre was located in what is now southern Lebanon on the Mediterranean Sea; Babylon was located in present day Iraq.

It is interesting to me that in the Old Testament, the kings of Tyre and Babylon both claimed worship as divine beings (Daniel 3:1-12). They made their people bow down to them because they wanted to be treated as gods. Isn't that a long-held ambition of Satan right from the beginning? Hasn't he always been attempting to be like God?

Remember, Satan's ambition will be temporarily satisfied when he, in the form of the Antichrist, will be worshipped by all who are left on the earth after the Rapture.

Ninth Name—"Son of Perdition"

The Antichrist is a man empowered by Satan. Among his many names in the Bible is the "son of perdition."

Let no man deceive you by any means: for that day shall not come, except there come a falling away first, and that man of sin be revealed, the son of perdition; who opposeth and exalteth himself above all that is called God, or that is worshipped; so that he as God sitteth in the temple of God, shewing himself that he is God.

2 Thessalonians 2:3-4

And every spirit that confesseth not that Jesus Christ is come in the flesh is not of God: and this is that spirit of antichrist, whereof ye have heard that it should come; and even now already is it in the world.

1 John 4:3

Another person in the Bible who is referred to as the son of perdition is Judas Iscariot. Some believe that it is possible the Antichrist may be Judas Iscariot returning to the earth in an action that counterfeits Jesus' return to earth. This idea is not often talked about, but because it is possible, let's look at some of the reasoning behind it.

A double prophecy in Psalm 55 shows both Judas' betrayal of Jesus and the Antichrist's betrayal of Israel, revealing them to be the same man. Luke 22:3 says, "Then entered Satan into Judas surnamed Iscariot." Jesus called Judas a devil, which suggests that Judas was more than a man: "Jesus answered them, Have I not chosen you twelve, and one of you is a devil?" (John 6:70).

The original Greek translation for the word Jesus used to describe Judas in this verse is *diabolos*, which means "false accuser" or "slanderer." It is one of the names of Satan.

Matthew Henry's Bible Commentary refers to Judas as the devil saying, "Hypocrites and betrayers of Christ are no better than devils. Judas not only had a devil, but he was a devil. One of you is a false accuser; so diabolos sometimes signifies (2 Tim. 3:3); and it is possible that Judas, when he sold his Master to the chief priests, represented him to them as a bad man, to justify himself in what he did. But I rather take it as we read it: He is a devil, a devil incarnate, a fallen apostle, as the devil a fallen angel. He is Satan, an adversary, an enemy to Christ. He is Abaddon, and Apollyon, a son of perdition. He was of his father the devil, did his lusts, was in his interests, as Cain, (1 John 3:12). Those whose bodies were possessed by the devil are never called devils (demoniacs, but not devils); but Judas, into whose heart Satan entered, and filled it, is called a devil."[8]

Was Judas the devil incarnate, just as the Lord Jesus was God incarnate? In John 17:12, Jesus himself calls Judas the "son of perdition."

> *While I was with them in the world, I kept them in thy name: those that thou gavest me I have kept, and none of them is lost, but the son of perdition; that the scripture might be fulfilled.*
>
> *John 17:12*

This is the same name Paul called the Antichrist in 2 Thessalonians 2:3, as we saw earlier.

Another interesting concept based upon Scripture is that the Antichrist will ascend from the same place Judas Iscariot went upon death.

And when they shall have finished their testimony, the beast that
ascendeth out of the bottomless pit shall make war against them,
and shall overcome them, and kill them.

Revelation 11:7

The Antichrist will come from hell and will be superhuman. In Revelation 11:7, he is seen coming out of the bottomless pit, which is the abode of lost spirits and wicked dead, the place of their incarceration and torment. (See also Luke 8:30-31, Revelation 20:1-3.) The Antichrist will come from the bottomless pit where Judas Iscariot was sent when he died.

Taking all this into consideration, I think it is possible that the Antichrist's history as Judas Iscariot is revealed in Revelation 17:8:

The beast that thou sawest was, and is not; and shall ascend out of
the bottomless pit, and go into perdition: and they that dwell on the
earth shall wonder, whose names were not written in the book of
life from the foundation of the world, when they behold the beast
that was, and is not, and yet is.

From the last line of the Scripture we can see that the Antichrist was once on earth (possibly in the form of Judas) and then, in John's day, he was not on earth possibly because he was dead (when Judas hanged himself.) He will ascend out of the bottomless pit at the time of his rebirth (as the Antichrist) and end up in perdition when Jesus casts him in the Lake of Fire at Armageddon.

Tenth Name—"The Chaldean"

I believe that Habakkuk gives quite a description of the Antichrist in this passage (symbolically speaking).

"Look among the nations! Observe! Be astonished! Wonder! Because I am doing something in your days--You would not believe if you were told.

"For behold, I am raising up the Chaldeans, that fierce and impetuous people who march throughout the earth to seize dwelling places which are not theirs.

"They are dreaded and feared; their justice and authority originate with themselves.

"Their horses are swifter than leopards and keener than wolves in the evening. Their horsemen come galloping; their horsemen come from afar; they fly like an eagle swooping down to devour.

"All of them come for violence. Their horde of faces moves forward. They collect captives like sand.

"They mock at kings and rulers are a laughing matter to them. They laugh at every fortress and heap up rubble to capture it.

"Then they will sweep through like the wind and pass on. But they will be held guilty. They whose strength is their god."

Are You not from everlasting, O Lord, my God, my Holy One? We will not die. You, O Lord, have appointed them to judge; and You, O Rock, have established them to correct.

Your eyes are too pure to approve evil, and You can not look on wickedness with favor. Why do You look with favor on those who deal treacherously? Why are You silent when the wicked swallow up those more righteous than they?

Why have You made men like the fish of the sea, like creeping things without a ruler over them?

The Chaldeans bring all of them up with a hook, drag them away with their net, and gather them together in their fishing net. Therefore they rejoice and are glad.

Therefore they offer a sacrifice to their net and burn incense to their fishing net; because through these things their catch is large, and their food is plentiful.

Will they therefore empty their net and continually slay nations without sparing?

Habakkuk 1:5-17 NASB

Chaldean and Babylonian refer to the same people. The Chaldeans are better known as the Babylonians, and we've already seen that "Babylonian" is another name for the Antichrist.

Habakkuk wrote this passage because he was very troubled about the evil and injustice overtaking his land at the hands of the Chaldeans. The violent Chaldean "nation," or end-time Antichrist figure, may have plans to bring calamity on our present world, but God has an intended end for every trial and an intended "after." There will be new life and blessings after Armageddon and the Tribulation because God can even use the wicked to bring His purposes forth.

Are you beginning to get a picture of the type of person the Antichrist will be? As we will see next, the Antichrist is a counterfeit of Jesus in every way.

Chapter 20

Portrait of Evil

The Antichrist is completely opposite of everything Jesus represents. Satan always tries to counterfeit everything that God does, only whatever he does is never of God; it's the devil's realm. According to the Bible, he even has a counterfeit trinity. Of course, God has the holy trinity—God the Father, God the Son (Jesus), and God the Holy Spirit. Well, the devil has his satanic trinity mentioned in Revelation 16:13, which is comprised of:

- The Dragon—Satan
- The Antichrist—the beast
- The False Prophet

Satan uses counterfeiting as a method to draw people off course. When we do not educate ourselves on exactly what the Word says, it is easy to miss the subtle differences. Deception is a very subtle thing, and we're going to see it more and more in our day. But if we cling to the Word, we won't be deceived.

When all the end-time events take place, it's going to be a tremendous testimony to the world that the Word of God is true. Satan has to come up with some big-time miraculous, counterfeit measures to try to overcome that.

Satan has always used the counterfeiting method to confuse the world of God's plan. We see this happen throughout the Bible. As watchers, we must stay focused on God to avoid confusion. Here's an example of what having the right focus can do.

I heard of a woman who swam the English Channel and wanted to set a record, but when she was a half-mile from the shore, she became exhausted. Her coach, her mom, and some friends were following her in a boat, so she called for them to bring the boat over to her so she could climb in. But they said to her, "Oh, don't stop now! You're only half a mile from the shore!"

She couldn't see the land because it was really foggy; she just saw the fog, and that's what she focused on. She said to them, "I think you're wrong. I think it's farther than a half a mile, and I see all that fog. I just can't go on."

When she got into the boat and discovered that it really was only a half a mile to shore, she said to them, "If I could have seen the land, I would not have stopped. But when I saw that fog I thought, *Oh it's much farther*, and I just didn't finish it." Instead of holding on until the end, standing to the end, swimming to the end, she lost it by just such a little margin because she had the wrong focus.

The next year she went into the contest and swam the English Channel again. It was foggy again, but she had a new strategy. This time she did not focus on the fog; she focused on finishing, and not only did she finish, but she beat all the records by two hours. She was the fastest one to swim the English Channel—she finished the course because she stayed focused.

God has a strategy for us to stay focused—stay saturated in the Word. That way, we will be able to recognize the enemy's counterfeits and finish our course victoriously—the way God has promised us we can finish.

There's a special Scripture passage that illustrates this so well. Matthew 13:26-30 tells how Jesus went forth to sow the good seed, and Satan's counterfeit was to immediately sow tares or weeds. The harvesters asked if they should pull the weeds, but the owner, who represents Jesus, tells the harvesters to let them grow together so that no wheat is uprooted with the weeds. With God's help, and by staying in His Word, the enemy will not be able to deceive us. As a child of God, it is God who works in us to His will, regardless of the counterfeits in the world:

For it is God which worketh in you both to will and to do of his good pleasure.

Philippians 2:13

Wherein in times past ye walked according to the course of this world, according to the prince of the power of the air, the spirit that now worketh in the children of disobedience.

Ephesians 2:2

Notice in Ephesians 2:2 who will be deceived. Those who follow the Antichrist and fall for his counterfeits are the children of disobedience. When someone refuses the truth (God's Word), what will they believe but a lie? In fact, one of Satan's counterfeits is what the Bible calls "another gospel."

Counterfeit Message

In the Scriptures to follow we can see that Jesus came to bring *the* Gospel, the Good News to humanity.

And Jesus went about all Galilee, teaching in their synagogues, and preaching the gospel of the kingdom, and healing all manner of sickness and all manner of disease among the people.

Matthew 4:23

And saying, The time is fulfilled, and the kingdom of God is at hand: repent ye, and believe the gospel.

Mark 1:15

Satan, however, has another gospel, or counterfeit message, he will seek to spread:

But I fear, lest by any means, as the serpent beguiled Eve through his subtilty, so your minds should be corrupted from the simplicity that is in Christ.

For if he that cometh preacheth another Jesus, whom we have not preached, or if ye receive another spirit, which ye have not received, or another gospel, which ye have not accepted, ye might well bear with him.

2 Corinthians 11:3-4

So the Antichrist will come with another gospel and as another Jesus. Empowered by Satan, the Antichrist will attempt to counterfeit the One true Savior.

We see this in the Antichrist's counterfeit of his followers. We know from the Word that Jesus led twelve disciples during His ministry on earth: "And when it was day, he called unto him his disciples: and *of them he chose twelve, whom also he names apostles*" (Luke 6:13).

But did you know that Satan has his "apostles" too:

And I will keep on doing what I am doing in order to cut the ground from under those who want an opportunity to be considered equal with us in the things they boast about. For such men are false apostles, deceitful workmen, masquerading as apostles of Christ. And no wonder, for Satan himself masquerades as an angel of light. It is not surprising, then, if his servants masquerade as servants of righteousness.

2 Corinthians 11:12-15 NIV

And thou hast tried them which say they are apostles, and are not, and has found them liars.

Revelation 2:2

Then in Revelation 9:4, the Bible states that God will seal His servants on the forehead: "And it was commanded them that they should not hurt the grass of the earth, neither any green thing, neither any tree, but only those men which have not *the seal of God in their foreheads.*"

Based on what we already know about the Antichrist, it should come as no surprise that he will have a counterfeit of this, requiring his followers to also take a seal, or mark, on their foreheads:

And the third angel followed them, saying with a loud voice, If any man worship the beast and his image, and receive his mark in their forehead, or in his hand, the same shall drink of the wine of the wrath of God.

Revelation 14:9-10

Why does Satan do all of this counterfeiting? He is jealous of God's kingdom and people. If he can confuse or persuade people to follow him, then he thinks he has won.

Many times the church only knows "enough to be dangerous" about the facts of the Bible. This makes it very easy for Satan to confuse and lead some away. As we've seen, that is why we must study and understand God's warnings and truths. The Bible is God's Word to mankind. It tells us who we are and how we should live, especially in this last hour. It comforts, guides, and instructs us daily. We can find wisdom, encouragement, and the answers we've been looking for in the Bible.

Remember, the Antichrist's personality is fundamentally opposed to Christ's. Satan himself is transformed into an angel of light. However, through Scripture we know that Jesus is the true Light of the world (John 8:12).

Big Mouth, Piercing Eyes

And of the ten horns that were in his head, and of the other which came up, and before whom three fell; even of that horn that had eyes, and a mouth that spake very great things, whose look was more stout than his fellows.

Daniel 7:20

This verse reveals to us that the Antichrist will exalt himself and speak tremendous things, but he won't speak the truth, and he will have a look that is "stout" or strong, firm, and forceful. This Old Testament scripture can be cross-compared with a New Testament scripture in Revelation: "And there was given him a mouth speaking great things and blasphemies; and power was given unto him to continue forty and two months" (Revelation 13:5).

This man will be an oratorical genius. Evidenced by his later successes in the political, economical, and warfare realms, the Antichrist will use his great speaking ability and charm to persuade nations to follow him.

Fierce and Intelligent

The Antichrist will possess great intelligence. In the book of Daniel, we read that he will have an intense expression that stands out. Daniel mentioned this from one of his many visions: "A king of fierce countenance, and understanding dark sentences, shall stand up" (Daniel 8:23).

The Hebrew word for "fierce" in this Scripture is *az*, which has several meanings—strong, fierce, mighty, power, greedy, and roughly. In this particular Scripture, it is being applied to a human—the Antichrist. When this word is applied to people, it seems invariably to denote enemies. Obviously, this "fierce countenance" characteristic of the Antichrist is an attribute of the enemies of God.

This verse also says that the Antichrist will understand dark sentences (referring to his skill in trickery, intrigue, and stratagem) and hard questions. In other words, he will be crafty, shrewd, seeking to make his way and to accomplish his purpose, not only by the terror that he will inspire, but by deceit and cunning.

Daniel's prophecies reveal the Antichrist's traits and God's plan for Israel's future. This great antagonist who will fill the world with wickedness will be so far above anyone else on earth that, as the next passage reveals, it will take divine intervention from God to stop him:

> *At the end of their rule, when their sin is at its height, a fierce king,*
> *a master of intrigue, will rise to power. He will become very strong,*

*but not by his own power. He will cause a shocking amount of de-
struction and succeed in everything he does. He will destroy powerful leaders and devastate the holy people. He will be a master of
deception and will become arrogant; he will destroy many without
warning. He will even take on the Prince of princes in battle, but
he will be broken, though not by human power.*

Daniel 8:23-25 NLT

This description of the Antichrist suggests that he will be wiser
than Daniel and Ezekiel because he will know the answers to great
secrets and possess unusual intelligence. Be assured that when the
Antichrist finally arises, he will be greatly admired for his extraordinary intellect. No wonder so many will be deceived if they don't know
the Word. Next, we will look at other areas illustrated in the Bible in
which the Antichrist will excel.

Seven Areas of Intelligence

The world will accept the Antichrist because he will be a genius in
seven areas. I'm going to unveil them through Scriptures:

Intellect

*Behold, thou art wiser than Daniel; there is no secret that they can
hide from thee.*

Ezekiel 28:3

*And in the latter time of their kingdom, when the transgressors are
come to the full, a king of fierce countenance, and understanding
dark sentences, shall stand up.*

Daniel 8:23

Oration

And of the ten horns that were in his head, and of the other which came up, and before whom three fell; even that horn that had eyes, and a mouth that spake very great things, whose look was more stout than his fellows.

Daniel 7:20

And the beast which I saw was like unto a leopard, and his feet were as the feet of a bear, and his mouth as the mouth of a lion: and the dragon gave him his power, and his seat, and great authority.

Revelation 13:2

Politics

And in his estate shall stand up a vile person, to whom they shall not give the honour of the kingdom: but he shall come in peaceably, and obtain the kingdom by flatteries.

Daniel 11:21

For God hath put in their hearts to fulfil his will, and to agree, and give their kingdom unto the beast, until the words of God shall be fulfilled.

Revelation 17:17

Commerce

With thy wisdom and with thine understanding thou hast gotten thee riches, and hast gotten gold and silver into thy treasures: by thy great wisdom and by thy traffick hast thou increased thy riches, and thine heart is lifted up because of thy riches.

Ezekiel 28:4-5

And through his policy also he shall cause craft to prosper in his hand; and he shall magnify himself in his heart, and by peace shall destroy many: he shall also stand up against the Prince of princes; but he shall be broken without hand.

Daniel 8:25

But in his estate shall he honour the God of forces: and a god whom his fathers knew not shall he honour with gold, and silver, and with precious stones, and pleasant things.

Daniel 11:38

But he shall have power over the treasures of gold and of silver, and over all the precious things of Egypt: and the Libyans and the Ethiopians shall be at his steps.

Daniel 11:43

Military Government

They that see thee shall narrowly look upon thee, and consider thee, saying, Is this the man that made the earth to tremble, that did shake kingdoms; that made the world as a wilderness, and destroyed the cities thereof; that opened not the house of his prisoners?

Isaiah 14:16-17

And his power shall be mighty, but not by his own power: and he shall destroy wonderfully, and shall prosper, and practise, and shall destroy the mighty and the holy people.

Daniel 8:24

Religion

Who opposeth and exalteth himself above all that is called God, or that is worshipped; so that he as God sitteth in the temple of God, shewing himself that he is God.

2 Thessalonians 2:4

When you read of all these awful attributes and exploits, you may think, *this is just terrible!* But when they begin to happen, they will just be signs that things are about to wrap up.

The Antichrist's Origin

Many people have asked me, "Where is the Antichrist going to come from?" Although there are several theories, I believe the book of Daniel is very specific on the origin of the Antichrist.

When considering the primary prophetic books of the Bible, Daniel is considered to be a strong book of prophecy to the nations. In contrast, the book of Zechariah is considered prophecy to the Jews, and the book of Revelation to the Church. All three books intermingle, but Daniel's dominate focus is the nations, so we're going to look at Daniel to unveil the future of the nations and the Antichrist's origin.

Daniel's Prophetic Dream

After Nebuchadnezzar's dream, Daniel also dreamed a prophetic dream. His dream coincided with the message of King Nebuchadnezzar's dream, only Daniel saw animals instead of the figure of metals. We find this recorded in Daniel 7:3-8:

And four great beasts came up from the sea, diverse one from another. The first was like a lion, and had eagle's wings: I beheld till the wings thereof were plucked, and it was lifted up from the earth, and made stand upon the feet as a man, and a man's heart was given to it. And behold another beast, a second, like to a bear, and it raised up itself on one side, and it had three ribs in the mouth of it between the teeth of it: and they said thus unto it, Arise, devour much flesh. After this I beheld, and lo another, like a leopard, which had upon the back of it four wings of a fowl; the beast had also four heads; and dominion was given to it. After this I saw in the night visions, and behold a fourth beast, dreadful and terrible, and strong exceedingly; and it had great iron teeth: it devoured and brake in pieces, and stamped the residue with the feet of it: and it was diverse from all the beasts that were before it; and it had ten horns. I considered the horns, and, behold, there came up among them another little horn, before whom there were three of the first horns plucked up by the roots: and, behold, in this horn were eyes like the eyes of man, and a mouth speaking great things.

In this passage, the animals Daniel sees are a golden-headed lion (Babylonians), a bear (Medes-Persians), a leopard (Greeks), and a fierce-looking iron creature (Romans). These animals are important to us because they are also listed in Revelation 17.

Previously I mentioned that out of the ten-toed kingdom (the revival of the Roman Empire) a horn will sprout out. This indicates the Antichrist will come from the area of the "fourth beast, dreadful and terrible," the Old Roman Empire. This is Europe, particularly the area around the Mediterranean. History tells that the Roman Empire died down for an extended period. However, this prophecy reveals that it will sprout up again in ten countries. Out of the ten countries that rise again, a little horn will arise that will be the Antichrist.

From the context of Daniel's visions, we know that the Antichrist is going to rise up and fight three of the smaller countries in this group. He will take them over, just as the little horn will overtake the others. Because he has great power to make war, after he conquers three of those ten major countries, the other seven will join him. In addition, much of the Antichrist's activities will take place in this area of the world—the Old Roman Empire.

After God gave Daniel this dream, He gave him a second pondering vision. This time, the dream narrowed down to two animals or nations—a ram and a he-goat:

> *Then I lifted up mine eyes, and saw, and, behold, there stood before the river a ram which had two horns: and the two horns were high; but one was higher than the other, and the higher came up last. I saw the ram pushing westward, and northward, and southward; so that no beasts might stand before him, neither was there any that could deliver out of his hand; but he did according to his will, and became great. And as I was considering, behold, an he goat came from the west on the face of the whole earth, and touched not the ground: and the goat had a notable horn between his eyes. And he came to the ram that had two horns, which I had seen standing before the river, and ran unto him in the fury of his power. And I saw him come close unto the ram, and he was moved with choler against him, and smote the ram, and brake his two horns: and there was no power in the ram to stand before him, but he cast him down to the ground, and stamped upon him: and there was none that could deliver the ram out of his hand. Therefore the he goat waxed very great: and when he was strong, the great horn was broken; and for it came up four notable ones toward the four winds of heaven. And out of one of them came forth a little horn, which waxed exceeding*

great, toward the south, and toward the east, and toward the pleas-
ant land.

Daniel 8:3-9

In this dream, the ram hits the he-goat, but the he-goat conquers him. The ram represents the Medo-Persian Empire. In biblical times a ram was the symbol of the Persians and had two horns or little kingdoms, namely Media and Persia. The he-goat represents the Greek Empire. A goat was a very proper symbol of the Greek or Macedonian people; in fact, two hundred years before the time of Daniel they were known as the goats' people.

From the he-goat's head stems a great horn. This great horn is the first Greek leader; most scholars agree that it is Alexander the Great. Suddenly, this great horn breaks off the he-goat and four notable horns spring forth. I believe these four horns represent Syria, Medo-Persia, Turkey, and Palestine.

Finally, from those four horns a smaller horn arises. Remember, this horn is the Antichrist. Interestingly, this small horn (or Antichrist) makes war with the south, east, and west. The south encompasses the area of Egypt, the east includes Palestine, and the west comprises Medo-Persia. The Antichrist does not make war with the north (Syria). Could this suggest that he is from the north, or from the area of Syria?

Daniel's second vision pinpoints the location of the Antichrist's origin even more so. Syria is part of the Old Roman Empire. Additionally, the Antichrist is the head of the northern army, which is referred to in Joel 2:20:

But I will remove far off from you the northern army, and will drive him into a land barren and desolate, with his face toward the east sea, and his hinder part toward the utmost sea, and his stink shall come up, and his ill savour shall come up, because he hath done great things.

He is called the king of Babylon in Isaiah 14:4 and the Assyrian in Isaiah 10:5. These Scriptures seem to point to the fact that the Antichrist comes from a country that is near the Black and Caspian seas, a country that was part of the former Babylonian and Assyrian empires, and is north of Israel. Again, these indicators seem to point to the area of Syria. Let's look at one more Bible passage on this.

At the End of Time

The Antichrist is alluded to in Daniel 11:21-39, which discusses Antiochus Epiphanes. He is the Syrian king who is considered a prototype of the Antichrist and his future dealings with the nation of Israel. Daniel 11 is considered by many to be a chapter of predominantly fulfilled prophecy. In one sense this is true. Daniel's prophecy in verses 1-39 was fulfilled in history by Antiochus; but events that will take place "at the end of time" are yet to come, as in verses 40-45:

Then at the time of the end, the king of the south will attack the king of the north. The king of the north will storm out with chariots, charioteers, and a vast navy. He will invade various lands and sweep through them like a flood. He will enter the glorious land of Israel, and many nations will fall, but Moab, Edom, and the best part of Ammon will escape. He will conquer many countries, and even Egypt will not escape. He will gain control over the gold, silver, and treasures of Egypt, and the Libyans and Ethiopians will be his servants.

But then news from the east and the north will alarm him, and he will set out in great anger to destroy and obliterate many. He will stop between the glorious holy mountain and the sea and will pitch his royal tents. But while he is there, his time will suddenly run out, and no one will help him. (NLT)

We're beginning to put the pieces to the end-times "puzzle" together with everything we've been looking at so far. I believe that it will cause your spiritual confidence and peace to dramatically increase as your understanding of end-time prophecy increases. As we go deeper into the Scriptures on the last days, we're going to continue to look at this major end-time personality. God put the Antichrist in His Word because He wanted us to know all about him.

Chapter 21

What Will the Antichrist Do?

So far we have an idea of where the Antichrist will come from—possibly around the Mediterranean area. We know what he'll look like—mean eyes, big mouth, "ugly" face. He will have smooth words that drip with honey at first. He'll be a great deceiver. And he'll be very smart. Now let's discuss what the Antichrist can do and how his character and his actions all flow together.

There are basically two kinds of rulers who lust for power: religious rulers and rulers of commerce or governments. Religious rulers want to rule over people, as with David Koresh, the leader of the Branch Davidian religious sect in Waco, Texas, in 1999 and with Jim Jones and his Jonestown cult in the 1970s, both ended in tragedy. Evil religious leaders want to rule over people's souls; they want to own people. Evil political rulers or rulers in the business world lust for power through material gain, land development, and economics.

The Antichrist will be both kind of ruler. He will want to rule the world and be worshipped as a god, and he will want to be the major "player" in commercial endeavors. At some point, he will rise up and be very powerful and very strong in war. During that time of great distress, or the Great Tribulation, he'll also be very experienced in commerce and making money. In Psalm 52:7 it says: "Lo, this is the man that made not God his strength; but trusted in the *abundance of his riches*, and strengthened himself in his wickedness."

One way the Antichrist will make money is by raising taxes. In Daniel 11, the angel explained Daniel's vision to him. In the explanation, the angel described the work of the Antichrist as a tax raiser: "Then shall stand up in his estate a *raiser of taxes* in the glory of the kingdom: but within few days he shall be destroyed, neither in anger, nor in battle" (Daniel 11:20).

While this verse is referring to Antiochus Epiphanes as we discussed earlier, it also represents the Antichrist and what he will do in the last days. I'm going to stir up your memory for a moment in reference to the Antichrist being a powerful moneymaker.

Earlier when we were going through the rooms in the "house" of Revelation, we saw two Bible chapters in the fifth room, or the satanic room—Revelation 17 and 18. These two chapters speak figuratively of two Babylons.

The first Babylon is ecclesiastical (church; religious). The ecclesiastical Babylon is the church system the Antichrist will build and of which he will declare himself god.

The second Babylon is commercial. The Antichrist is going to build a tremendous commercial center on the base of ancient Babylon. That is what Daniel 8:25 means when it states "…he shall cause craft to prosper." From Scripture, we know that this commercial Babylon will be very prosperous. For example, the following passage tells us when Babylon does finally fall, all the merchants weep and cry:

> *And he cried mightily with a strong voice, saying, Babylon the great is fallen, is fallen...and the fruits that thy soul lusted after are departed from thee, and all things which were dainty and goodly are departed from thee, and thou shalt find them no more at all... The merchants of these things, which were made rich by her, shall stand afar off for the fear of her torment, weeping and wailing... and cried when they saw the smoke of her burning, saying, What city is like unto this great city! And they cast dust on their heads, and cried, weeping and wailing, saying, Alas, alas that great city, wherein were made rich all that had ships in the sea by reason of her costliness! for in one hour is she made desolate.*
> *Revelation 18:2, 14-15, 18-19*

These merchants are really sad! For this much weeping, the Antichrist surely will build a mighty, powerful, and prosperous commercial Babylon. This passage truly fits right in with Daniel 8:25.

Deceive, Deceive, Deceive

After the Antichrist's war, he puts himself up in a high position by using his ability to deceive. The Bible says that his method of deception is so effective that if it were possible, even the elect (believers) could be deceived: "For there shall arise false Christs, and false prophets, and shall shew great signs and wonders; insomuch that, if it were possible, *they shall deceive the very elect*" (Matthew 24:24).

We will not be deceived if we cling to the Word, saturate ourselves with it, and understand end-time prophecy. That is our key to victory in these last days.

Declare Peace

After the Antichrist enters the scene, makes war, and conquers nations, he will usher in peace. According to Paul, when the Antichrist comes on the scene in a position of power, he will deceive the people worldwide into thinking it is a time of peace and safety, but "then sudden destruction cometh upon them, as travail upon a woman with child; and they shall not escape" (1 Thessalonians 5:3).

During this peacetime, the Antichrist will accomplish a seemingly miraculous feat: he will solve the Israeli/Arab conflict by creating peace between them. It will amaze and astound many and cause the Jews to enter into a (temporary) covenant with him, thinking that he is their long-awaited Messiah. The peace, however, is temporary and will only last for a short time.

Establish a Religious System

Even though the Antichrist will convince the entire world to follow him, his hunger for glory will continue to increase. This is the same sin that caused Satan to be exiled from heaven. (See Isaiah 14:12 and Ezekiel 28:12-18). In an attempt to satisfy this hunger, the Antichrist will establish a false religious system designed to bring worship to himself, as revealed through the symbolism in Revelation 17:1: "And there came one of the seven angels which had the seven vials, and talked with me, saying unto me, Come hither; I will shew unto thee the judgment of the great whore that sitteth upon many waters."

According to *The Wycliffe Bible Commentary*, the "great whore" mentioned here represents the false religious system of the Antichrist: "She is definitely some vast spiritual system that persecutes the saints of God, betraying that to which she was called. She enters into relations with the governments of this earth, and for a while rules them. I think the closest we can come to an identification is to understand this harlot as symbolic of a vast spiritual power arising at the end of the age, which enters into a league with the world and compromises with worldly forces. Instead of being spiritually true, she is spiritually false, and thus exercises an evil influence in the name of religion."

In Revelation 17:1 this harlot, "the great whore," is seen sitting upon "many waters," which means she has many people under her power. Verse 2 details explicitly nations following this mass false religion: "With whom the kings of the earth have committed fornication, and the inhabitants of the earth have been made drunk with the wine of her fornication."

In the next Scripture, the "whore" sits upon a "scarlet beast." Remember, earlier we established that one of the Antichrist's many names is beast. When we see the woman in this passage, she appears very rich. Arrayed in purple and scarlet color, adorned with gold, precious stones, and pearls, the woman pictures a wealthy false church.

So he carried me away in the spirit into the wilderness: and I saw a woman sit upon a scarlet coloured beast, full of names of blasphemy, having seven heads and ten horns.

Revelation 17:3

The reference to "ten horns" represents the ten kingdoms the Antichrist will unite. These were also pictured as "ten toes" in Nebuchadnezzar's dream. The beast enters again with the seven heads and ten horns, which conveys these ten kingdoms will be subdued under him. What are the "seven heads?"

This false religious system did not start with the Antichrist. This system's roots trace back to the story of Cain and Abel found in Genesis 4:1-7 when Cain tried to offer his own works to God instead of a blood sacrifice.

Throughout history, this false religious system is exposed through stories like Nimrod and the tower of Babel. In the Old Testament many of the kings practiced idolatry, the Egyptians worshiped the Nile River (among other things), and the Canaanites participated in satanism. The false church will sit on top of the end-time nations. Historically, the false church began with the building of Babel by Nimrod. It started in sin.

And Cush begat Nimrod: he began to be a mighty one in the earth. He was a mighty hunter before the Lord: wherefore it is said, Even as Nimrod the mighty hunter before the Lord. And the beginning of his kingdom was Babel, and Erech, and Accad, and Calneh, in the land of Shinar.

Genesis 10:8-10

The purpose for building the tower of Babel was to make a name for the builders. They tried to begin a new and idolatrous religion. The word *Babel* has several meanings, including "confusion" and "gate of god." When the builders attempted to reach heaven via their tower, God confused their tongues and scattered them. These builders fit the description that Paul referred to in the book of Romans:

Because that, when they knew God, they glorified him not as God, neither were thankful; but became vain in their imaginations, and their foolish heart was darkened. Professing themselves to be wise, they became fools, and changed the glory of the uncorruptible God into an image made like to corruptible man, and to birds, and four-

footed beasts, and creeping things…And even as they did not like to retain God in their knowledge, God gave them over to a reprobate mind, to do those things which are not convenient.

Romans 1:21-23, 28

False religion was the reason God called Abraham out of the Babylonian area. Idolatry was common there.

And Joshua said unto all the people, Thus saith the LORD God of Israel, Your fathers dwelt on the other side of the flood in old time, even Terah, the father of Abraham, and the father of Nachor: and they served other gods.

Joshua 24:2

God desired to establish Abraham as a holy nation, one that only worshiped Him, and He knew this idol worship would eventually affect Abraham if he didn't leave. Matthew Henry wrote, "His [Abraham's] country had become idolatrous, his kindred and his father's house were a constant temptation to him, and he could not continue with them without danger of being infected by them."[9]

The seriousness of practicing Satan's false religion can be seen in the story of Achan. After the Israelites victory at Jericho, he stole a Babylonian garment and some silver and gold (spoils of the war that the Bible calls "the accursed thing") in disobedience to Joshua's command. (See Joshua 6:18-19.) Achan paid a heavy price for his actions—he was stoned to death.

And Achan answered Joshua, and said, Indeed I have sinned against the LORD God of Israel, and thus have I done: When I saw among the spoils a goodly Babylonish garment, and two hundred shekels of silver, and a wedge of gold of fifty shekels weight, then I coveted them, and took them; and, behold, they are hid in the earth in the midst of my tent, and the silver under it…And Joshua said, Why hast thou troubled us? the LORD shall trouble thee this day. And all Israel stoned him with stones, and burned them with fire, after they had stoned them with stones.

Joshua 7:20-21, 25

The Israelites placed a high level of seriousness on false religions. They knew idol worship is a serious sin against God. Israel had often fallen into idolatry, even after ages of warnings against this practice by the Old Testament prophets, and eventually the Israelites were carried away to Babylon. During their captivity, King Nebuchadnezzar of Babylon made a golden image to worship, and his grandson profaned the vessels of God's house. Eventually, Babylon was judged and passed into the hands of Darius the Mede.

The term "Mystery, Babylon" from Revelation 17:5 represents false religion, which has been around through the ages: "And upon her forehead was a name written, Mystery, Babylon the Great, The Mother of Harlots and Abominations of the Earth." It is Satan's substitute for true Christianity. Anything that is against the blood sacrifice—is cultish.

False religion has always competed with the truth of God, but in the Antichrist's reign, it will come to a head.

Create an Abomination

After making war, the Antichrist will establish the "abomination of desolation." The Bible mentions this three times in the book Daniel:

And he shall confirm the covenant with many for one week: and in the midst of the week he shall cause the sacrifice and the oblation to cease, and for the overspreading of abominations he shall make it desolate, even until the consummation, and that determined shall be poured upon the desolate.

Daniel 9:27

And arms shall stand on his part, and they shall pollute the sanctuary of strength, and shall take away the daily sacrifice, and they shall place the abomination that maketh desolate.

Daniel 11:31

And from the time that the daily sacrifice shall be taken away, and the abomination that maketh desolate set up, there shall be a thousand two hundred and ninety days.

Daniel 12:11

Daniel 11:31 prophesied that Antiochus Epiphanes, a type or shadow of the Antichrist, would build an altar to Zeus in the temple. This is called the "abomination that causes desolation" (NIV), a desecration of the altar which destroys its true purpose. Similarly, the Antichrist will establish an abomination, or demonic counterfeit worship, in the sanctuary.

Set Himself Up as an Idol

It will not be enough for the Antichrist to have a universal religion and united world under his control. His hunger for power will cause him to promote himself as a god demanding worship. He will do something inconceivable—he will build an idol of himself in the Holy of Holies of the temple. Incredibly, that idol will begin to speak and many will be amazed. However, one particular group that will not be amazed is the Jews. Through this forced idol worship, they will realize this Antichrist cannot be their promised Messiah. Idol worship contradicts everything their Lord Jehovah has established. This will cause the Jewish people to turn against the Antichrist.

In this time period, the Antichrist is killed. However, he somehow arises from the dead, completing Revelation 17:11 that says, "The beast that was, and is not, even he is...." This verse means the beast "was" alive, then "is not" alive, and then "he is" alive again.

Why does he do this? What is the purpose? His goal, as always, is to counterfeit Christ. Jesus died, rose again, and now reigns. The Antichrist's ulterior motive in completing this feat will be to confuse people into following him as the one true god.

Cause the Jews to Return to God

When the Antichrist sets himself as an idol in the temple of Jerusalem, it will drive the Jews to consider that this is wrong. They will realize he is falsely personifying the long awaited Messiah and has committed an abomination (the abomination of desolation) by setting himself as a false idol in the Holy of Holies. As it becomes clear to the Jews they have been serving the wrong master, they will turn away from him, rebelling against his leadership, and begin to turn back to God.

The Antichrist, however, will become enraged and will turn his fury towards them. He will begin to lead a major campaign against the Jews and their Promised Land. This is another aspiration of the Antichrist's leadership: to control the Promised Land—Israel. Remembering the atrocities of the past, scores of Jews will begin to return to their homeland of Israel.

During this time of the Tribulation, a great revival will break out among the Jewish people. Many will repent and be "sealed" by God for evangelizing the world—144,000 according to the Bible. These same Jews are responsible for turning great numbers of the Jewish people back to God. In the end many Jews will lead all of heaven in wonderful praises to the Lamb. (See Revelation 7:9-17; 14:1-5.)

Control "The Pleasant Land"

You may be wondering why everyone wants the Promised Land. After much study, I discovered an area of politics called geopolitics that I believe has much to do with the desire of various nations to gain control of this area of the world.

Geo is associated with the earth. *Politics* is the art or science of conducting governments. *Geopolitics* is defined by *Merriam-Webster* as "a study of the influence of such factors as geography, economics, and demography on the politics and especially the foreign policy of a state; a governmental policy guided by geopolitics; a combination of political and geographic factors relating to something (as a state or particular resources)." Basically, we could say geopolitics is the art of governing the earth, or segments of the earth.

With that in mind, I believe the geopolitics of the end times has three basic premises:

1. He who rules Eastern Europe commands the heartland (the Middle East).

2. He who rules the heartland commands the world island (Palestine).

3. He who rules the world island commands the world.

The geopolitics of this region teaches that if anyone can truly rule Palestine, he can command the world. Thus, he who rules Europe controls the Middle East, commands Palestine, and reigns over the world. It seems obvious that this principle is the reason for the international hunger to control the Middle East. The Antichrist is no exception to the temptation. He will desire to manage the Promised Land. Daniel predicted this thousands of years before in Daniel 8:9: "And out of one of them came forth a little horn, which waxed exceeding great, toward the south, and toward the east, and toward the pleasant land."

The word "pleasant land" in the above passage represents the Holy Land, or Israel. The original Hebrew for the word "pleasant" in this verse is *tsebiy*, which means "splendor, beauty, or beautiful." The land of Israel has often been described in this way—a land of beauty, a land flowing with milk and honey. It is not surprising that Daniel, who was an exile from his beloved country, used this term to describe it.

Declare War

As the Antichrist gains popularity among the world, he will begin to counsel with the nations and secure a temporary peace. His hunger for power will drive him to desire more than simply being the counselor to the world; he will want to own the world.

The Antichrist will begin to raise himself up. This coincides with the four seals we read about in Revelation. These seals all lead to the returning of Christ.

The red horse is spoken about in Revelation 6 when referring to war. In the same chapter of Revelation as the red horse of war, another horse is mentioned—the pale horse representing death. As the Antichrist rises up in power, he will cause war, which will lead to great death and martyrdom upon the earth. He will do this by stirring up the international political arena.

Eventually, the Jews' return to Jehovah will enrage the Antichrist, and he will decide to extinguish the Jews for the last time. So he will rally all the nations of the world against Israel, and they will march from the valley of Megiddo to Jerusalem. Thus, the Antichrist will declare the greatest war of all time—Armageddon.

Draw the Nations to Fight

Among other catastrophes, the Antichrist remains in leadership. During the last few years of the Tribulation, various events (including the Jews' return to God) will cause the Antichrist's fury to increase. His fury will motivate him to unite the nations in league with him to gather for the greatest war of all time. The nations will gather in the valley of Megiddo to attack the nation of Israel.

Three spirits will be released during the last half of the Tribulation, which will motivate the Antichrist to take this action.

> *And I saw three unclean spirits like frogs come out of the mouth of the dragon, and out of the mouth of the beast, and out of the mouth of the false prophet. For they are the spirits of devils, working miracles, which go forth unto the kings of the earth and of the whole world, to gather them to the battle of that great day of God Almighty.*
>
> *Revelation 16:13-14*

The prophet Ezekiel explained in his prophecies of the end times that the three spirits of Revelation 16:13 are sent out to gather the kings of (1) Meshech and Tubal; (2) Persia, Ethiopia, and Libya; and (3) Gomer and Togarmah. (See Ezekiel 38-39.)

Meshech and Tubal

Originally Meshech and Tubal were not the names of countries, but sons of Japheth, Noah's son. God showed Ezekiel the nations would constantly change over the centuries, so He called the areas by the names of Noah's descendents who settled there.

Japheth became the father of the Caucasian people. (See Genesis 10:2,5.) Historical records show Meshech and Tubal (Russian and Slavic peoples) settled near the Black and Caspian seas. These bodies of water are currently bound by Turkey, Romania, Bulgaria, the Ukraine, Iran, and former Soviet southern republics such as Georgia, Azerbaijan, and Kazakhstan.

Persia, Ethiopia, Libya

Today, Ethiopia and Libya are the same nations that they were during Ezekiel's time, but much smaller. Persia reached from modern day India to Greece, encompassing what is now Iran and part of Afghanistan. During the end times, these countries will grow in might, power, and size. This is not only possible but is highly probable because each country sits on reserves of oil, natural gas, and other minerals.

For example, Ethiopia has left its natural resources untapped for decades. Ethiopia, which is now poor and reliant on other countries for financial and military aid, will become a major world power because the world will turn to her for resources.

Gomer and Togarmah

Gomer, son of Japheth, and Togarmah, Japheth's grandson, settled farther west and north in Europe. Their descendants now live in several countries, including Austria, Italy, France, Sweden, Germany, and the former Yugoslavia.

The kings of these three federations will be part of the Antichrist's confederate nations and will have the biggest armed forces. Because they will doubt the Antichrist, he will have to lure them into action by using the supernatural powers of the three unclean spirits. Although the Antichrist's other allied nations will be part of this army that converges on Israel at Armageddon, Ezekiel's three countries will be the major forces.

The Antichrist's Confederacy

Since national boundaries and forms of government change often, I would probably be wrong within a year if I gave the current names of the countries that will be a part of the Antichrist's confederacy. For instance, what was Yugoslavia became Bosnia-Herzegovina, Serbia, Croatia, Slovenia, Macedonia, and others in 1992. West and East Germany were reunited as one nation in 1990. Additionally in 1991, the Soviet Union broke off into more than a dozen independent states.

What I can say is the Antichrist's confederacy of ten nations (whether they are ten nations we can recognize today or ten new nations) will come out of the area surrounding the Mediterranean Sea, covering Europe, the Middle East, and northern Africa.

Daniel's prophecies provide this information. Nebuchadnezzar's dream of an image with a golden head, silver arms and chest, brass stomach and thighs, iron legs, and feet of iron and clay, was the same as Daniel's dream of four beasts, a lion, bear, leopard, and iron image that had ten horns.

The gold head/lion represents Babylon; the silver arms and chest/bear represent the Medo-Persians; the brass stomach and thighs/leopard represent Greece; the iron legs/iron image represent Rome; and the iron and clay toes/ten horns represent the Antichrist's kingdom.

These visions correspond with the beast in Revelation 13, which is described as having seven heads and ten horns that are each crowned. They also correspond with the beast of Revelation 17, which is described as having seven heads and ten horns. This beast is the Antichrist.

John explains in this last book of the Bible the beast's seven heads, "...are seven kings: five are fallen, one is, and the other is not yet come; and when he cometh, he must continue a short space" (Revelation 17:10). The seven kingdoms are those that afflicted the Jews when they were a nation. The first five kings are Egypt, Assyria, Babylon, the Medo-Persians, and Greece. The one that "is" in John's day was Rome. And the one that is yet to come and will "continue a short space" is the Antichrist.

The ten horns represent the ten counties that ally with the Antichrist. They come out of the boundaries of these seven kingdoms.

Will America Join the Antichrist?

Will America be a part of the Antichrist's confederacy and end-time army? No, the Antichrist does not conquer the whole world, only the part of the world that was once the Roman Empire. America was not part of any of the seven world empires that afflicted Israel.

American, the countries that were once part of the British Empire, and various other nations will revolt against the Antichrist as he becomes more aggressive against Israel. Ezekiel calls these countries, "Sheba, and Dedan, and the merchants of Tarshish, with all the young lions thereof…" (Ezekiel 38:13). Again, Ezekiel uses the descendants of Noah to describe the nations.

Dedan and Sheba are both descendants of Ham. Dedan's people settled on the northwest shores of the Persian Gulf, including northern Saudi Arabia and Kuwait. (See Genesis 10:7.) Sheba and his family settled on the southwest shores of the Persian Gulf. This area includes southern Saudi Arabia, Oman, and the United Arab Emirates. Today the peoples of Sheba and Dedan consist mostly of Arabs and are generally considered to be enemies of Israel. However, when the Antichrist creates a peace treaty between the Arabs and Israel, these countries will keep their word and protect Israel.

Tarshish was Noah's great-grandson who settled in the western Mediterranean Sea near the Rock of Gibraltar in Spain. (See Genesis 10:4.) The merchants of Tarshish were famous for their ships, and their homes were considered the farthest point in the world. Because Tarshish was as far away as one could possibly go at that time (which is shown by Jonah's attempt to flee there when he was running away from God), it represented a distant but unknown land. This land will have a worldwide influence in the last days. The "young lions" are offshoots of that country and commonwealth.

Although Tarshish was in what is now Spain and the Spanish Empire had many branches, I believe God is referring to Great Britain and her former colonies. These countries, including the United States, have greater worldwide influence than the former Spanish colonies. However, even if the prophecy did refer to Spain, many parts of the United States were originally part of the former Spanish Empire. Therefore, they would be part of the armies that revolt against the Antichrist.

The Ultimate Victory

Although the Antichrist's leadership will create horrible conditions upon the earth, God can, and will, transform these actions into a good result.

This aspect of God's personality is seen in the story of Joseph being sold into slavery by his brothers. After Joseph was sent into Egypt, God opened doors of promotion to him. Later, when Joseph reunited with his brothers, he told them, "As for you, you meant evil against me, but God meant it for good in order to bring about this present result, to preserve as many people alive" (Genesis 50:20 NASB).

In the same way, God will ultimately have the victory over the Antichrist's deeds. One of His major victories will be fulfilling the covenant He made with His chosen people—the Jews.

Bright and Bleak Future

Although the Antichrist seemingly accomplishes great feats during his time of leadership on earth, God, in His infinite wisdom, inspired the ancient Bible prophecies we study today. That means God knew and preplanned the end times even before we were born. While He does not cause the Antichrist's rise to power, He does allow this rise and ultimately utilizes Satan's tool for His plan. God allows the false "christ's" evil ways to contrast Jesus' love for mankind in the eyes of the whole world. Ultimately, many will turn to the one true Messiah—Jesus Christ.

What does the future hold for the Antichrist? God's final plan for him includes total annihilation. In Revelation 19:20, we see that the beast and the false prophet will be taken and cast into the lake of fire.

Unfortunately, there is no salvation for those people who took his mark—the deceived. Verse 21 records what will come to pass—they will be "slain by the sword of him that sat upon the horse, which sword proceeded out of his mouth: and all the fowls were filled with their flesh." At this point, Jesus' victory will be complete.

We've seen some of the things that will help make the way for the Antichrist to come and what he does once he's here and in power. But that is only one side of the story. This present world is going to end and a new day is coming, one in which the prince of the power of the air will be destroyed, and the Prince of Peace will set up His kingdom and reign for all eternity.

Chapter 22

Why All the Sixes?

…and his number is Six hundred threescore and six.

—Revelation 13:18

M any people who know nothing else about the end times have heard of the number "666." People wonder what it stands for. Why all sixes? What will it be used for? I've heard some very interesting explanations for this number, but the Bible gives the true meaning.

In the book of Revelation, six represents several things. According to Revelation 13:16-18, it represents an evil number or satanic number ("the number of the beast"), and it represents "the number of man." Man was created on the sixth day (Genesis 1:26, 31), and in Matthew 16:23, Jesus said that Satan is man-centered, that he thinks as people think.

Three (the amount of numerals in the number 666) represents trinity. *The Wycliffe Bible Commentary* calls 666 "the trinity of six." I, too, believe this is Satan's sign for his unholy trinity. It's no surprise his mark in the end times will be "666."

In biblical times, the method was practiced of representing numbers in words, names, and phrases by letters of the alphabet. With that in mind, it is probable the Greek name of the beast will contain the number 666. For people who receive Jesus as their Savior after the Rapture, this will help them to determine who the Antichrist is.

The fact that no one will be able to buy or sell without receiving the mark is often emphasized over other aspects of 666, but that is not the mark's main purpose. One of Satan's primary purposes for writing his mark on his followers is that it's a counterfeit of God. Remember, Satan's ultimate goal and ambition is to "be like the most High" (Isaiah 14:14).

Satan likes to mimic the works of God. God has a Son, so Satan has a "son" (the Antichrist). God has a system of worship, so Satan has a system of worship. God manifests Himself in the form of a Trinity, so Satan has an unholy trinity. God has set a seal, or mark, on His people, and so does Satan.

Several Hebrew words for "mark" are used in Scripture. One of those words, *tav*, means "a sign" and was used by the prophet Ezekiel in Ezekiel 9:4, 6, which told of his vision of the destruction of the wicked. Those sealed on their foreheads with the seal, or mark, of the living God would be kept from harm and protected in the same way that the blood of the lamb was sprinkled on the doorposts of the homes of the Israelites (Exodus 12:22-23).

Satan's attempts to counterfeit God will come to a head when he sets a mark on his "children" or followers to be like God. This is evident in the New Testament use of the word "mark." The Greek meaning of this word in Revelation 13:16-17 (which refers to the mark of the beast) is *charagma*, meaning "a stamp" or "imprinted mark." According to Scripture, this mark in some form of the number 666, will be the badge of the followers of the Antichrist and will be stamped on their forehead or their right hand.

In the same way owners of cattle brand and mark their stock, the people who take the mark of the beast will be branded under the Antichrist. Taking this mark upon their foreheads or hands will actually be the sign and seal they belong to the devil and his henchmen.

Opinions differ on whether or not the mark of the beast is an actual mark or is symbolic in some way. But the reality is while those who do not take this mark will suffer deadly consequences on earth, the fate of those with the mark will be much worse.

> *Then a third angel followed them, shouting, "Anyone who worships the beast and his statue or who accepts his mark on the forehead or on the hand must drink the wine of God's anger. It has been poured full strength into God's cup of wrath. And they will be tormented with fire and burning sulfur in the presence of the holy angels and the Lamb. The smoke of their torment will rise forever and ever, and they will have no relief day or night, for they have worshiped the beast and his statue and have accepted the mark of his name."*
> *Revelation 14:9-11 NLT*

In the well-known exposition on Revelation by Bible scholar Joseph Seiss, he described the fate of those who take the mark as helpless slaves and cattle who submit themselves to the devil's branding iron, "and yielding, to perish everlastingly, for there is no more salvation for anyone upon whom is this 'mark....'"[10]

Those who take the mark of the beast will not be simply receiving a mark; it will not really be about buying and selling. This passage reveals it will be much more serious than that because whoever receives the mark will be worshiping the beast and rejecting God. That is the most important aspect of 666.

The False Prophet

And he had power to give life unto the image of the beast, that the image of the beast should both speak, and cause that as many as would not worship the image of the beast should be killed.

Revelation 13:15

What will the living conditions be like when taking the mark will be enforced? During the Tribulation, Satan will introduce a new evil character, the third member of his unholy trinity, the False Prophet. This second beast will arrive on the scene with the power to perform signs and wonders. He will cause people to worship the Antichrist and make a talking idol of the beast, which he will place in the temple. The False Prophet will order the death of anyone who refuses to worship the Antichrist. In fact, he will lead many people of the world to worship him by controlling the wealth.

Israel will lose its spiritual protection when it temporarily makes an alliance with the devil, so it will be powerless to stop the assault of the False Prophet and the Antichrist. From all of the death and famine in the world during the end times, Israel's economy and agriculture will fail.

Lament like a virgin girded with sackcloth for the husband of her youth. The meat offering and the drink offering is cut off from the house of the Lord; the priests, the Lord's ministers, mourn. The field is wasted, the land mourneth; for the corn is wasted: the new wine is dried up, the oil languisheth.

Joel 1:8-10

The Antichrist will strip the country of all its other valuables. The prophet Joel gave a picture of this destruction in Joel 1:4, saying it will be like the palmerworm, locust, cankerworm, and caterpillar invasions of ancient days, when each new bug eats a part of the crops until even the seeds are gone.

From this economic failure, the Antichrist will seize the opportunity to force the world to follow his system. Instituting an international embargo on food, goods, and staples, the Antichrist will attempt to "starve out" rebels against his cause. Therefore, no one will be allowed to buy or sell unless they do it within the Antichrist's system, which is pictured in Revelation 6:5 as the black horseman who is released by the opening of the third seal. Basically, the Antichrist will control the world with his mark.

You may be thinking, *That is out of the question.* But as one Bible scholar says, controlling the world may not be as impossible as it sounds: "When you combine political power with economic power and all religion, you have a formula for controlling the whole world. But the lost world worships money and power, so the task will not be too difficult."[11]

Mark-of-the-Beast Technology

Many systems are currently in place that would make control of world trade possible. Computers, cable systems, microchips, and transportation are advancing quickly. Computer chips have been invented which, when inserted under the skin, can carry a person's vital information, such as name, address, credit history, banking informa-tion, employment, medical records, and so forth.

Our governments are also relying more and more on a one-world trade system. All of Europe and the three countries of North America are working jointly to bolster their economies.

I'm not trying to say any of these will be the technology from which the mark will come. Right now no one knows what the Antichrist will use. I believe all of this is a foreshadowing of events in Revelation 13 and will allow the Antichrist to take over easily and manage a world-wide economy.

From present-day world conditions and the picture the Scriptures paint of the end times, it seems likely the time will shortly come for these events to take place. Revelation 13:6 says it's wisdom to un-derstand about the number of the name of the future Antichrist. The wisdom we need is not so much to try to figure out what his name will be. We will be taken up in the Rapture before the Antichrist is revealed. We need wisdom now to detect and discern the signs of the times through the bad principles of the antichrist spirit that is at work in the world today.

There are people who do not know, or who refuse, Jesus. They will most likely become victims to the lies and deceits of the devil. Yet God in His mercy has shown ahead of time in His Word where their unbelief is leading them so that they can learn and change before it's too late. We as believers need to get the message out before the Rap-ture comes. People who reject God's Son Jesus are opening their souls to the devil's "messiah," the Antichrist.

Part of being a "watcher" is to bring into the kingdom as many souls as we can *now*. No one should have to suffer at the hands of Satan's evil accomplices. We see many instances in the Bible where God has protected His people from harm. Christ's work on the cross was the ultimate example of this protection—Jesus paid the price for our sins so we might not die in our iniquity. He shed His blood so ours would not have to flow.

Chapter 23

The Catching Away

*The Master himself will give the command. Archangel thunder!
God's trumpet blast! He'll come down from heaven and the dead
in Christ will rise—they'll go first. Then the rest of us who are still
alive at the time will be caught up with them into the clouds to meet
the Master.*

—*1 Thessalonians 4:16–17 MSG*

Earlier I told you that one of the major themes of Revelation
and the end times is regeneration. During the Tribulation,
God will restore this world to its original pre-curse condition using fire, earthquakes, and floods. These "birthing pains" will
cause great torment to the people on earth. Many will die; others
will wish they were dead.

God does not want His children to experience these horrors. In a
tender act of protection, much like a father pulling his child from the
dangers of deep water, God's Son Jesus will gather us in His arms. This
gathering together to Christ is the Rapture.

There is more than one Rapture, but in this chapter we will look at
the first Rapture. When that occurs, Jesus will not return to earth to

retrieve us; instead, the Christians who are both living and dead will meet Him in the clouds. Let's read about it from the *King James Bible* version:

> *For the Lord himself shall descend from heaven with a shout, with the voice of the archangel, and with the trump of God: and the dead in Christ shall rise first: then we which are alive and remain shall be caught up together with them in the clouds, to meet the Lord in the air: and so shall we ever be with the Lord.*
>
> 1 Thessalonians 4:16-17

The phrase "caught up" in this verse is translated from the Greek word *harpazo*, which means "…pluck, pull, take (by force.)" This same idea of a physical rescue was expressed by Daniel when he prophesied, "…and there shall be a time of trouble, such as never was since there was a nation even to that same time: and at that time thy people shall be delivered, every one that shall be found written in the book" (Daniel 12:1).

In this verse from Daniel, the Hebrew word for "delivered," is *malat*, which means to "release or rescue…speedily." Daniel's prophecy has to do with the Jews in the end times, but it gives encouragement to every believer to know that God is in control and will accomplish His purposes in spite of Satan's evil forces. The Lord assured Daniel (and us) that those believers who are alive in that day will be delivered.

Daniel 12:2 continues to encourage with the assurance that the ones who will die will be resurrected to be with the Lord in glory: "And many of them that sleep in the dust of the earth shall awake, some to everlasting life."

While there are references to the Rapture in the Scriptures, the word *Rapture* does not appear in the Bible in talking about this catching away. *Merriam-Webster* defines the word as "a state of ecstasy." While this English meaning can refer to our being in an eternal state of ecstasy when we are finally with our Lord, the term is actually derived from the Latin word *rapere*, which means "to seize." Thus, our being "seized" into heaven became known as the Rapture.

In the Twinkling of an Eye

The world will neither see nor hear Christ when the Rapture occurs—they won't even know anything like that has happened. All they'll know is a multitude of people are missing. The Word says only Christians can hear the trumpet of God and the shout of Jesus as this first seal of the title deed of the earth is opened. (See 1 Thessalonians 4:16; Revelation 4:1, 6:1-2.) All the world will experience is one second we will be on earth standing side-by-side with our co-workers, friends, or loved ones, and the next second we will be gone. Luke 17:35-36 reveals this occurrence: "Two women shall be grinding together; the one shall be taken, and the other left. Two men shall be in the field; the one shall be taken, and the other left."

The Rapture will happen incredibly fast—in a moment, in the twinkling of an eye according to 1 Corinthians 15:52. In this verse, the Greek word for "moment" is *atomos*, which means "uncut, i.e. (by implication) indivisible [an 'atom' of time]."

When something is indivisible, it is so microscopically small it cannot become any smaller. Imagine a measure of time that is so fast it could not be any faster—much like the speed of light. The Rapture of the Church will be even faster!

The world will not see what happens to us on that day, but they will come up with many reasons for our departure, including a mass conspiracy or abduction by UFOs. Only a few people on earth will comprehend what has really happened and turn to God as a result.

In 1 Thessalonians 4:16, we saw during the Rapture the dead in Christ will rise first. We can read about the Rapture in more than one place in the Bible. Here are some other Scriptures referring to the dead in Christ rising first during this divine event:

As for me, I will behold thy face in righteousness: I shall be satisfied, when I awake, with thy likeness.

Psalm 17:15

Verily, verily, I say unto you, The hour is coming, and now is, when the dead shall hear the voice of the Son of God: and they that hear shall live.

John 5:25

For as in Adam all die, even so in Christ shall all be made alive. But every man in his own order: Christ the firstfruits; afterward they that are Christ's at his coming.

1 Corinthians 15:22–23

In a moment, in the twinkling of an eye, at the last trump: for the trumpet shall sound, and the dead shall be raised incorruptible, and we shall be changed.

1 Corinthians 15:52

As soon as the dead in Christ rise up, the living will be physically caught up into the clouds to meet our Lord for the first time. Revelation 12:5 symbolically reveals this "catching away:"

And she brought forth a man child, who was to rule all nations with a rod of iron: and her child was caught up unto God, and to his throne.

The "man child" spoken of here represents the whole body of the "true saints." For we who will be "caught up unto God," it will involve the greatest change and be the most monumental, magnificent event of our lives.[12] After that occurs, we will begin our eternal fellowship and worship of Christ.

Who Will Go?

Anyone who does not believe in God or who has not made Christ their Lord and Savior will not go in this Rapture. We covered this in depth earlier in this book, but it is important to understand that not every person who goes to church and calls themselves a Christian will be involved in this pre-Tribulation Rapture. For one thing, we need to have a relationship with God through daily time spent in fellowship (or talking) with Him and in reading the Scriptures.

Revelation 12 pictures the Rapture as a woman travailing in child-birth. The baby boy she delivers has the authority to "rule all nations with a rod of iron" and is seen being "caught up unto God, and to his throne." (Revelation 12:5).

We know that the woman is the entire Christian Church because she is clothed with the sun and wearing a crown of twelve stars. (See Revelation 12:1.) The sun shows that she is the light of the world; the twelve stars represent the twelve apostles. The moon under her feet shows she has the powers of darkness under her. And as we just saw, the child she delivers is the overcoming church.

Similarly, in Revelation 3, Christ calls the churches by name. The Laodicean church is left behind at the Rapture basically because these people do not know Christ. God has an interesting way of describing this: "So then because thou art lukewarm, and neither cold nor hot, I will spue thee out of my mouth" (v. 16).

I believe God is addressing the backsliders and lukewarm Christians who warm the pews. They neither love nor hate Christ—they are indifferent. As Matthew Henry explains, "They thought they were very well already, and therefore they were very indifferent whether they grew better or not."[13] When these kinds of people gather for services, they do not invite God into their midst. Yet He still tries to get their attention as shown in Revelation 3:20:

> *Behold, I stand at the door, and knock: if any man hear my voice, and open the door, I will come in to him, and will sup with him, and he with me.*

On the other hand, the overcoming Christians are the Philadelphian church type of believers mentioned in this chapter. They are the ones who keep God's Word and stand on it in patience and faith. Christ promised them He would keep them "from the hour of temptation [the Tribulation], which shall come upon all the world" (Revelation 3:10). That promise is for us too—He will deliver us from the wrath of the Tribulation that is to come.

Safe from the Enemy's Attack

Satan will try to keep the Church from entering into heaven, engaging in a battle with the archangel Michael. The dragon won't be able to keep the saints from gathering with Christ, and his bitter contest will end with his expulsion from the heavens and the end of his reign as prince of the power of the air. (See Ezekiel 28:18; Daniel 8:10-13; Revelation 12:7-10.)

In anger, Satan will set out to destroy the remnant Church—the lukewarm Christians who turn to God after the Rapture as recorded in Revelation 12:

> *Therefore rejoice, ye heavens, and ye that dwell in them. Woe to the inhabiters of the earth and of the sea! for the devil is come down unto you, having great wrath, because he knoweth that he hath but a short time. And when the dragon saw that he was cast unto the earth, he persecuted the woman which brought forth the man child. And to the woman were given two wings of a great eagle, that she might fly into the wilderness, into her place, where she is nourished for a time, and times, and half a time, from the face of the serpent. And the serpent cast out of his mouth water as a flood after the woman, that he might cause her to be carried away of the flood. And the earth helped the woman, and the earth opened her mouth, and swallowed up the flood which the dragon cast out of his mouth. And the dragon was wroth with the woman, and went to make war with the remnant of her seed, which keep the commandments of God, and have the testimony of Jesus Christ.*
>
> *Revelation 12:12-17*

Verse 16 suggests nature will somehow protect these new Christians. Perhaps they will flee to the mountains or some kind of divine intervention could happen. They could be helped in some unexpected way. Flooding or overflowing water is often seen in Scriptures as a type of strong enemy as in Psalm 18:16 that says, "He sent from above, he took me, he drew me out of many waters."

Whatever the source of help, in John's end-time vision, he saw that the remnant Church will be safe from the enemy's attack and that to preserve and protect it, something will take place as wonderful as if the earth would suddenly open and swallow up a powerful flood.

Chapter 24

Seven Years of Trouble
Part 1

The Tribulation begins after the Rapture. Its source is found in the conflict between God and Satan, described in Genesis 3:15, but it does not just happen. It is triggered by the Antichrist's rise out of the revived Roman Empire. Ironically, his push for peace with the nations of the world marks the beginning of this seven-year period of trouble, anguish, and eventual war.

The actual term "tribulation" is used only a handful of times in the Bible in referring to this final episode of world history (as we know it), but it is described in many Scriptures (Exodus 15, Matthew 24, and Mark 13, to name a few.) Other terms the Bible uses to depict it are punishment (Isaiah 24:20-23), trouble (Jeremiah 30:7), destruction (Joel 1:15), and darkness (Joel 2:2).

The entire Tribulation period will be seven years long and is broken down into two time periods of three and a half years. The first three and a half years will be marked by a false sense of peace (although it will still be a time of trouble) as the master deceiver causes the world to believe he has achieved world peace among the nations. The second half, or the Great Tribulation, will definitely be "a trying experience." We have seen that certain events will cause the Antichrist to break this covenant of peace. This will lead to the second three and a half years of colossal scenes of trouble and turmoil in a magnitude never before experienced on earth.

Many people have wondered how we know that the Tribulation period only lasts for seven years. The secret is revealed in a numbering pattern representing time. This pattern is found in the book of Daniel and is often referred to as Daniel's Seventy Weeks. In fact, the prophet Daniel called the period of the Tribulation the final week in his Seventy Weeks vision.

Daniel's Seventy Weeks

Seventy weeks are determined upon thy people and upon thy holy city, to finish the transgression, and to make an end of sins, and to make reconciliation for iniquity, and to bring in everlasting righteousness, and to seal up the vision and prophecy, and to anoint the most Holy. Know therefore and understand, that from the going forth of the commandment to restore and to build Jerusalem unto the Messiah the Prince shall be seven weeks, and threescore and two weeks: the street shall be built again, and the wall, even in troublous times. And after threescore and two weeks shall Messiah be cut off, but not for himself: and the people of the prince that shall come shall destroy the city and the sanctuary; and the end thereof shall be with a flood, and unto the end of the war desolations are determined. And he shall confirm the covenant with many for one week: and in the midst of the week he shall cause the sacrifice and the oblation to cease, and for the overspreading of abominations

he shall make it desolate, even until the consummation, and that
determined shall be poured upon the desolate.

Daniel 9:24-27

In this passage Daniel said seventy "weeks," or years, would elapse between the Israelites' return to Jerusalem to rebuild the city and temple and the advent of the Messiah to rule this world. One week (7 days) counts for seven years (1 day of the week = 1 year) in this prophecy. Therefore 70 weeks would multiply by 7 to yield a total of 490 years. This time period is called the Jewish Age and lasts for 490 years (70 times 7).

Jesus arrived 483 years after the temple's rebuilding. When the Jews rejected Him, the Jewish Age was suspended and the Church Age began. The Jewish Age will resume again when the Church is raptured, but only one week remains on the clock. This means the time between the Rapture of the Church and the advent of the Messiah as Prince of this world is only seven years (483 plus 7 = 490).

Daniel described this final week in Daniel 9:27 as a time when the sacrifices and feasts will cease and the Antichrist will erect his idol, the "abomination of desolation," in the temple.

This passage indicates that at the end of the Tribulation, which is the end of the Jewish Age, the Lord will return from heaven with His saints and angels to make an end of sins, to make reconciliation for iniquity, to bring in everlasting righteousness, to seal up the vision and prophecy, and to anoint the most Holy.

This "reconciliation for iniquity" is what Jesus was referring to in Matthew 13:40 when He said, "As therefore the tares are gathered and burned in the fire; so shall it be in the end of this world." The *world* in this verse does mean "world" in English. It is the Greek word *aion*, which means "age," as in a period of time. From these Scriptures we can see that at the end of the Jewish Age will come the judgment of the sinners (tares).

The Antichrist

We have already covered the Antichrist—his names, the area where he may come from, what army he will head, the countries he will rule, his role in the last days, the havoc he will wreak. But remember that all this takes place during the Tribulation period. That's when Satan's power will finally be unleashed in full force and take shape in the person of this major end-time figure, because just prior to that time our prayers and authority will be taken from the earth due to the Rapture.

Angelic Sermons

Humankind will be so preoccupied with its pain caused by the Antichrist's rule during this time that what little energy people will have will be conserved for the mere act of surviving. The Gospel message will be preached, however, in a unique move of God—the preaching will come from an angel who declares the Gospel from heaven to people on earth. This angel will prophesy the fall of the Antichrist's kingdom and religion, telling people not to take the mark of the beast.

> *And I saw another angel fly in the midst of heaven, having the everlasting gospel to preach unto them that dwell on the earth, and to every nation, and kindred, and tongue, and people, saying with a loud voice, Fear God, and give glory to him; for the hour of his judgment is come: and worship him that made heaven, and earth, and the sea, and the fountains of waters. And there followed another angel, saying, Babylon is fallen, is fallen, that great city, be-*

cause she made all nations drink of the wine of the wrath of her fornication. And the third angel followed them, saying with a loud voice, If any man worship the beast and his image, and receive his mark in his forehead, or in his hand, the same shall drink of the wine of the wrath of God, which is poured out without mixture into the cup of his indignation; and he shall be tormented with fire and brimstone in the presence of the holy angels, and in the presence of the Lamb: And the smoke of their torment ascendeth up for ever and ever: and they have no rest day nor night, who worship the beast and his image, and whosoever receiveth the mark of his name. Here is the patience of the saints: here are they that keep the commandments of God, and the faith of Jesus. And I heard a voice from heaven saying unto me, Write, Blessed are the dead which die in the Lord from henceforth: Yea, saith the Spirit, that they may rest from their labours; and their works do follow them.

Revelation 14:6-13

Some people believe the Holy Spirit will be removed from the earth at the Rapture. That theory does not follow the Bible's words, because it is through the Holy Spirit's drawing that we come to know Christ. (See John 12:32; 16:7-11.) Without the Holy Spirit's drawing power, people could not be saved during the Tribulation.

In fact, the Holy Spirit will move in incredible ways because the greatest time of evangelism on this earth will be during the Tribulation period.

End-Time Revival

Masses of people will turn to the Lord in the end times. The masses will be so great that they will populate the earth during the beginning of the Millennium.

The Bible doesn't give a number of how many people will be saved during this early part of the Tribulation, but Revelation 7:9 says the amount of people saved will be more than a man could count: "After this I beheld, and, lo, a great multitude, which no man could number, of all nations, and kindreds, and people, and tongues, stood before the throne, and before the Lamb, clothed with white robes, and palms in their hands."

Notice the Scripture says these Tribulation saints are of "all nations, and kindreds, and people, and tongues." That means this revival will spread throughout the entire world during the Tribulation.

In this book we have seen the first few seals opened and what they represent. When Christ opens the fifth seal of the title deed to the earth, we see those Tribulation saints raptured into heaven, standing before the Lamb, dressed in garments washed white as snow and holding palm leaves. (See Revelation 6:9-11; 7:9,14; 14:12-13.)

These palm leaves the saints carry in Revelation 7:9 are very important because they represent victory. In the Bible, the Israelites used palm leaves to remind them of the victories God gave them over their enemies in battles and storms. These Tribulation saints standing before Jesus will wave their palms to honor the victory God gives over death and hell.

Hiding in Caves

The final event before the end of the first three and a half years of the Tribulation is the opening of the sixth seal. Up to this point, heaven had orchestrated the Antichrist's rise to power and mankind's positioning to make a decision between God or Satan. With the sixth seal comes the beginning of God's powerful forces moving violently on the earth.

And I beheld when he had opened the sixth seal, and, lo, there was a great earthquake; and the sun became black as sackcloth of hair, and the moon became as blood; And the stars of heaven fell unto the earth, even as a fig tree casteth her untimely figs, when she is shaken of a mighty wind. And the heaven departed as a scroll when it is rolled together; and every mountain and island were moved out of their places. And the kings of the earth, and the great men, and the rich men, and the chief captains, and the mighty men, and every bondman, and every free man, hid themselves in the dens and in the rocks of the mountains; And said to the mountains and rocks, Fall on us, and hide us from the face of him that sitteth on the throne, and from the wrath of the Lamb: For the great day of his wrath is come; and who shall be able to stand?

Revelation 6:12-17

The sixth seal will bring great natural catastrophes:

- Incredible earthquakes
- The sun becomes black
- The moon turns red
- The stars fall
- The wind ravages trees and fields
- The mountains and islands are moved out of place

People will hide in caves and ask the rocks to kill them so they can be saved from God's wrath. (See Matthew 24:29-31,38,39; Luke 21:25-26; Revelation 6:12-17.)

As the devastation of the sixth seal indicates, the second half of the Tribulation will be much worse. It will be an intense time of distress and suffering. In fact, God calls it the "Great Tribulation," meaning the horrors will increase for man and the devil. (See Matthew 24:21; Revelation 2:22.) It is very similar to the last three and a half years of Daniel's final week in his Seventy Weeks prophecy.

The Second Half

Just before the seventh seal is opened, everything will fall silent in heaven for a half-hour while God prepares and delivers His people before the devastating judgments of the final seal are unleashed on the earth. The whole earth will stand in awe: "And when he had opened the seventh seal, there was silence in heaven about the space of half an hour" (Revelation 8:1).

The last three and a half years of the Tribulation, called the "Great Tribulation," will be filled with much pain, death, and destruction for people, animals, earth, and the heavens. Before this begins, however, God will perform a great act of love for His people.

First, the angel holding God's seal will instruct the four angels in charge of the north, south, east, and west winds to have their destruction. Before these angels carry out the judgments on the earth, God's loving mercy will seal 144,000 people.

> *Saying, Hurt not the earth, neither the sea, nor the trees, till we have sealed the servants of our God in their foreheads. And I heard the number of them which were sealed: and there were sealed an hundred and forty and four thousand of all the tribes of the children of Israel.*
>
> *Revelation 7:3–4*

We have seen that these 144,000 people are Jews, 12,000 from each of the twelve tribes of Israel (Revelation 7:5-8). God will write

His name on their foreheads with a mark: "And I looked, and, lo, a Lamb stood on the mount Sion, and with him an hundred forty and four thousand, having his Father's name written in their foreheads" (Revelation 14:1).

I believe this mark will be as real and visible as the mark of the beast in Revelation 13:16-17.

Secondly, God will resurrect the dead in Christ and rapture the Tribulation saints who are still alive. This is sometimes referred to as the Great Harvest Rapture. During this activity, God will separate the wheat from the tares as we saw Jesus talk about in Matthew 13. An act of God's mercy, this Rapture will rescue the Gentiles who accepted Christ during the first three and a half years of great torture, despair, and trouble.

After this I beheld, and, lo, a great multitude, which no man could number, of all nations, and kindreds, and people, and tongues, stood before the throne, and before the Lamb, clothed with white robes, and palms in their hands; And cried with a loud voice, saying, Salvation to our God which sitteth upon the throne, and unto the Lamb. And all the angels stood round about the throne, and about the elders and the four beasts, and fell before the throne on their faces, and worshipped God, saying, Amen: Blessing, and glory, and wisdom, and thanksgiving, and honour, and power, and might, be unto our God for ever and ever. Amen. And one of the elders answered, saying unto me, What are these which are arrayed in white robes? and whence came they? And I said unto him, Sir, thou knowest. And he said to me, These are they which came out of great tribulation, and have washed their robes, and made them white in the blood of the Lamb. Therefore are they before the throne of God, and serve him day and night in his temple: and he that sitteth on the throne shall dwell among them. They shall hunger no more, neither thirst any more; neither shall the sun light on them, nor any heat. For the Lamb which is in the midst of the throne shall feed them, and shall lead them unto living fountains of waters: and God shall wipe away all tears from their eyes.

Revelation 7:9-17

What is the difference between these two groups (the Gentiles who accept Christ during this time and the 144,000)? Why would God leave one group of His people on earth while He takes the other group into heaven?

Gospel Messengers

God does this because His full attention is now being turned to the Jews. He will send them as messengers of the Gospel. These 144,000 Jews will be protected from the coming plagues and the wrath of the Antichrist so they can witness to the world and to Israel.

The 144,000 are the first fruits of the Jews, people who are spiritual "virgins," having never dabbled in a religion that was not from God nor worshiped or followed the beast. Revelation 14:4 describes them as being "...not defiled with women; for they are virgins... [they] follow the Lamb whithersoever he goeth...[and] were redeemed from among men, being the first-fruits unto God and to the Lamb."

The Bible often uses adultery and fornication as a picture for spiritual unfaithfulness. Because the 144,000 stayed true to God and waited for Him to fulfill their desires in life, they are referred to as "virgins" in this verse.

"Virgin" can also be taken literally to mean that these people had not been defiled by sexual indiscretions. The reason this may be taken literally is that Jesus said, "As the days of Noah were, so shall also the coming of the Son of man be" (Matthew 24:37). He explained that people will eat and drink, marry, and give in marriage, fulfilling their every desire without respect for self, others, or God—just as people did before the flood in Noah's time.

This carnality will be rampant during the Tribulation. Sex and every form of physical indulgence will have free reign. However, God always has a remnant. He will set these 144,000 people apart because (1) they are Jewish; (2) they have remained true to God; (3) they have accepted Christ; and (4) they are physically pure.

Eventually, we see them on Mt. Sion singing "a new song" before Jesus and with the other saints in heaven, a song that no one else on earth can learn:

> And I looked, and, lo, a Lamb stood on the mount Sion, and with him an hundred forty and four thousand, having his Father's name written in their foreheads. And I heard a voice from heaven, as the voice of many waters, and as the voice of a great thunder: and I heard the voice of harpers harping with their harps: And they sung as it were a new song before the throne, and before the four beasts, and the elders: and no man could learn that song but the hundred and forty and four thousand, which were redeemed from the earth. These are they which were not defiled with women; for they are virgins. These are they which follow the Lamb whithersoever he goeth. These were redeemed from among men, being the firstfruits unto God and to the Lamb. And in their mouth was found no guile: for they are without fault before the throne of God.
>
> Revelation 14:1-5

Harps will play in heaven, and all in heaven will join in this service of incredible worship. The 144,000 will have a special relationship with the Lamb because they will recognize He is their Messiah, Savior, and Redeemer.

The Tribulation Saints

The Tribulation saints will be part of the worship service of the 144,000, but this event will take place after they have already held a private service in heaven following their Rapture. They will stand before the Lord dressed in robes that have been washed white by the blood of the Lamb, playing harps and singing a very important song: "And they sing the song of Moses the servant of God, and the song of the Lamb, saying, Great and marvellous are thy works, Lord God Almighty; just and true are thy ways, thou King of saints" (Revelation 15:3).

This isn't the "new song" of the 144,000; in fact, it is a very ancient song. Moses wrote it after God parted the Red Sea, allowing the Israelites to pass into safety, and then brought the waters back together, destroying Pharaoh and his army. Notice how Moses' song of victory tells the story of the Tribulation saints:

> *Then sang Moses and the children of Israel this song unto the Lord, and spake, saying, I will sing unto the Lord, for he hath triumphed gloriously: the horse and his rider hath he thrown into the sea. The Lord is my strength and song, and he is become my salvation: he is my God, and I will prepare him an habitation; my father's God, and I will exalt him. The Lord is a man of war: the Lord is his name...Thy right hand, O Lord, is become glorious in power: thy right hand, O Lord, hath dashed in pieces the enemy. And in the*

greatness of thine excellency thou hast overthrown them that rose
up against thee: thou sentest forth thy wrath, which consumed them
as stubble...The enemy said, I will pursue, I will overtake, I will
divide the spoil; my lust shall be satisfied upon them; I will draw
my sword, my hand shall destroy them...Who is like unto thee, O
Lord, among the gods? who is like thee, glorious in holiness, fear-
ful in praises, doing wonders?...Thou in thy mercy hast led forth
the people which thou hast redeemed: thou hast guided them in thy
strength unto thy holy habitation...Thou shalt bring them in, and
plant them in the mountain of thine inheritance, in the place, O
Lord, which thou hast made for thee to dwell in, in the Sanctuary,
O Lord, which thy hands have established. The Lord shall reign
for ever and ever.

Exodus 15:1-3, 6-7, 9, 11, 13, 17-18

The Israelites still had many trials and battles to face before they could enter and claim the Promised Land, but their song praised God for fulfilling all His promises in their lives. Similarly, the Tribulation saints in heaven will rejoice because of their victory over the Antichrist through God's unusual deliverance. These saints will praise the Lord for His complete work giving His chosen their full inheritance.

Picture of the End Times

The story of the Exodus, God's delivery of the Israelites out of bondage and into a land of promise, is a beautiful picture of the end times. In Exodus, Pharaoh represents a foreshadowing of the Antichrist, and the plaques provide a glimpse of what the trumpet/vial judgments in the book of Revelation will be like.

With the plagues in Exodus, God utilized nature to speak to man. These plagues of nature showed man where he was deceived. They served as judgment for man and showed the Egyptians their gods were false and powerless. (See Exodus 9,10,11.) Because they worshiped such things as the Nile, frogs, locusts, and their firstborn children, God used those very things against the Egyptians to discredit their gods.

As the *International Standard Bible Encyclopedia* explains, "The magicians who claimed to represent the gods of Egypt were defeated, Pharaoh himself, who was accounted divine, was humbled, the great god, the Nile, was polluted, frogs defiled the temples and, at last, the sun, the greatest god of Egypt, was blotted out in darkness."

If you are familiar with this story, you'll remember that those who paid attention to the message of God's plagues found deliverance out of Egypt. Those who placed the mark of God (the blood of a slain lamb) on their doors were spared death in their families during the final plague:

And thus shall ye eat it; with your loins girded, your shoes on your feet, and your staff in your hand; and ye shall eat it in haste: it is the Lord's passover. For I will pass through the land of Egypt this night, and will smite all the firstborn in the land of Egypt, both man and beast; and against all the gods of Egypt I will execute judgment: I am the Lord. And the blood shall be to you for a token upon the houses where ye are: and when I see the blood, I will pass over you, and the plague shall not be upon you to destroy you, when I smite the land of Egypt.

Exodus 12:11-13

Although it was mainly God's chosen people, the Israelites, who understood the lesson, the plagues, and followed God's commandments, a few Egyptians understood and left during the Exodus.

The same will happen during the Tribulation. The people who understand the message of the seven trumpets/vial judgments will realize that the devil's power counts for nothing when compared with God's (Revelation 8). Each plague that falls on man and the earth will prove that Satan ultimately has no control over the world and is unworthy of their worship.

Remember, people who have listened to the messages from heaven and to the many signs that have come from the previous six seals will be delivered from the earth in the mid-Tribulation Rapture.

The Two Witnesses

And I will give power unto my two witnesses, and they shall prophesy a thousand two hundred and threescore days, clothed in sackcloth.

Revelation 11:3

Soon after God "catches away" the Tribulation saints and seals the 144,000, He will exemplify His everlasting love for people again. This time, He will bring two men into Israel to preach His Word and empower them to prophesy. These men are known as the two witnesses.

I believe these two witnesses will be Moses and Elijah because they were on the mount of Transfiguration with Jesus. (See Matthew 17:1-3.) Their miracles were identical to the ones the two witnesses will perform—they will cause fire to rain down, turn water into blood, and bring other plagues. (See Revelation 11:3-12; Exodus 7:20; 9:23; 2 Kings 1:12.)

Their purpose in the Tribulation will be to harass the Antichrist and call the Jews to worship Jesus. They will remain in Israel for 1,260 days, or almost three and a half years. (See Revelation 11:3.)

Zechariah prophesied of these two men in his vision of a gold candlestick and two olive trees:

And the angel that talked with me came again, and waked me, as a man that is wakened out of his sleep. And said unto me, What seest thou? And I said, I have looked, and behold a candlestick all of gold, with a bowl upon the top of it, and his seven lamps thereon, and seven pipes to the seven lamps, which are upon the top thereof: And two olive trees by it, one upon the right side of the bowl, and the other upon the left side thereof.

Zechariah 4:1-3

He saw two witnesses as olive trees. The olive tree is a symbol of the Jews' spiritual heritage: "Then said he, These are the two anointed ones, that stand by the LORD of the whole earth" (vs. 14).

In the Bible, oil is often symbolic of the anointing. In Zechariah 4:12, we see the two witnesses pour their oil, or their anointing, into the candlestick, which is the symbol for the Church in Revelation: "And I answered again, and said unto him, What be these two olive branches which through the two golden pipes empty the golden oil out of themselves?"

In his well-known commentary, Matthew Henry gave a vivid description of what the oil represented, saying, "God gave them the oil of holy zeal, and courage, and strength, and comfort; he made them olive-trees, and their lamps of profession were kept burning by the oil of the inward gracious principles, which they received from God. They had oil not only in their lamps, but in their vessels—habits of spiritual life, light, and zeal."[14]

As the two witnesses zealously preach the Word during the Tribulation, their anointing will bring more and more people into Christ's Church.

In the next chapter we will see what happens to the two witnesses and look at the seven trumpet/vial judgments, which give us a bird's-eye view of heaven's judgments on mankind and the devil. As we continue to unveil the end-time mysteries and get the whole picture, it's so evident God is in complete control of the last days and the Tribulation period.

Chapter 25

Seven Years of Trouble
Part 2

Once God's people are protected, the seventh seal on the title deed of the earth will be opened. Out of this seal will come seven judgments—four upon the earth and three upon mankind.

Viewing these seven judgments from heaven, we see them as trumpets blown by angels, but from earth's perspective, the trumpets look like vials. Compare Revelation, chapters 6-11, with Revelation, chapters 12-16, and you will see these chapters tell the same story—the first version is seen from heaven, and the second from earth.

For instance, according to the version seen from heaven, when the second trumpet sounds, "...a great mountain burning with fire was cast into the sea: and the third part of the sea became blood; and the third part of the creatures which were in the sea, and had life, died; and the third part of the ships were destroyed" (Revelation 8:8-9). Likewise, in the version of this event seen from the earth, the second vial is poured out upon the earth and affects the sea, making it "as the blood of a dead man: and every living soul died in the sea" (Revelation 16:3).

The trumpet judgment shows only a third of the sea dying, but the vial judgment shows all in the sea dying. Why would the same event have two different outcomes? The difference is the event is seen from two different perspectives. From heaven's vantage point, we can see the whole earth and that not everything is affected. But when we stand on earth, our view is limited, and it appears that the whole earth is affected.

The seven trumpet/vial judgments are discussed several times in the Bible. God describes them in Acts 2:19-20 saying, "And I will shew wonders in heaven above, and signs in the earth beneath; blood, and fire, and vapour of smoke: the sun shall be turned into darkness, and the moon into blood, before the great and notable day of the Lord come."

In Haggai 2:6-7, God says, "Yet once, it is a little while, and I will shake the heavens, and the earth, and the sea, and the dry land; and I will shake all nations."

These words echo Christ's prophecy of the Great Tribulation in the book of Matthew:

Immediately after the tribulation of those days shall the sun be darkened, and the moon shall not give her light, and the stars shall fall from heaven, and the powers of the heavens shall be shaken.
Matthew 24:29

When Jesus opens the seventh seal, these much-prophesied wonders will begin with the sounding of the trumpets in heaven. Let's look at the first one, the fiery hail.

First Trumpet—Hail on Fire

The first trumpet/vial will send hail mixed with fire and blood to the earth. It will fall in the same way fire and brimstone fell on Sodom and Gomorrah in Genesis.

Then the Lord rained upon Sodom and Gomorrah brimstone and fire from the Lord out of heaven.

Genesis 19:24

The first angel sounded, and there followed hail and fire mingled with blood, and they were cast upon the earth: and the third part of trees was burnt up, and all green grass was burnt up.

Revelation 8:7

This fire will have a serious effect on the people who have taken the mark of the beast.

And the first went, and poured out his vial upon the earth; and there fell a noisome and grievous sore upon the men which had the mark of the beast, and upon them which worshipped his image.

Revelation 16:2

The Greek word for "noisome"—*kakos*—means "bad, evil" and is used in this verse to pinpoint the plague referred to here as being terribly painful and dangerous. The Greek word for "grievous"—*poneros*—means "causing pain and trouble, bad." It is added to emphasize the blistering gravity of the sores and to distinguish this plague as being exceptionally severe.

Second Trumpet—Ocean Life Dies

The second trumpet/vial will affect the water of the seas, turning it to blood much the same as the Nile was judged in Exodus 7:20. As a result, most of the sea life (including seafood) will die within the ocean. People will no longer be able to rely on the natural resource for food. We have already seen Revelation 8:8 and 16:3 that refer to this. Notice their similarity to Exodus 7:20:

And Moses and Aaron did so, as the LORD commanded; and he lifted up the rod, and smote the waters that were in the river, in the sight of Pharaoh, and in the sight of his servants; and all the waters that were in the river were turned to blood.

The waters became so corrupt that not only did the fish die, but there was a terrible offensive odor. Can you imagine this happening in the Tribulation? These first two prophecies alone should propel you to get right with God now if you feel that you aren't. Yet there are more detestable plagues to come.

Third Trumpet—Drinking Water Spoiled

The third trumpet/vial will also affect the water, but this time the fire will fall on fresh water, poisoning the drinking water with wormwood.

Basically, wormwood is a plant that yields a bitter dark green oil. *Merriam-Webster* actually defines "wormwood" as "something bitter." It is often associated with gall, which is also connected to bitterness in relation to the idea of poison. This will be a huge devastation since most of the world's water supply will be come contaminated and there will be deadly consequences for those who drink it.

And the third angel sounded, and there fell a great star from heaven, burning as it were a lamp, and it fell upon the third part of the rivers, and upon the fountains of waters; and the name of the star is called Wormwood: and the third part of the waters became wormwood; and many men died of the waters, because they were made bitter.

Revelation 8:10-11

Revelation 16 reveals this contamination will turn the water into blood.

And the third angel poured out his vial upon the rivers and fountains of waters; and they became blood. And I heard the angel of the waters say, Thou art righteous, O Lord, which art, and wast, and shalt be, because thou hast judged thus. For they have shed the blood of saints and prophets, and thou hast given them blood to drink; for they are worthy. And I heard another out of the altar say, Even so, Lord God Almighty, true and righteous are thy judgments.

Revelation 16:4-7

This is similar to the punishment God promised to followers of Baal (a false god worshiped by the inhabitants of Canaan) in Jeremiah 9:15 when He said, "...I will feed them...with wormwood, and give them water of gall to drink."

Fourth Trumpet—Extreme Darkness and Heat

The fourth trumpet/vial will cause a third part of the sun, moon, and stars to darken.

And the fourth angel sounded, and the third part of the sun was smitten, and the third part of the moon, and the third part of the stars; so as the third part of them was darkened, and the day shone not for a third part of it, and the night likewise.

Revelation 8:12

The change in the sun's light will somehow increase its heat and scorch men with an intense burning.

And the fourth angel poured out his vial upon the sun; and power was given unto him to scorch men with fire. And men were scorched with great heat, and blasphemed the name of God, which hath power over these plagues: and they repented not to give him glory.

Revelation 16:8-9

God similarly judged the sun in Egypt when he caused darkness to fall over the land. The darkness was so profound that the Bible says it could even be felt.

And the LORD said unto Moses, Stretch out thine hand toward heaven, that there may be darkness over the land of Egypt, even darkness which may be felt. And Moses stretched forth his hand toward heaven; and there was a thick darkness in all the land of Egypt three days.

Exodus 10:21-22

Can you believe what we've seen so far? These first four trumpets/vials have brought great judgments upon the earth, water, and sky. We've seen a world on fire, thirsty, and scorched. Even though man will be terribly tortured by these events, these judgments were meant mainly for nature in order to cleanse the earth of the curse. But it's not over yet.

The next three trumpet/vials will be directed toward mankind exclusively. The pain and torment will be so great with these plagues that just before, an angel in heaven will warn those left on earth crying out, "Woe, woe, woe, to the inhabiters of the earth" (Revelation 8:13).

Fifth Trumpet—"Locusts" From Hell

When the fifth trumpet sounds, an angel from heaven who has been given the enormous responsibility of keeping the key to the bottomless pit will open the pit and loose "locusts" upon the earth. These "locusts" are actually demons who will have the power to torment like scorpions. They will have bodies like horses, heads like men, hair like women, crowns of gold, teeth like lions, breastplates of iron, wings that sound like chariots running to battle, and tails with scorpion stings. They can't hurt vegetation or the 144,000 Jews; and they aren't allowed to kill men, only torture them to the point where they beg to die.

And the fifth angel sounded, and I saw a star fall from heaven unto the earth: and to him was given the key of the bottomless pit. And he opened the bottomless pit; and there arose a smoke out of the pit, as the smoke of a great furnace; and the sun and the air were darkened by reason of the smoke of the pit. And there came out of the smoke locusts upon the earth: and unto them was given power, as the scorpions of the earth have power. And it was commanded them that they should not hurt the grass of the earth, neither any green thing, neither any tree; but only those men which have not the seal of God in their foreheads. And to them it was given that they should not kill them, but that they should be tormented five months: and their torment was as the torment of a scorpion, when he striketh a man. And in those days shall men seek death, and shall not find it; and shall desire to die, and death shall flee from them.

*And the shapes of the locusts were like unto horses prepared unto
battle; and on their heads were as it were crowns like gold, and
their faces were as the faces of men. And they had hair as the hair
of women, and their teeth were as the teeth of lions. And they had
breastplates, as it were breastplates of iron; and the sound of their
wings was as the sound of chariots of many horses running to battle. And they had tails like unto scorpions, and there were stings in
their tails: and their power was to hurt men five months. And they
had a king over them, which is the angel of the bottomless pit, whose
name in the Hebrew tongue is Abaddon, but in the Greek tongue
hath his name Apollyon.*

Revelation 9:1-11

We see here that the leader of the demon locust is Apollyon, or the
destroyer, whose name is Satan. For five months, people covered with
the sores produced by these demon locusts will be forced to live in the
darkness caused by the smoke from hell covering the sun and moon.

*And the fifth angel poured out his vial upon the seat of the beast; and
his kingdom was full of darkness; and they gnawed their tongues for
pain, and blasphemed the God of heaven because of their pains and
their sores, and repented not of their deeds.*

Revelation 16:10-11

People will speak contemptuously of God because of their pain
during this horrible time, but incredibly they will not repent.

Unstoppable Plagues

As the plagues plunge the world into chaos, the Antichrist's followers will begin to doubt him. Remember, the Jews will turn against

him at the end of the first three and a half years of his reign, and the nations of the world will then begin to question him. His marvelous miracles cannot quench the fires, his tricks cannot cleanse the waters, and his charm cannot take the pain away.

At this point, his grip on the world is loosening. Two of his confederate nations will turn against him—the king of the south, probably Egypt, will war against him—the king of the north, probably Turkey, will fiercely "come against him," bent on destroying him.

> *And at the time of the end shall the king of the south push at him: and the king of the north shall come against him like a whirlwind, with chariots, and with horsemen, and with many ships; and he shall enter into the countries, and shall overflow and pass over.*
>
> *Daniel 11:40*

The Antichrist will fight against them and win, but his fury will grow because of their uprisings. He will aim his fury at Israel, and when the sixth angel sounds his trumpet, the Antichrist will take advantage of the situation to begin the March to Armageddon.

Sixth Trumpet—A Third of Humanity Killed

With the sixth trumpet/vial, the Euphrates River (in modern day Iraq) will dry up, freeing four fallen angels who had been bound in the river. These angels will be commanders of 200 million demon horsemen who have breastplates of fire and brimstone. The heads of their horses will be like the heads of lions, out of which come fire, smoke, and brimstone.

The horsemen will spend thirteen months on earth, killing one-third of the earth's already dwindling population with the fire, smoke, and brimstone from their own mouths.

They also will torture people with their horses' tails. Revelation 9:19 TLB describes those tails as being similar to serpents' heads, which strike and bite with fatal wounds.

The mayhem caused by the seals and the trumpet/vials judgments will greatly please the devil. He will think the demons God has set free increase his power against God. And with the Euphrates River dried up, a pathway will be opened for the kings of the east to ride into Israel for the final battle. Thus Satan will act on the opportunities opening to him and send out three unclean spirits to gather the kings of the world together for a war against God. (See Revelation 16:12-16.)

The Valley of Megiddo

The world's final battle, the Battle of Armageddon, will begin in the valley of Megiddo; but it will not be fought there. Megiddo is only a gathering place.

Once assembled there, the Antichrist's demon-powered army will march in absolute precision down the Valley of Jezreel toward the Jordan River valley, then head south. They will turn west near Jericho and head to Jerusalem, where the final battle will take place. Many Bible scholars believe that this is the Valley of Jehoshaphat.

Jesus Claims the Earth

While the Antichrist is luring the world's armies to Armageddon for the final showdown, the scene in heaven will be triumphant. In Revelation 10, Jesus plants one foot on the earth and the other on the sea.

And I saw another mighty angel come down from heaven, clothed with a cloud: and a rainbow was upon his head, and his face was as it were the sun, and his feet as pillars of fire: and he had in his hand a little book open: and he set his right foot upon the sea, and his left foot on the earth.

Revelation 10:1-2

I believe this will not be His physical return to the earth. It will be a figurative, symbolic move that will be very significant. He will make this distinct, deliberate act in order to show He has command of each and His power is universal, all things being under His feet. It expresses the purpose that He is going to take possession of the whole world and restore it to its rightful owners—mankind.

Seventh Trumpet—Law of the Inheritance Fulfilled

And the seventh angel sounded; and there were great voices in heaven, saying, The kingdoms of this world are become the kingdoms of our Lord, and of his Christ; and he shall reign for ever and ever. And the four and twenty elders, which sat before God on their seats, fell upon their faces, and worshipped God, Saying, We give thee thanks, O LORD God Almighty, which art, and wast, and art to come; because thou hast taken to thee thy great power, and hast reigned. And the nations were angry, and thy wrath is come, and the time of the dead, that they should be judged, and that thou shouldest give reward unto thy servants the prophets, and to the saints, and them that fear thy name, small and great; and shouldest destroy them which destroy the earth. And the temple of God was opened in heaven, and there was seen in his temple the ark of his testament: and there were lightnings, and voices, and thunderings, and an earthquake, and great hail.

Revelation 11:15-19

With the opening of the seventh and final seal, Jesus will fulfill the law of inheritance, proving He is the rightful Heir to the world. By setting His foot upon the earth, He will legally claim the right to kick the trespasser, the devil, off His property.

The earth is the Lord's, and the fulness thereof; the world, and they that dwell therein.

Psalm 24:1

In another figurative move, Jesus will give the title deed of the earth to John and instruct him to eat it. This will symbolize mankind's legal inheritance to the earth. By eating it and finding it to be bitter in his stomach, John will exemplify that the possession of the world is sweet, but the events that lead up to this moment will cause great sorrow to the human race. (See Ephesians 1:11-14; Revelation 10:10.)

What this means is that people usually feel pleasure in being able to see or be foretold future events by receiving a word from God, whatever it may be. However, as Bible scholar Matthew Henry explains, "...when this book of prophecy was more thoroughly digested by the apostle [John], the contents would be bitter; these were things so awful and terrible, such grievous persecutions of the people of God, and such desolation made in the earth, that the foresight and foreknowledge of them would not be pleasant, but painful to the mind of the apostle...."[15]

The Two Witnesses Raptured

The Antichrist will observe as his empire crumbles. In his fury, he will attack those who have attacked him—particularly the two witnesses we saw earlier. He will kill them in Jerusalem and leave their bodies lying on the street for all the world to see. This will last for three and a half days for the world to observe.

And when they shall have finished their testimony, the beast that ascendeth out of the bottomless pit shall make war against them, and shall overcome them, and kill them. And their dead bodies shall lie in the street of the great city, which spiritually is called Sodom and Egypt, where also our Lord was crucified. And they of the people and kindreds and tongues and nations shall see their dead bodies three days and an half, and shall not suffer their dead bodies to be put in graves. And they that dwell upon the earth shall rejoice over them, and make merry, and shall send gifts one to another; because these two prophets tormented them that dwelt on the earth.

Revelation 11:7-10

As the people watch these events unfold on television, they will rejoice at the death of the two witnesses because their praying, preaching, and courage in persecution will have caused many to feel self-condemned and scared stiff. However, more will be amazed as the two witnesses resurrect and ascend into heaven.

And after three days and an half the spirit of life from God entered into them, and they stood upon their feet; and great fear fell upon them which saw them. And they heard a great voice from heaven saying unto them, Come up hither. And they ascended up to heaven in a cloud; and their enemies beheld them.

Revelation 11:11-12

During the two witnesses' rapture, an earthquake in Jerusalem will kill 7,000 of the city's inhabitants.

And the same hour was there a great earthquake, and the tenth part of the city fell, and in the earthquake were slain of men seven

thousand: and the remnant were affrighted, and gave glory to the
God of heaven.

Revelation 11:13

To see this incredible event of the two witnesses' resurrection and its aftermath of destruction on the earth will stun those left in that evil day. They will be so amazed, convicted, and terrified that for the moment they will acknowledge the power of God is in it all.

Now the stage will finally be set for Armageddon.

A War Without Fighting

No other aspect of the end times is as misunderstood as Armageddon. While it strikes fear in the hearts of some, to others, the word Armageddon has become nothing more than a term signifying the struggle between good and evil, or a bloody battle. Used to describe the destruction of the world and the end of humankind, Armageddon has been called a war without winners.

Armageddon is the final rebellion of Satan and man against God. It will be a terrible battle that will create a river of blood. But, in one sense, it will be a war without fighting.

The Antichrist will gather a global army, pillaging cities and killing thousands. Not once, however, will Satan and his servants lift a sword against the Lord. When Christ returns with His bride to earth, Satan's army will be destroyed with the voice of our Savior. (See Revelation 19:15,21.) Therefore, there will be no real struggle between good and evil because Christ will overcome without lifting a finger.

Rescue and Defeat

While all we've covered so far is happening on earth, a great event will be unfolding in heaven—the Marriage Supper of the Lamb. (See Revelation 19:9.) The saints and angels will gather to witness this awesome event.

The bride of Christ will be arrayed in the linen of righteousness, washed clean and white by the blood of the Lamb (Revelation 19:7-8). The bride will include all the believers who awaited His first coming, those who accepted Him after His death and resurrection, and the ones who asked Him into their hearts during the Tribulation.

Christ will enter the chapel on a white horse. His eyes will be as a flame of fire, and many crowns will be on His head. His robe will be dipped in blood (Revelation 19:11-13).

And here is the mind which hath wisdom. The seven heads are seven mountains, on which the woman sitteth. And there are seven kings: five are fallen, and one is, and the other is not yet come; and when he cometh, he must continue a short space. And the beast that was, and is not, even he is the eighth, and is of the seven, and goeth into perdition. And the ten horns which thou sawest are ten kings, which have received no kingdom as yet; but receive power as kings one hour with the beast. These have one mind, and shall give their power and strength unto the beast. These shall make war with the Lamb, and the Lamb shall overcome them: for he is Lord of lords, and King of kings: and they that are with him are called, and chosen, and faithful.

Revelation 17:9-14

As this passage indicates, the ceremony is a call to war. When it is finished, His saints will mount white horses to follow him and be part of Satan's ultimate defeat. (See Revelation 19:14.)

I'm convinced that the greatest days are ahead and that what God is going to do with this earth and His people at that time will be pure "dynamite."

Under Christ's supervision, and with the saints' help, people of the earth will begin the reconstruction of their homes. They will cleanse the earth of the dead, plant their fields, and clothe their bodies.

God's righteous—Christians and Jews who believe Jesus is their Messiah—will receive the title deed to the earth. They will live without evil in their midst and will be part of the divine process of restoring this world into the paradise it was before man's fall from grace.

In bodies that will not die and with hearts that won't break, mankind will begin an eternity of praise and fellowship with our Father, our Savior, the Holy Spirit, and our brethren in Christ. This extraordinary time will mark the start of new beginnings that will be filled with the greatest days we've ever known on earth.

Epilogue

by Sarah Bowling

I have many awesome memories growing up as the daughter of Marilyn Hickey and I'd like to share a few with you to give you a little insight into what a remarkable lady she is.

I remember a family vacation we took to Europe over Christmas using a Eurail pass and a guidebook that told us how to travel Europe on $20 a day. Using our train passes, we went to several different countries. Mom's job was to figure out the best hotel options for the dollar, interfacing with the hotel clerks using broken English, French, and some Spanish. She was great and it was a fun family vacation.

Once, we took a cruise on the Nile River as a family. Mom loved it. We were able to climb around Abu Simbel and even got to see some mummified crocodiles.

Mom also enjoys having a nice meal. She likes almost every kind of food, but particularly appreciates a fine Mediterranean dish. She's also keen on Mexican cuisine. And I think she likes my cooking—or she's polite enough not to point out my culinary mistakes!

Mom is a busy lady, but she really likes going to a nice place, having a good meal, and relaxing with a good book—even fiction or international history. Over the years, I can see she is more intentional with her time and with whom and how she interfaces. She is very purposeful about pouring into the next generation. Her heart is to see the next generation grow in the Word and be effective in their ministries.

Life Lessons

One of the life lessons I learned while growing up is to watch and listen—I've watched my mom move with tremendous grace and wisdom through conflicts, tension-filled situations, hardships, and struggles. From watching her, I've seen her remain calm and quiet, waiting for the right things to say or do, at the right time. She has worked to relate to many different kinds of people—Christians, Muslims, Hindus, all kinds of religious leaders, government leaders, secular media, and more. She has consistently maintained her poise and remained unflustered.

Another life lesson I've learned from my mom is to trust in God's Word to be effective in my life. I remember back in fifth grade when we were coming to the end of the school year, and the dreaded field day was around the corner. I always hated field day because I never did well. I always came in last and thoroughly failed at everything. But that year my mom encouraged me to do something different—to begin saying what the Bible says about me, rather than saying the normal failure stuff. So everyday for about two weeks before field day, I would say what the Bible says about me: I'm the head and not the tail, above and not beneath (Deuteronomy 28); I can do all things through Christ who strengthens me (Philippians 4:13); and other scriptures. When field day finally arrived, I came home with *only* first and second place in every event I entered! Compared to my preceding years, this was a total miracle—the exact opposite of what I had done in the past four years.

Another life lesson I learned from my mom was to trust the Voice in my heart. I remember a time when I was about ten-years-old and travelling with Mom on one of her speaking engagements. A woman picked us up from the airport and I could tell right away that she was a flake. It was all I could do to keep my mouth shut until we got to the hotel room because I had such strong alarms going off in my heart about her. Once we got to the hotel room, I told my mom the woman was flakey. My mom reserved her own judgment to see what would happen, but after a day or so, my mom let me know I was right—the woman was not right spiritually. Mom encouraged me that it was okay to listen to my heart with such intensity.

My mom also taught me I could do anything. Whenever I came up with a crazy idea about growing up to be America's first woman astronaut, she never quelled my ideas. My first major at university was physics. Now when I look back on it, that was a really crazy major for me—but she never put me down or told me something I wanted was impossible. She has always been supportive and encouraging, affirming that I could do anything in life.

Health Challenges

One of the challenges Mom faced not too long ago was a physical attack of intestinal parasites. It totally sapped her energy and really set her back for about four months. This was very hard for her because she wasn't able to keep up her normal activities and schedule. She was initially frustrated and then became almost depressed as she continued to get physically weaker. The doctors couldn't figure out what the problem was and this just added to her frustration. She and Dad would come for dinner and while she didn't eat much, she found it helpful to be around our kids and their energy. She struggled to keep her focus and had difficulty getting settled into the Bible, where she normally finds her strength. After some time, we encouraged her to go for some counseling and her doctor decided to put her on some high power antibiotics to knock out any potential parasites. Both tactics were immensely helpful to her and over a few months she regained her strength, energy, and focus. From that season, she will tell you she has much more compassion for people who struggle with depression and emotional hardships.

Family Struggles

Growing up, Mom and Dad had some challenges with my brother and me for different reasons. My brother unfortunately got into the wrong crowd in junior high and started dabbling in illegal drugs. He continued on this path for a number of years. During that period, Mom would have times of struggling and times of grace. She kept anchored in the Word of God and that gave her power to endure longer than the hardship. She always took God's truth to be louder and stronger than the facts she heard and saw.

When it comes to me, Mom struggled when I went through a faith crisis in my early twenties. She maintained her confidence in God regardless of what I said and she did her best to keep our relationship stable without freaking out about my religious explorations. I think she'd say she had to consistently decide to put more confidence in God than in what her kids were saying or doing. And God was faithful to bring all of us through those difficult times.

One thing about Mom is her determination and strength of character. I don't know of any negative habits she's had to overcome. She's always maintained her daily Bible memorizing and has always been disciplined in how she uses her time and in studying. Recently she has become increasingly committed to consistently working out. She has always been an advocate of eating healthy and fresh food, so growing up our family always had fresh vegetables, fruit, and meat.

A Little Fun

I would like to share that when Mom was younger, she had a side to her that enjoyed pulling off practical jokes. She taught me how to short sheet a bed and took me to TP (toilet paper) my teacher's house in junior high! She also enjoyed turning the lights out on people in the bathroom when she left. So if you ever meet her in the bathroom....

One of our fun family traditions has to do with Mom's punch bowl that she brings out every year at Christmas. We all tease her about it because it's pretty old and tired, but it's fun to remember during the holidays. Another tradition is Mom always makes a special black cherry Jell-O over the holidays and it is always everyone's favorite.

Looking Toward the Future

When I think of my mom, I can say we both relate to each other on so many levels. We both cheer for each other to run the race God has set before us. We both want to hear God's voice clearly and obey Him quickly. I know we both want to get to heaven and hear God say to us individually, "Well done." We both have a passion for the Bible and see it as an integral essential in a believer's daily living. For my part, I'm pursuing some deeper studies in Biblical languages so I can better understand and communicate relevance from the Bible to our daily living. Since Mom is a student of languages herself, she's pretty excited about that.

Something I probably work hard to dispel is the vocabulary chasm that exists in today's world as it relates to spiritual terms and application. It's no secret that the American population is largely illiterate in Biblical terminology. This deficiency can leave us vulnerable to settling for a superficial existence and trying to snuff out the beckoning of our hearts for greater depth and a rich, sustaining interior life. There's tremendous spiritual poverty everywhere, but the greatest tragedy is that we rarely recognize it for what it is—poverty in our hearts. We are so very rich and poor at the same time. It's no wonder that people are confused and restless.

Of course Mom and I want to use all the avenues available today to minister to people (Web, social media, television, text messaging, and whatever new technology is yet to come), but in every facet, we both want Jesus to speak through us to people's hearts. We don't need more humanity when what we're really hungry for is authentic Divinity. Now that's something I can say Mom and I both would like you to consider.

Prayer of Salvation

God loves you—no matter who you are, no matter what your past. God loves you so much that He gave His one and only begotten Son for you. The Bible tells us that "…whoever believes in him shall not perish but have eternal life" (John 3:16 NIV). Jesus laid down His life and rose again so that we could spend eternity with Him in heaven and experience His absolute best on earth. If you would like to receive Jesus into your life, say the following prayer out loud and mean it from your heart.

> *Heavenly Father, I come to You admitting that I am a sinner. Right now, I choose to turn away from sin, and I ask You to cleanse me of all unrighteousness. I believe that Your Son, Jesus, died on the cross to take away my sins. I also believe that He rose again from the dead so that I might be forgiven of my sins and made righteous through faith in Him. I call upon the name of Jesus Christ to be the Savior and Lord of my life. Jesus, I choose to follow You and ask that You fill me with the power of the Holy Spirit. I declare that right now I am a child of God. I am free from sin and full of the righteousness of God. I am saved in Jesus' name. Amen.*

If you prayed this prayer to receive Jesus Christ as your Savior for the first time, please contact us on the web at www.harrisonhouse.com to receive a free book. Or you may write to us at:

Harrison House
P.O. Box 35035
Tulsa, Oklahoma 74153

Other Books by Marilyn Hickey

Breaking Free from Fear

Breaking Generational Curses

God's Benefit: Healing

Watcher

Winning Over Weight

Your Miracle Source

These books available at
fine bookstores everywhere
or at www.harrisonhouse.com.

To contact Marilyn Hickey
please write to:

Marilyn Hickey Ministries
P.O. Box 17340
Denver, CO 80217
Please include your prayer requests
and comments when you write.

About the Author

Marilyn Hickey is no stranger to impacting the lives of millions worldwide. As founder and president of Marilyn Hickey Ministries, Marilyn is being used by God to help "cover the earth with the Word." Her mission has been effectively accomplished through various avenues of ministry such as partnering with other ministries to ship thousands of Bibles into Communist countries; holding crusades in places like Ethiopia, the Philippines, Korea, Haiti, Brazil, Malaysia, Japan, and Honduras; and reaching individuals worldwide through television broadcasts seen on networks such as Black Entertainment Television (BET) and Trinity Broadcasting Network (TBN). In addition, Marilyn Hickey Ministries has established a fully accredited 2-year Bible college to raise up Christian leaders to carry out God's mission. Marilyn also serves the body of Christ as the Chairman of the Board of Regents for Oral Roberts University, and is the only woman serving on the Board of Directors for Dr. Davie Yonggi Cho (pastor of the world's largest congregation, Yoido Full Gospel Church).

In addition to her ministry, Marilyn is also a busy wife and mother of two grown children. She is married to Wallace Hickey, pastor of Orchard Road Christian Center in Greenwood Village, Colorado.

Endnotes

1   Arthur Bloomfield, *All Things New* (Minneapolis, Minnesota: Bethany House Publishers, 1971.)

2   Charles E. Pfeiffer and Everett F. Harrison, editors, *The Wycliffe Bible Commentary*, (Electronic Database: Moody Press, 1962), s.v. "Daniel 8:9-14." All rights reserved.

3   Based on a notes section from Spiros Zodhiates, Th. D., *The Complete Word Dictionary: Old Testament* (Chattanooga: AMG Publishers, 1994), P. 2101, s.v. "Daniel 2:31-45."

4   Adam Clarke, *Adam Clarke's Commentary on the Bible*, (Nashville, TN: Thomas Reference, 1997). s.v. "Daniel 2:33."

5   Jamison, Fausset, and Brown, *Bible Commentary*, (Peabody, MA: Hendrickson Publishers, 1997). s.v. "Daniel 2:34."

6   Spiros Zodhiates, Th. D., *The Complete Word Dictionary: Old Testament*, p. 2133, s.v. "[Daniel] 11:21-35."

7   International Standard Bible Encyclopaedia, original James Orr 1915 Edition (Electronic Database: Biblesoft, 1995-1996), s.v. "MAGOG."

8   *Matthew Henry's Commentary on the Whole Bible: New Modern Edition* (Electronic Database: Hendrickson Publishers, Inc., 1991), s.v. "John 6:60-71, Christ's discourse with His disciples."

9   Matthew Henry, s.v. "Genesis 12:1-3, The Call of Abram."

10 Joseph A. Seiss, *The Apocalypse: Exposition of the Book of Revelation* (Biblesoft: Electronic Database, 1998), s.v. "Revelation 12:1-2," "Revelation 13:13-18."

11 Warren W. Wiersbe, *The Essential Everyday Bible Commentary* (Nashville: Thomas Nelson Publishers, 1991), s.v. "Revelation 13:11-18."

12 Joseph A. Seiss, s.v. "Revelation 12:5."

13 Matthew Henry, s.v. "Revelation 3:14-22."

14 Matthew Henry, s.v. "Revelation 11:3-13, The two witnesses."

15 Matthew Henry, s.v. "Revelation 10:8-11, The charge to further prophecy."